Cruelty and Deception

Cruelty and Deception

::

THE CONTROVERSY OVER
DIRTY HANDS IN POLITICS

::

EDITED BY
Paul Rynard & David P. Shugarman

broadview press

::

Pluto Press

CANADIAN CATALOGUING IN PUBLICATION DATA

Main entry under title:

Cruelty and deception: the controversy over dirty hands in politics

Co-published by Pluto Press, Australia. ISBN 1-86403-107-7   CIP no. C99-932236-2
Includes bibliographical references.
ISBN 1-55111-196-9

1. Political ethics.   2. Political Corruption.
I. Rynard, Paul, 1963–   II. Shugarman, David P., 1943–

JA79.C78 1999   172   C99-930708-8

BROADVIEW PRESS, LTD.
is an independent, international publishing house, incorporated in 1985.

North America
Post Office Box 1243, Peterborough, Ontario, Canada K9J 7H5
3576 California Road, Orchard Park, New York, USA 14127
TEL (705) 743-8990; FAX (705) 743-8353; E-MAIL customerservice@broadviewpress.com

United Kingdom and Europe
Turpin Distribution Services, Ltd., Blackhorse Rd.,
Letchworth, Hertfordshire, SG6 1HN
TEL (1462) 672555; FAX (1462) 480947; E-MAIL turpin@rsc.org

Australia
St. Clair Press, Post Office Box 287, Rozelle, NSW 2039
TEL (612) 818-1942; FAX (612) 418-1923

www.broadviewpress.com

Broadview Press gratefully acknowledges the financial support of the Book Publishing Industry Development Program, Ministry of Canadian Heritage, Government of Canada.

Cover design by Zack Taylor, Black Eye Design. Cover photograph © 1999 PhotoDisc, Inc. Typeset by Zack Taylor, Black Eye Design.

The publisher has made every attempt to locate the authors of the copyrighted material or their heirs and assigns, and would be grateful for any information which would allow correction of any errors or omissions in subsequent editions of the work.

Printed in Canada

Contents

Preface and Acknowledgments 7

Introduction: The Controversy Over Dirty Hands 11
David P. Shugarman

PART ONE   **DEFENDING DIRTY HANDS**

Introduction to Part One 23

1   Dirty Hands and Ordinary Life 27
Michael Stocker

2   Missionaries and Mercenaries 43
Ronald Beiner

3   Bernard Shaw and Dirty-Hands Politics:
A Comparison of *Mrs Warren's Profession*
and *Major Barbara* 51
John Allett

4   Politics, Power, and Partisanship 67
Tom Sorell

5   Principles and Politics 87
Leah Bradshaw

6   Justice, Expediency, and Practices of Thinking 101
Evan Simpson

7   Democratic Legitimacy and Official Discretion 111
Arthur Applbaum

PART TWO   **REJECTING DIRTY HANDS**

Introduction to Part Two 135

8   There is No Dilemma of Dirty Hands 139
     Kai Nielsen

9   On the One Hand and On the Other 157
     Michael Yeo

10   Bribery, Business, and The Problem of Dirty Hands 175
     A.W. Cragg

11   Hands: Clean and Tied or Dirty and Bloody 187
     Michael McDonald

12   Ethical Politics and the Clinton Affair 199
     Ian Greene and David P. Shugarman

13   Retrospection and Democracy: Bringing
     Political Conduct under the Constitution 207
     S.L. Sutherland

14   Democratic Dirty Hands? 229
     David P. Shugarman

     Appendix: Selected Classic Statements
     on Dirty Hands: Excerpts from Machiavelli,
     Weber, Trotsky, Sartre, and Walzer 251

     Selective Bibliography 263

     Contributors 271

     Sources 275

     Index 277

Preface

AND ACKNOWLEDGEMENTS

This book is about a major controversy affecting ethical governance and morality in politics: what is the best way to approach and answer the question of whether or not actions that involve cruelty and/or deception—actions which we normally regard as immoral—are obligatory or acceptable as social and political practices? The "dirty-hands" issue raises a classic problem of how we or our politicians should act when various of our moral commitments seem to be at cross-purposes. Arguments about the acceptability of dirty hands are arguments about what to do when moral positions conflict, when it seems that in order to so something which is clearly right, one has also to do something that is clearly wrong. Thus, this book explores key moral considerations that arise in political decision-making and in social life generally.

The problem of dirty hands is one which also raises the difficulty of maintaining integrity in government on the one hand, and securing the enjoyment of other highly regarded values and political practices on the other. While citizens in liberal democracies may be becoming more cynical about the honesty and trustworthiness of their politicians, they nevertheless are concerned about ethical issues in public life and about how their representatives and fellow citizens ought to be addressing these issues. The pros and cons of euthanasia, abortion, capital punishment, affirmative action, and Aboriginal rights are continually debated in academic journals, the popular press, and radio and television phone-in shows. In all these cases there are differences over which of our deeply held moral principles should take priority when there is conflict between them and whether exceptional circumstances require or allow us to alter moral positions that we would otherwise regard as sacrosanct. The essays in this book contribute to a growing body of literature in the fields of practical ethics, political theory, and policy studies that seeks to clarify such highly charged moral issues and their public policy ramifications. It should prove useful to students in philosophy, politics, sociology, psychology, public administration, and ethics generally.

Does the term "dirty hands" adequately conceptualize the problems of reconciling ethics and power? Is politics—including democratic politics—a dirty business much of the time? And if so, does that mean that even good politicians sometimes need to get their hands dirty if they are to accomplish anything worthwhile and challenge the dirty dealings of the unscrupulous? These questions have both theoretical and practical components: they address how we can best understand, explain, and conceptualize political realities as well as the ethical considerations that are applicable to those realities. Our essayists, specialists in areas of philosophy, political theory, and ethics, offer different answers to these questions.

In preparing the book for publication we saw that the dirty-hands controversy could not be simplified into a dispute between idealists and realists or consequentialists and their opponents. We nevertheless felt it was useful to divide various arguments, while acknowledging the nuances of their positions, into two broad categories: the authors in Part One argue in defense of the ethics of dirty hands; those in Part Two challenge that defense and reject the explanatory pull of the dirty-hands dilemma.

Most of the papers in the collection are, at our urging, expanded reworkings of presentations first delivered to a workshop on dirty hands held at York University in December 1993. Several others involve abridgement and revision of previously published essays. In all these cases our debts to the authors for their patience, willingness to rewrite, and agreement to suggested changes are, of course, substantial. Our debts to others are also considerable.

From its inception the book as a research project was importantly aided by a grant from the Social Sciences and Humanities Research Council of Canada for a series of workshops on ethics in public life organized by Ian Greene and David Shugarman.

In many respects this book is a more philosophically oriented sequel to one of the major themes treated in Greene and Shugarman's *Honest Politics* (James Lorimer & Co., 1997) and owes a great deal to their collaborative efforts over the years. Time constraints on Greene as a result of his involvement in co-authoring two other recent works on ethics in Canadian politics and his responsibilities as an administrator at York meant that, unfortunately, he had to relinquish his role as one of the co-editors. Nevertheless, without his involvement as a co-researcher and co-organizer in the research project funded by the SSHRC, this book would not have been possible.

During the book's gestation a number of students from York's Graduate Program in Political Science have been very helpful. Sue Ferguson helped organize the original workshop and provided a reflective summary of some of the key issues raised; Brenda Lyshaug, Graham Longford, Tami Jacobi, and Pamela Leach helped with bibliographical research along the way. John Simoulidis joined the project in its final stages and played an important role in bringing it to a conclusion by helping in the preparation of the appendices and assisting in the editing of several articles.

One graduate student's contribution was absolutely crucial: Paul Rynard's willingness once again to interrupt the completion of his doctoral dissertation to contribute his skill of superior editorial assistance proved so substantial that it made sense to include his name on the cover as a full co-editor.

The editors wish to thank Don LePan and Michael Harrison of Broadview Press for agreeing to publish the collection and Broadview's editor Barbara Conolly for her support and patience. We also want to express our gratitude to Les Jacobs, Les Green, David Bell, and Peter Penz for their comments on various drafts of selected papers. We appreciate the support provided by McLaughlin College's secretarial staff throughout the project.

Finally, members of our families were generous with their assistance and understanding. In this respect we wish to thank Julie Shugarman for her suggestions on portions of the introduction; Linda Scott for typing, proofing, and commenting on portions of several papers in draft stages; and Michelle Sweet whose hard work made Rynard's participation in the project possible.

The Controversy Over Dirty Hands

DAVID P. SHUGARMAN

It is often said that politics is a dirty business and that those who engage in it can't help but get their hands dirty. Many people who have a cynical view of politicians regard them as clever and unscrupulous manipulators who have no compunction about dirtying their hands in pursuit of their own interests. From this perspective, the world of politics is a sinister and corrupt place, where people seek power and advantage for selfish ends: ethics and politics are polar opposites. A diametrically opposed view, often associated with the teachings of Socrates and Kant, holds that honest politics is not an oxymoron, that public life can and should be shaped by leaders committed to truth and dedicated to serving the public interest; that good politicians need not and will not dishonour themselves or others. In this view, ethical leaders disavow cruelty and deception and practice what they preach. However, there is an influential current in contemporary political theorizing which departs from both cynicism and its honest-politics opposite. This third view treats dirty-handed conduct as indeed unsavoury and incriminating, but as necessary and praiseworthy nevertheless. The proponents of this view claim that, paradoxically, moral leadership sometimes requires doing wrong in order to do right, and that understanding this marks a practical appreciation, on the parts of both political actors and objective observers, of an awkward, limited, but realistic pairing of ethics and politics. Scrutiny and reassessment of this third view is the subject of this book.

This collection of essays deals with the appropriateness of "dirty hands" in politics. It explores the meaning of the term and its implications: whether "dirty hands" is useful as a description of the way public figures actually behave in crisis, and whether it is acceptable as a model for guiding ethical and efficacious conduct. Our authors present differing appreciations both of the extent to which there are dirty hands in political decision-making and actions, and of the justifiability of such conduct if and when it presents itself. Defenders of dirty hands make the argument (in various ways) that sometimes cruelty and/or deception are necessary means to achieve a desirable end. The desirable goal may be the advancement of the greater good, or the prevention of a considerable evil. On the other hand, there are a variety of strong arguments for rejecting the practice, as well as the theoretical justifications, of dirty-handed activity. The book presents arguments and analyses pro and con using normally repugnant methods to advance political causes. This is a major area of concern and controversy in the theory and practice of ethical politics. Some of our authors pit Socratic and/or Kantian insights against those who make a case for the use of cruelty and deception. Others focus on the tension between principles and procedures that support democracy and those that support dirty hands. The dirty-hands problem sets ethicists, political theorists, and social philosophers against one another on empirical, logical, and normative grounds.

The dirt in question is not the kind one gets on one's hands from a day's honest labour on the farm, or in the factory, or through working in one's garden, or repairing the plumbing; rather, it is the sort that makes one's character and actions morally suspect and unsettling. It is the dirt one gets on one's hands from doing something sleazy and often cruel, cruel to the point of hurting people—often innocent people—and even killing them, so that the dirty hands are actually bloody. And unlike hands dirty from honest labour, which can be displayed proudly before washing, a politician's dirty or bloody hands may not at first be seen, because the very nature of the dirty-handed act is that it is deceptive, not visible to most. The hands involved are those of a trickster; they move quickly while the attention of the spectator is diverted elsewhere. The dirt that comes from unethical conduct is in an important sense metaphorical, because there is often literally no dirt to be seen. The authority figure appears to have clean hands, but this is part of the deception; the hands have been covered by gloves, or they have been washed off before anyone can see the evidence, or the dirt attaches to subordinates given dirty jobs to do.

It is generally held that Machiavelli, writing about the vagaries and corruption of Italian principalities in the sixteenth century, was either the first major European theorist to make the case for nastiness in political leadership or the most articulate spokesman for it, though some historians of political thought have suggested that the current goes as far back as the ancients – back to Plato's defense of the noble lying and mythmaking of virtuous guardians of the commonwealth. But what sets Plato clearly apart from both Machiavelli and contemporary advocates of cruelty and deception is that the advocated deceit in *The Republic* did not entail, as far as Plato was concerned, the suffering or injury of anyone. It was meant to contribute to harmony *without* recourse to violence and was certainly not a cover for violent or despicable acts.

Indeed, when Plato's Socrates reflected on the difficulties of following a life of philosophy in a corrupt society, he confronted the problem of dirty hands. He held that if a lover of truth finds that "there is no soundness in the conduct of public life, nowhere an ally at whose side a champion of justice could hope to escape destruction," he will keep quiet and go his own way, for, "seeing lawlessness spreading on all sides," he should be content "if he can keep his hands clean from iniquity while this life lasts." In the midst of disorder and lawlessness a philosopher is like a fish out of water, or as Socrates put it, "like a man fallen among wild beasts." Such a man "should refuse to take part in their misdeeds." It is important to note that this is not a recommendation to avoid public life *per se*: it is rather advice to reject *corrupt* public life, for Socrates quickly adds that while maintaining one's integrity is no small achievement, if a philosopher could find a society congenial to his nature, his accomplishments would be even greater, both for his country and himself.[1]

This argument does not favour the sanctity and calm serenity of the private over the inevitably fractious public, or opt for solitude over social relations. Rather, it emphasizes that where good government is lacking, neither philosophy nor civil relationships can be properly enjoyed. It is power-hungry politicians and the struggle for power which are inimical to all three. So while Socrates acknowledged that politics may degenerate into dirty business, he denied such business legitimacy. He seems to have held that, while one should not participate in ruling where ruling requires dirty hands, ruling does not necessarily require dirty hands; for when he scornfully responds, in the *Apology*, to the Athenian Assembly's charges against him of breaking their laws, he clearly does so as a citizen of Athens who prides himself on having acted ethically and consistently in private and public life.

For Machiavelli, however, there are things which must be done to restore, establish, and preserve order, and securing these ends overrides commitments to ethical proprieties:

> A wise man will never criticize someone for an extralegal action undertaken to organize a kingdom or establish a republic. He will agree that if his deed accuses him, its consequences excuse him.... For it is those who are violent in order to destroy who should be found guilty not those who are violent in order to build anew...[2]

Furthermore, and in sharp contrast to Socrates's position that a good man, whether in or out of political office, does not harm others, Machiavelli maintains that "it is necessary for a ruler …to learn how not to be good, and to know when it is and when it is not necessary to use this knowledge," and that "A ruler … cannot conform to all those rules that men who are thought good are expected to respect, for he is often obliged, in order to hold on to power, to break his word, to be uncharitable, inhumane, and irreligious."[3]

In a similar vein, four hundred years later, the German sociologist Max Weber held that to engage in politics is to make a contract with the devil: one accepts "power and force as means," in return for the chance to accomplish something worthwhile; and one needs to understand that in politics "it is not true that good can follow only from good and evil only from evil, but that often the opposite is true. Anyone who fails to see this is, indeed, a political infant."[4]

And Hoederer, the revolutionary hero of Jean-Paul Sartre's mid-twentieth century play *Dirty Hands*, scolds a young idealist for not understanding that the pursuit of justice requires "using every means at hand to abolish classes," that "all means are good when they're effective," that one cannot avoid having soiled hands if anything worthwhile is to be accomplished, and that anyone who thinks otherwise is hopelessly impractical:

> Purity is an idea for a yogi or a monk. You intellectuals and bourgeois anarchists use it as a pretext for doing nothing…. Well I have dirty hands. Right up to the elbows. I've plunged them in filth and blood. But what do you hope? Do you think you can govern innocently?[5]

In an influential article published in 1971, Michael Walzer drew on these views of Machiavelli, Weber, and Sartre in an attempt to explore the "conventional wisdom" that dirty hands and politics were intertwined.[6] Walzer's essay generated a considerable amount of supplementary commentary, criticism, and controversy. It was the catalyst for discussion at a workshop at York University, which proved enormously helpful to me in the preparation of an earlier co-authored work that focused on applied ethics in Canadian politics,[7] and that led to the present collection.

In his essay, Walzer made it clear that he shared the Hoederer response. He, too, took the view that no one can govern innocently. And in contrast to Machiavelli, who thought it a difficult task to get good men to do "necessarily" wicked things, Walzer declared: "It is easy to get one's hands dirty in politics and it is often right to do so."[8] To Walzer, a dirty-handed leader is neither aberrant, embarrassing, nor evil, but rather the quintessentially moral politician. How can we tell if we're dealing with a moral politician? "It is *by his dirty hands* that we know him," answers Walzer.[9] Walzer claims that the moral politician is one who is not only willing to get his hands dirty, but does so, who is aware of and troubled by the fact that he must commit wrong acts, but nevertheless does so for the greater good. He—and, as several of our essayists point out, dirty-handedness seems to be associated with masculine characters and characteristics—is someone who wrestles with the application of conflicting moral obligations to concrete situations and comes up with the right, though morally troubling, solution.

What characterizes the dirty-handed politician, says Walzer, is his experience of "a painful process of having to weigh the wrong he is willing to do in order to do right, which leaves pain behind, and should do so, even after the decision has been made."[10] What is new in contemporary defenses of generally dirty measures is conveyed in Walzer's emphasis on the importance for both leaders and citizens to recognize that immoral acts cannot be canceled out or forgotten, and that some form of retribution is due. It is necessary that the wrongfulness be absorbed and addressed socially. The trouble with Machiavelli, Walzer contends, is not that he recommends using cruelty and deception, but that "he does not specify the state of mind appropriate" to a ruler who does so.[11] The trouble with some latter-day Machiavellians who do raise the matter of the suffering public servant is that they don't go beyond the individual's angst. According to Walzer, the public actor who acknowledges no wrong and feels no remorse in getting his hands dirty is just a politician—not a moral one—and the person who refuses ever to get his or her hands dirty may remain moral, but cannot be a political actor. From this view, when a political actor lies, tortures, and even kills on behalf of citizens, it is crucial that they "make sure he pays the price," and because they too are complicit, *they* must also pay a price.

Here, by way of a preview and a background to the discussions to come, is a brief summary of the main features of the dirty-hands theorists' approach to ethics. This is followed by an outline of some of the key questions and objections that are raised against it. Dirty-hands features can be set out as propositions: (1) the crucial reasons for acting are the protection and/or promotion of public good, which can mean reasons of state (*raison d'état*) or revolution; (2) when it comes to considering as well as judging a public act, the criterion is the consequence(s); (3) violence and deception, "wicked means," even cruelty can be employed for beneficial as well as destructive ends; (4) when normally reprehensible means are used for "good" purposes, their use is morally defensible; (5) public life is carried on in an atmosphere akin to warfare, where social relations are marked by intense rivalry, duplicity, and violence; (6) public life requires heroic leadership; and (7) genuinely ethical practitioners of cruelty and deception understand the dualism and ambivalence of their actions and feel guilty about the moral wrong they discharge.[12]

Not all defenders of dirty hands would subscribe to every one of these propositions and, as has been mentioned above, the last one is a relatively new addition to the case being made. For some analysts of moral conflict in politics, another proposition should figure prominently in the list, namely, that there is a great divide between public and private moralities. This belief was certainly important in Machiavelli's reflections, is evident in Weber's writings, and plays a major role in the theories of many international relations "realists."[13] But theorists like Walzer, Stephen Lukes, and Thomas Nagel hold that, while the dirty-hands dilemma may be "posed most dramatically in politics,"[14] it is a general problem "arising in all spheres of life,"[15] and while public morality may not be derivable from private, the two are not mutually exclusive.[16] On the other hand, except for the seventh, the propositions listed are widely shared by highly disparate political actors and theorists, who would otherwise fundamentally disagree on public policy matters and on the extent of the gap between the private and the public.

In this regard one of the remarkable items of dirty-hands advocacy is that it spans ideological categories. From the revolutionary left, there is Leon Trotsky's contention that *anything* done in support of working-class mobilization and the goal of liberation is not only "permissible" but "obligatory."[17] From the ultra-conservative right comes American Senator Barry Goldwater's declaration that "extremism in defense of liberty is no vice."[18] As rationales for dirty hands these are, at one level, indistinguishable from each other. At another level, each would hold that the other's substantive social morality—as concerns the meaning of liberty, for example—is so seriously deficient as to be bogus and dangerous, providing yet further justification for anything done to disable the other. But dirty hands are not advocated only by those on the extreme ends of the ideological spectrum. Many democratic socialists and liberal democrats also conceive of dirty-hands issues as a staple of politics.[19] "States and their agents are licensed, in liberal theory," says Stanley Benn, "to set aside moral principles for the sake of good outcomes (or more usually to avoid bad ones)."[20] Furthermore, liberal democrats like Benn, Walzer, Martin Hollis, Bernard Williams, and Stuart Hampshire (to some extent) have not only made arguments in support of cruelty and deception, they have linked such measures to democracy. Yet while moral Machiavellism and its contemporary variations may not be restricted to any particular position on the left-right continuum, there are ideological aspects of dirty hands (as several of our contributors point out) that are important and that seem to have considerable bearing on the question of how democracy can accommodate such actions.

Debate between defenders of dirty hands and their critics has often been characterized as a debate between consequentialists, especially the utilitarian variety, and deontologists. Very briefly summarized, the former focus on engineering the best policy outcomes possible in difficult circumstances. The latter focus on the importance of preserving one's integrity and acting with respect for the rights of others. In this regard, it is assumed that arguments over what is the right thing to do in a particular circumstance are between those who judge the worth of an act or policy on the basis of its expected outcome or utility—its overall contribution to the particular, desirable end being sought—and those who believe that certain acts are right or wrong in themselves and that a person has a duty to refrain from doing what is wrong in itself, no matter how much it may contribute to a goal that is morally esteemed. The latter challenge to consequentialist ethics holds that in social relations it is wrong, morally and logically, to separate means and ends by categorizing some people and their interests as "means" and others as ends. Kant's maxim, "Act always so that you treat humanity whether in your person or in that of another always as an end, but never as a means only," can thus be understood as providing the polar alternative to moral Machiavellism.

Highlighting the utilitarian-versus-Kantian debate is useful inasmuch as this is the way the moral Machiavellians often account for the differences between their position and that of their critics, and because they also emphasize what they take to be the rigidity and impracticality of Kant's further proposition that applied ethics must be universal and absolute. It is also important because it sheds light on why those influenced by Kant express worry and caution that making excuses and exceptions for the indecent treatment of people encourages amoral or immoral politics. However, it is by no means a fully adequate characterization of what is at issue in the defense of dirty hands and its repudiation. To say that the disagreement is really about the choice between ends or means, or the ethics of consequences versus the ethics of intention, blurs the fact that there are consequences involved in effecting both means and ends. For example, using violence to deal with unruly dissenters has consequences for the dissenters just as it has consequences for people and officials who want orderly dissent and peaceful streets. So the consequentialist case may often be less a matter of trumping non-consequentialist morality than one of choosing which consequence or set of consequences is superior to another and on what grounds.

There are consequentialist utilitarians who see the resolution of conflicting moral demands through lenses other than those of the moral Machiavellians and who hold that, in order to advance the probabilities of successful moral outcomes, conscientious and wise politicians will make choices that involve transgressing some rights in order to uphold others, without being tainted or having to do penance. Furthermore, the Kantian-utilitarian dialectic tends to skip lightly over major concerns raised from a demanding democratic perspective. A fixatation on imputed contradictions between the two moralities deflects attention from those democratic theories and practices which may call for their reconciliation or transcendence. But can they be reconciled or transcended? And if, for instance, procedural fairness, accountability, equality, and respect for individual and minority rights are undermined to support "good" causes or ends, how can moral Machiavellism be squared with democracy?

In what follows, readers will be presented with a variety of nuanced, informative, and provocative answers to these and other questions raised in the controversy over dirty hands in politics. They can then decide for themselves if cruelty and deception are genuinely defensible as bulwarks of ethical politics.

Notes

1 Plato, *The Republic*, ed. F. M. Cornford (London: Oxford, 1941) 496d & e. This and the next four paragraphs are borrowed from an earlier article, David Shugarman, "The Use and Abuse of Politics," in *Moral Expertise: Studies in Practical and Professional Ethics,* ed. Don MacNiven (New York: Routledge, 1990).

2 Machiavelli, *Selected Political Writings,* ed. David Wootton (Indianapolis: Hackett, 1995) 108.

3 Machiavelli, "The Prince," *Selected Political Writings,* Ch. 15 and 18: 48, 55.

4 *From Max Weber,* ed. and trans. H. H. Gerth and C. Wright Mills (New York: Oxford, 1958) 123.

5 Sartre, *No Exit: And Other Plays,* trans. Lionel Abel (New York: Vintage Books, 1955) 223-4.

6 Michael Walzer, "Political Action: The Problem of Dirty Hands," *Philosophy and Public Affairs* 2:2 (Winter 1973).

7 Ian Greene and David P. Shugarman, *Honest Politics: Seeking Integrity in Canadian Public Life* (Toronto: James Lorimer, 1997).

8 Walzer 174.

9 Walzer 168 (emphasis added).

10 Walzer 174.

11 Walzer 176.

12 An earlier version of these propositions was set out and elaborated in Shugarman, 208-210.

13 To Reinhold Niebuhr there was a sharp distinction that must be drawn between "the moral and social behaviour of individuals and social groups…[which] justifies and necessitates political policies which a purely individualistic ethic must always find embarrassing." *Moral Man and Immoral Society* (New York: C. Scribner's Sons, 1952) xi. This is emphasized in recent writings of various moral philosophers, e.g., Hampshire and Hollis, among others.

14 Walzer 174.

15 Stephen Lukes, *Moral Conflict and Politics* (Oxford: Clarendon Press, 1991) 193.

16 Thomas Nagel, "Ruthlessness in Public Life," *Public and Private Morality,* ed. S. Hampshire (Cambridge: Cambridge University Press, 1978).

17 Leon Trotsky, John Dewey, and George Novack, *Their Morals and Ours: Marxist versus Liberal Views on Morality. Four Essays* (New York: Merit Publishers, 1969) 37.

18 Theodore White, *The Making of the President 1964* (Toronto: Signet Books, 1965) 261.

19 Lukes, esp.193, 196.

20 Stanley Benn, "Private and Public Morality: Clean Living and Dirty Hands,"*Public and Private in Social Life,* ed. S. Benn and G.F. Gauss (New York: St. Martins Press, 1983) 167.

Defending Dirty Hands

Introduction

The authors in Part One share the belief that ethical politics and serving the public will sometimes require committing egregiously immoral acts; that the complex demands of social life produce situations where moral rules conflict, and some must be broken in the service of others. Building on the work of Machiavelli, most treatments of the problem of dirty hands emphasize its origins in the urgent and unique realm of politics or statecraft, yet several of the essays here assert that the need to break rules while pursuing morally defensible goals is an unfortunate aspect of moral life in general—although it is worth emphasizing that these authors are not counselling amorality and are very much concerned with ethics and justice.

Michael Stocker argues that we should reconsider dirty-hands cases as moral conflicts from which we can learn about the difficulty of acting rightly in both social and political life, although he does not dispute that dirty-hands dilemmas arise more naturally and frequently in politics. For him, "the immorality of the world can irredeemably stain our acts and lives," meaning that, in difficult circumstances, we cannot be both innocent and good since we must choose between ignoring moral obligations to act or committing a justifiable wrong. Yet, says Stocker, this paradox is not adequately addressed by most theoretical approaches. Instead, he seeks to show that dirty hands are *morally* challenging but not *conceptually* problematic: their troubling and conflicting nature must be recognized, but this can be done without sacrificing theoretical consistency.

Ronald Beiner aims to correct what he calls an imbalance in the literature dealing with dirty hands. Those who support such methods over-estimate the moral uniqueness of the political realm, since we can be confronted with the dirty-hands paradox in any realm of social life when confronting difficult circumstances. What Conor Cruise O'Brien's *Katanga and Back* illustrates, Beiner argues, is that the pull of dirty hands is "a universal human dilemma" such that even resolutely non-political actors can find themselves in situations "where the dirty-hands problem is inescapable."

For John Allett the moral questions raised by dirty-hands cases also extend well beyond the political. He finds Walzer's treatment of the dirty-hands dilemma very insightful and applies it to the thought of the great British playwright George Bernard Shaw, in a discussion of the exploration of dirty hands in plays written at different points in Shaw's career. Allett concludes on a cautionary note. He argues that Shaw departed from an earlier appreciation of the lessons of legitimate dirty-hands reasoning to move to an extreme defence of immorality for higher purposes. As a result, democratic sensibilities were eclipsed. So, while he is generally affirmative of much of Walzer's approach, Allett also has much in common with our Part Two authors because he uses Shaw's development to illustrate the dangers of one version of dirty-hands advocacy.

Tom Sorell's defence of dirty hands is in several respects at a midway point between Michael Walzer's arguments and those of Kai Nielsen in Part Two. He notes that utilitarian reasoning *can* acknowledge the feelings of dirty hands and that "one can get dirt on one's hands even from choosing the lesser of two evils." He claims that, because public morality is sufficiently different from private politics, it is therefore unique enough to be well-served by consequentialist approaches to ethical problems which will sometimes endorse dirty tactics. He also believes that citizens of a democracy may likely view dirty-hands politicians wrestling with their dilemmas with empathy rather than condemnation. Although Sorell is concerned that we not draw too large a gulf between public and personal considerations of morality and emphasizes the importance of personal responsibility in choosing to go into politics, he concludes that "it may be that the divide between public and private life does coincide with the boundary between utilitarian and non-utilitarian theories." In this respect his essay is reminiscent of traditional distinctions made by political realists about the differences between the moral obligations appropriate in public life and those in ordinary morality.

Leah Bradshaw also argues a case for dirty hands based on a distinction between the public and private realms, and she puts forth a particular interpretation of the writings of Hannah Arendt as support in this regard. For Arendt, according to Bradshaw, lying is not a symptom of corrupt politics, rather "it is politics"; though, paradoxically, "systematic lying always fails." We need political leaders who understand the difference between public and private realms and who will employ practical judgement rather than moral absolutes. Bradshaw goes on to make the provocative claim that a recognition of the legitimate place of dirty hands in politics is part of the tradition of western political thought stretching back to Plato and Aristotle and on to Arendt, for whom dirty acts are "the price one pays for human freedom. " The significance of all this, says Bradshaw, has been missed by contemporary feminist and post-modernist theorists.

The problem of extreme situations is a central theme in both Evan Simpson's and Arthur Applbaum's contributions. We must normally respect rights, as required by justice, says Simpson; yet, when the exigencies of public life justify an emphasis on expediency, our leaders ought to be prepared to countenance the harm that attends their making painful choices. What is called for, then, is what he calls hybrid thinking—a combination of deontological and utilitarian considerations—which can give us a better understanding of the "threshold" when extreme circumstances replace normality. Simpson's argument here places great store in perspicacious, independent judgement as to when a social context is such that "serious good beckons or evil threatens." When appropriate thresholds are recognized, it becomes clear when rights or utility should prevail, and the supposed moral conflict between the two options disappears.

The questions of if, when, and how violating rules can be justified is central to Arthur Applbaum's discussion. In fact he is critical of the sweeping rationalizations which are sometimes advanced by dirty-hands defenders and therefore has much in common with our Part Two authors. However, he suggests that under certain precise conditions, particularly when democratic institutions are not functioning well, and only after applying an elaborate set of moral tests, political actors can justifiably employ deception. While not in fact addressing directly the controversy over dirty hands, Applbaum raises questions about the ambiguous nature of democratic legitimacy. His conclusions are provocative in light of the imperatives of democracy as they are discussed in Part Two in essays by Yeo, Sutherland, and Shugarman.

Finally, readers should keep in mind that there are significant disagreements among the authors within each part of the book. And on many questions there is agreement between authors who are nevertheless on different sides of the issue. Our division of essays into different sides of the controversy over dirty-hands advocacy should not exaggerate the differences between them.

ONE

Dirty Hands and Ordinary Life

MICHAEL STOCKER

Can there be acts of dirty hands—acts that are justified, even obligatory, but nonetheless wrong and shameful? To borrow an example from Michael Walzer, can it be justified, even obligatory, for an official to torture someone to force him to tell where his fellows have hidden a time bomb among the innocent populace? And if, as Walzer suggests, it can be justified, even obligatory, to do this, can it also be wrong and shameful? This question has recently attracted much attention, but little agreement.[1]

More accurately, although there has been little agreement over the question of whether there can be cases of dirty hands, there has been widespread agreement that dirty-hands cases are conceptually problematic, even to the point of being contradictory. I will argue that they are conceptually unproblematic and are, indeed, instances of ordinary, everyday, evaluative phenomena. I will also argue that they have been thought problematic only because our ethical theories have over-concentrated on act evaluations and have misunderstood even these.

My goal, then, is at once to correct our ethical theories and also to show dirty hands as conceptually unproblematic. I will use each to accomplish the other. Thus, at times I will be concerned with general structures of action, choice, and evaluation, and at times with particularities of dirty hands.

The dirty-hands cases I am concerned with are (1) justified, even obligatory, but (2) nonetheless somehow wrong. Some call such situations dilemmas. But I reserve "dilemma" for cases where there is no right act open to the agent, and where every option is simply wrong. Others call acts that satisfy (1) and (2) conflicts. They are, indeed, conflicts. But they are a special sort of conflict—special even beyond what is given by (1) and (2). For they involve dirty acts, and not every wrong act is also a dirty act, nor does every conflict involving wrong acts involve dirty hands. These distinctions will come out below.

Some Structures of Overall, Action-Guiding Evaluations

Many think it impossible that an act be at once (1) justified, even obligatory, but also (2) none the less somehow wrong. I will argue that this seems problematic only because of serious errors made by our ethical theories. They over-concentrate on overall, action-guiding act evaluations, e.g. "ought," "right," and "duty."[2] Further, they misunderstand both what they over-concentrate on and other large portions of our evaluative world.

Much recent work in ethics has been on how to characterize action-guiding evaluations. We can ignore the controversies over these characterizations. What is of importance for us are two interrelated points of general agreement about such evaluations: that they are action-guiding, and that they are overall evaluations.

Let us turn first to action-guidingness. These evaluations say of acts whether they are or are not to be done. It is thus natural to restrict these evaluations to acts we can do and to hold that "ought" implies "can."[3] Usually, the "can" is understood causally. However, as is especially important for conflicts in general and dirty hands in particular, it must also be understood morally. This is to understand it in terms of what is morally possible—i.e., what is morally permissible.

Whether "can" is taken causally or morally, if "ought" implies "can" and if evaluations are action-guiding, what one cannot do cannot be what one ought to do. Turning now from act evaluations to agent evaluations, many take the doctrine that "ought" implies "can" as showing that an agent cannot be criticized for not doing what cannot be done. Thus, in these ways, to hold that "ought" implies "can" is to hold that doing exactly what is to be done—which some see as perfect practice—makes for a perfect act, or at least one such that neither it nor its agent can be faulted.

These understandings of the "ought" implies "can" doctrine thus deny moral relevance to impossible oughts—oughts we are unable to obey. Dirty hands, however, involve impossible oughts. What is morally unavoidable is said to tell against act and agent. In Walzer's example, even if the torture is justified, perhaps obligatory, it nonetheless stains both the act and the agent.

It is, of course, controversial whether torture in such a case, or ever, can be justified, let alone obligatory. But the same points can be made about not torturing the prisoner. Even if not torturing is justified, perhaps obligatory, what this involves can still tell against both the act and agent. Even if morality requires that the injuries and deaths of the innocents must be endured, they are matters of moral moment and matters for extreme regret.

Let us now turn to the second point of general agreement: that the act evaluations we are interested in are overall evaluations. These may, of course, be based on partial considerations, some of which tell for, and some against, doing some act. The evaluations we are interested in, however, speak with one unambivalent voice, telling us simply, for example, that we ought, or ought not, do a given act.

Dirty-hands cases, however, involve more than an overall, action-guiding evaluation. The partial, constituting values retain their moral relevance. So, in Walzer's example, the disvalue of the torture is not taken into account only in determining the overall value of authorizing it. (Nor is the disvalue of the deaths and injuries of the innocents taken into account only in determining the overall value of refusing to authorize it.) It remains as a disvalue even within that justified, perhaps obligatory, whole—a disvalue which is still there to be noted and regretted. As Bernard Williams says in "Ethical Consistency," the dirty feature is a remainder within the act.[4]

The dirty feature is taken into account first in determining the overall value of the act and again on its own. It is thus double-counted. Further, when it is taken up again on its own, it is taken up in an evaluation that is not action-guiding. Despite the dirty feature, the act is to be done. Nonetheless, because of the feature, the act is regrettable.

Dirty hands, thus, involve double-counted impossible oughts and non-action-guiding act evaluations. For these reasons, it is charged that dirty hands are impossible, or at the very least, involve severe conceptual problems.

Thomas Nagel, Walzer, Williams, and others hold that despite these conceptual problems, we must recognize that there are dirty hands. Richard Brandt, R. M. Hare, and others, in large measure because of these problems, hold that claims about dirty hands must be explained away—e.g., as a bad mixture of heuristics and ethics. They hold that people must be alive to moral costs, but that if an act is right overall and if the agent is justified in thinking it right overall, then this is all there is to think about it morally. The act is wholly unexceptionable, and the agent has nothing to regret or feel shame or guilt about.

I will present a third option. Even though dirty hands are morally problematic, they are conceptually unproblematic. Double-counted impossible oughts and non-action-guiding act evaluations are perfectly general and conceptually unproblematic features of our acts. Further, the reasons advanced to show their incoherence, instead of embodying good moral or conceptual sense, depend on radically implausible views of value and action. Thus, to be adequate, ethical theories must allow for dirty hands, for impossible oughts, and for non-action-guiding act evaluations.

Some Foundational Features of Choice and Action

We can begin to show why adequate theories must allow for these by examining two features of dirty hands: they are cases of moral conflict, and they are cases where one is morally compromised in doing what is morally justified, perhaps required.

Consider, then, a current account of conflict given in terms of incompossibility:[5] there is a conflict of value where (1) x has value, (2) y has value, and (3) it is possible for either x or y, but not both, to be actualized. Correlatively, there is a conflict of desire where (1) x is desired, (2) y is desired, and (3) it is possible to get either x or y but not both.

However, a foundational point about choice, and thus about action, is that a choice is a choice of which values and desires to satisfy and which not to satisfy. For, except in the rarest of cases, there are evaluative and desiderative considerations for doing each of the jointly impossible acts. Thus, in the sense given by the incompossibility account, virtually every choice and act involves conflict. But unless one's life is unfortunate beyond description, it is false that almost every choice and act is conflicting or problematic. Similarly, nearly every choice and act requires a compromise between values, even moral values. But again, unless one's life is unfortunate beyond description, not all such compromises are compromising. Thus, the incompossibility account does not show what is problematic, or even that there is anything problematic, about conflicts. Similarly for dirty hands and being compromised in doing what is justified.[6]

A cost considered qua cost, and not qua what it is a cost for, is better not endured than endured. But what it is a cost for can, despite its having a cost, be better had than not had. Thus, the general structure of choice involves having to forgo what is valued and in this way suffering losses.

My claim so far is that it is perfectly general and conceptually unproblematic that almost every act has costs and that these can be seen at once as costs and also as justified. This, of course, is to say that it is perfectly general and conceptually unproblematic to double-count those costs: once in taking them as costs and once in holding that despite their being costs, what they are costs for is justified. It is also to make a non-action-guiding act evaluation. That the cost is to be borne is an action-guiding act evaluation. That the act none the less has a cost is, or grounds, a non-action-guiding act evaluation.

Thus, double-counted unavoidable costs and non-action-guiding act evaluations are perfectly general and conceptually unproblematic. Why, then, would we think dirty hands problematic, much less incoherent?

How Are These Costs Taken Up?

Whether or not the parallel between ordinary acts and dirty hands is accepted, the common and non-dirty features—double-counted unavoidable costs and non-action-guiding act evaluations—can play many of the structural roles which lead philosophers to hold that dirty hands are conceptually problematic, if not incoherent. (Nonetheless, as will be discussed, dirty-hands acts are not simply ordinary acts and the dirty part is not just one cost, or one source of disvalue, among others).

To see this, we can start by noting that many justified costs are also regretted. Sometimes regretting them is justified, even required, as will be taken up below. But sometimes it is not justified. Some people regret what should not bother any reasonable person: e.g. having to pay a completely reasonable charge for a dinner in a restaurant, rather than being given it as a present by the proprietor. Consider also what we might call a taxi-meter sensibility of accurately noting the cost of everything. For someone with such a sensibility, there would be intertwined with the pleasure of giving a present to a child a full awareness of its cost.

Clearly, we must go beyond the empirical issue of which conflicts and double-counted costs and oughts are noted. We must confront the issues of which should be taken up and how they should be taken up. We must, that is, turn to an ethics and a moral psychology of attention and involvement—as found in Aristotle, Weil, and Murdoch.

As these theorists show, some conflicts and some double-counted costs and oughts should not be taken up at all, and certainly not with regret. But some others, despite its being permissible or even obligatory to bear them, are quite properly taken up, and with regret. Here we might consider the following cases: (1) jettisoning goods in a storm to save the ship and crew (as in the *Nicomachean Ethics* 3.1), (2) paying taxes, (3) the pain caused by filling a cavity, (4) giving up one's education to take a job in order to support one's family, (5) choosing between a job and a family.

The Special Moral Nature of Dirty Features

An obvious reply to my argument is that in dirty-hands cases, unlike in ordinary ones, what is double-counted has a particular moral character which makes dirty hands problematic. The dirtying features of dirty hands—the double-counted impossible oughts, the remainders—are in important ways moral costs. But so is the loss of an education.

As a second attempt, we might thus qualify the claim about the dirty features and say that these are absolutely wrong in the sense of being always wrong: their wrongness is not overridden. What does get overridden in dirty-hands cases, is the action-guidingness of the dirty features. Ethicists have focused so exclusively on what is action-guiding that they fail to distinguish it from wrongness and have thus been unable to allow for or understand dirty hands.[7] But giving up one's education to support one's family may also always be wrong in a way that grounds compunction. So we still need a way to characterize dirty-hands cases.

Let us start by noting that among the dirty features of dirty hands are people being wronged. They and their trust, integrity, and status as ends are violated, dishonoured, and betrayed; innocents are killed, tortured, lied to, deceived. Dirty hands can also involve other sorts of harms and wrongs— e.g., the destruction of a holy place or a great work of art. They sometimes involve the violation of a principle rather than a person: e.g., agreeing not to prosecute terrorists in order to end a hijacking.

I think we can get at the special nature of these dirty moral costs—and show that they are not simply costs, nor even simply moral costs—by examining what sort of moral conflicts they involve.[8] So for example, not benefiting someone and, more clearly, harming someone—perhaps most clearly, harming a friend or loved one—may always be ground for conflict and regret. But the wrong that is the ground of the conflict of dirty hands goes beyond not benefiting or harming. As said already, it is a violation and a betrayal of a person, value, or principle.

In paradigm cases of dirty hands, the costs are important moral costs: e.g. to save one's country in a desperate war, one betrays an innocent person, perhaps even an innocent friend, to those trying to kill him. But dirty hands, or at least slightly soiled fingers, can involve less important wrongs—e.g., to deceive the enemy into thinking that his loyalties have changed, a secret agent publicly insults his old teacher.

These, it might be remarked, all involve political, or at least institutional, and public immoralities. This might suggest that dirty hands are morally peculiar because they involve politics and, indeed, that they are morally peculiar in just the ways that politics are. After all, we always knew that politics is a particularly dirty business. As Walzer reminds us,[9] Machiavelli argued that rulers must learn not to be good, and Hoederer, in Sartre's play *Dirty Hands*, holds that it is not possible to govern both well and innocently. Thus, politics is not a home for ethics and shows little about ethics—except its limits.

However, the non-political, including the personal, also allows for dirty hands. Suppose that the marriage of my cousin has been seriously troubled but is now on the mend. Pleased for the couple, I offer to do whatever I can. Drawing me aside, my cousin says there is something I can do. As her husband suspects, she had been having an affair. Unless his suspicions are allayed, there will be no chance of reconciliation. For both her sake and his, she asks me to help convince him that she did not have the affair. She asks me to help her keep the truth from him, perhaps even to deceive or lie to him. This, I suggest, can involve dirty hands.

Some Features of Dirty Hands and Similar Acts

If dirty hands involve a violation of a person, principle, or value, two related issues must be addressed. It must be shown how, given that it is a violation, it can be justified, and also how, given that it is justified, even necessary, it can be a violation.

We can make some headway on both questions by starting with the fact that, at least in many cases, the circumstances which justify the dirty hands are themselves immoral. In Aristotle's case of having to do what is base to save one's family, there are the tyrant's immoral threats.[10] In Walzer's torture case and in Nagel's case of bombing enemy civilians to break their country's will, there are the immoralities of war. And in another of Walzer's cases, that of acceding to a corrupt ward boss's demands for a bribe, there are the immoral demands and implied threats.

I think it difficult to overestimate the importance of the role of immorality in creating situations which necessitate and justify acting with dirty hands. In at least many cases, including those just mentioned, were it not for the immorality, there would be no need or room for dirty hands. The issue is important enough to stop and show that the immorality of the circumstances can provide the specific difference between cases of dirty hands and other cases.

Consider a case presented by Patricia Greenspan: a doctor who, through no one's fault, has to choose between saving one patient or the other or—what is unthinkable for the doctor—letting them both die. The choice clearly can involve regrets, perhaps even anguish. But it does not seem to involve dirty hands. Contrast this with the case of Sophie from Styron's *Sophie's Choice*. Upon entering a Nazi concentration camp with her two children, she is told by an officer that only one of the children will be allowed to live, that she must choose which of them this will be, and that if she does not choose, both will be killed. She picks one. And does so with dirty hands.

The contrast with the doctor's case is not only that Sophie has strong, special obligations. Doctors have such obligations to their patients. Nor is the contrast due to the fact that she is the child's mother. For if, simply through natural calamity, people have to choose which of their desperately undernourished children will get the required food and which will not—i.e., which will live and which will die—the death can be double-counted

33

and a source of continuing anguish. But this does not seem to involve dirty hands.

I think it is not enough to say simply that the justifying and necessitating circumstances of these cases of dirty hands are themselves immoral. They are violations of moral autonomy and selfhood—and this in a particularly vicious way. The agent is immorally coerced to take part in, perhaps even to help implement, an immoral project.

Many of the clearest cases of dirty hands involve such immoral coercion. And, as just seen, immoral coercion is the specific difference between at least some acts of dirty hands and other similar acts which do not involve dirty hands, even though they too are justified but nonetheless somehow wrong. Some further comments and examples would be useful here.

Suppose that someone has embezzled from my account, leaving me enough to pay only some of my creditors. Repaying those to whom I have the strongest obligation and not repaying the others would be justified, even obligatory. But this act does not seem a case of dirty hands. One way to put this is that the relevant ought-judgment here is more clearly of the situation than of my act: "It ought to be that I be able to repay them" or "I ought to be able to repay them" rather than "I ought to repay them." Yet this act is similar in important ways to the paradigm of dirty hands—the case where one agent is morally forced by someone else's immorality to do what is, or otherwise would be, wrong.

Even though I was forced by another's immorality to choose not to repay some creditors, I was not forced to choose to help implement that person's evil project. For, as the case is naturally taken, the embezzler wants my money simply to have it to spend. Had the embezzler instead been intent on immorally harming those I would thus be unable to repay—and more clearly, intent on forcing me to help implement this immoral project—my non-repayment would then be, or come very close to being, an act of dirty hands. It is important here that it is another's immoral plan that is to be implemented. Note also that it is the circumstances of dirty hands which at once necessitate and also justify the wrongful act.

These, then, are some considerations in favour of the suggestion that what is special about dirty hands, setting them apart from other conflicts where one is unable to avoid doing what is wrong, is that they involve being coerced to help implement another's evil project. Even if this claim is right about only some important cases of dirty hands, it is important in at least the following five ways.

First, it helps show why dirty hands, despite being morally very problematic, are not conceptually problematic. For whatever can be said about being immorally coerced to help another's immoral project, it cannot be said that it is conceptually incoherent or even problematic.

Second, we can see in what way Nagel is right to hold that in dirty-hands cases we are prevented from engaging in the proper reaction to evil—fighting it—and are, rather, forced to help implement it. It is not that we, even temporarily, have adopted an evil end, much less adopted evil as our end.

Third, we see why politics is so naturally a home for dirty hands—if, as many hold, it is also the natural home of immorality and immoral coercion. We also see why dirty hands are also found outside politics.

Fourth, insofar as immoral circumstances are important for dirty hands, it is only to be expected that dirty hands are morally so difficult. As we know, one of the most intractable moral problems is how to act morally in immoral situations.[11]

Fifth, dirty hands remind us of the perhaps archaic view that the immorality of the world can irredeemably stain our acts and lives. They show that not only one's own immoralities, but also another's immoralities, can make it impossible to avoid doing what is immoral. They show, contrary to a Kantian theme, that our acts are not always fresh moral starts. Their moral nature depends sometimes not only on us and what we can do at the time of the act, but also on what we have done previously. It can also depend on others and what they do. (We thus see that the moral nature of our acts is in the same mixed category as meaningfulness and Aristotelian *eudaimonia*: importantly within our control but also importantly outside our control.)

These five points clearly show the importance of the connection between dirty hands and being coerced to implement another person's evil plans. But for a fuller understanding of dirty hands, some other points should be made—some supporting and some taking away from that connection.

I earlier said that "the wrong and the ground of conflict of acts of dirty hands goes beyond not benefiting or harming ... it is a violation and a betrayal of a person, value, or principle." However it is clear that there can be violations and betrayals which are justified, but not because they involve being morally coerced into helping implement another's evil project.

To modify a case already mentioned, if people stupidly—only stupidly, not immorally—waste their money, they may have no choice but to let down, even betray, others and the trust others have placed in them, and thus to violate important principles. We might here consider parents who have been stupid with their money, and who are thus unable to help pay for a child's education, but must instead spend their remaining money on necessities and on re-paying serious and pressing debts.

However, this does not seem to be a case of dirty hands despite the fact that what is done is—although justified or even obligatory—regrettable, shameful, and perhaps even morally humiliating. Thus, instead of showing that justified betrayals and violations do not require immoral coercion, this case may rather show that not all justified betrayals and violations involve dirty hands.

Perhaps, however, some justified betrayals and violations which do not involve immoral coercion are cases of dirty hands. In particular, perhaps circumstances which are only very difficult, and do not involve immoral coercion, can justify betrayals and violations which are cases of dirty hands.

Consider these three situations: first, that of a military commander who, through stupidity or simple bad luck, orders his men into an untenable situation and then, to avoid still greater damage to the pursuit of the battle, has to abandon them to their fate. Second, a case in which, to get the best candidate appointed, one allows immoral (e.g., racist or sexist) jokes about other candidates to go unchallenged. Third, circumstances under which to do useful research, one accepts dirty money.[12]

It is clear that these acts involve harms, perhaps wrongs, and also betrayals and violations. It is also clear that they involve, perhaps require, regrets and even compunction. I have found considerable agreement that these cases do involve dirty hands.

If immoral coercion is not necessary in all cases of dirty hands, we might wonder why it is so important, perhaps even necessary, in others. And if it is not always necessary, we might wonder why it is so difficult to construct very serious—i.e., very immoral—cases of dirty hands which do not involve immoral coercion and so easy to construct very serious cases of dirty hands which do involve immoral coercion.

At least the beginnings of a general answer has, in effect, already been given. Dirty-hands cases do not simply involve mere bads and harms. Nor, therefore, are they wrong simply because they involve these. Rather, they involve betrayals and violations of people, principles, or values.

It should also be remembered that an evil person can make it near enough impossible for others who are moved by moral considerations to avoid moral violations. Also, that an act that will help implement an evil plan is, itself, a strong moral reason not to do it. Morality requires us not to co-operate with evil and often to help fight it. It is, itself, a violation to do what one is immorally coerced into doing. Yet to have to do what is a violation because one has been immorally coerced to do it seems an evil which goes beyond the mere combination of being coerced by an evil person with having to act so as to help implement an evil plan. What I mean is suggested by a related sort of case. Simply because we do not want to do it, it can be painful to do what, on its own, we do not want to do. So too, simply because we hate the person, it can be painful to do what someone we hate tells, or simply wants, us to do. But the pain of these combined can exceed by far the "sum" of these pains. I mean the pain of doing what, on its own, we do not want to do when, further, we have been made to do it by someone we hate.

To the extent that these last suggestions are well taken, we can see why immoral coercion may well not be necessary for dirty hands. But we can also see why it is so important for dirty hands, especially for serious cases of dirty hands.

After all, being dirty is not peculiar to cases of dirty hands. Many other acts are dirty in just the ways that dirty-hands cases are dirty. What is special about cases of dirty hands then is not that they are dirty, but that they are nonetheless justified or even obligatory. And the reasons they are justified or even obligatory are the usual sorts of reasons that other acts are justified. Nor are dirty-hands cases special because they involve costs, remainders, or conflicts. Many other acts involve these, too.

Put generally, then, it is unclear why non-action-guiding act evaluations of double-counted impossible oughts should be thought conceptually problematic. Put more particularly, it is unclear why dirty-hands cases should be thought conceptually problematic.

As with worlds and lives, so with acts: there is no need to confuse what is here and now best or right with what is perfectly good or wholly right. Even what is best or right can have features that are, and remain, bad or wrong. One can be justified in doing an act that ineliminably has a part which be wrong to do on its own—and, more importantly for us, remains a wrong, albeit a justified wrong, when done in doing what is right.

Moral Emotions and Dirty Hands

Moral remainders do not give the whole story of dirty hands. Double-counted impossible oughts are not only had by acts of dirty hands; they are also taken up and noted, for example, with regret. Further, acting with dirty hands is said to rob us of our innocence and to require shame and guilt. Some comments on how this is possible and, again, unproblematic will be useful. This will advance our understanding of dirty hands, and more generally of non-action-guiding act evaluations.

We can see how acts which are justified or even obligatory can provide the ground of regret, shame, or guilt. (For our purposes, we need not distinguish shame and guilt.) Those acts can contain the objects of those emotions—namely, the double-counted remainders. These, of course, are also the grounds of the non-action-guiding act evaluations. And here it must be remembered that those who act with dirty hands do not merely cause what is terrible. They have chosen, even if coerced, to bring about what is terrible.

Even if it is agreed that there are objects for those emotions, two reasons might be advanced to show that it is pernicious to think that those emotions could be warranted. First, it might seem that if an act merits regret, shame, or guilt, it should not be done wholeheartedly, if done at all. Thus it would seem that dirty hands could be done only with vacillation and uncertainty. But if such acts are to be done, it may well be better that they be done well—i.e., resolutely and wholeheartedly.

This worry is not pointless. Some people faced with mixed considerations do vacillate. To act resolutely, they need to see an act as being of only one clear moral sort. But other people are able to act resolutely, and in this sense wholeheartedly, even where they see moral mixtures, and in this sense are not wholehearted. They are able to form a unified view of a whole, even though they still see the parts of the whole as parts.

The second charge of moral perniciousness starts from the fact that shame and guilt involve retributive negative feelings, which the agent and others can take to be deserved. These can involve the desire for atonement and cleansing, e.g., by punishment. The charge continues that just as it would be immoral to exact judicial punishment on agents of dirty acts—after all, they are doing what is right, even obligatory—so it is a moral error for anyone, including the agents themselves, to think they deserve blame and other punishment.

The reason guilt or shame would be mistaken, we are told, is that they require a connection between agents and the grounds of the guilt or shame: I cannot be ashamed of or feel guilty about something unless, as I take things, I am connected with it in such a way that it reflects poorly on me. But, as just noted, the agents we are concerned with are not culpable for the dirty part of the dirty act. Therefore, it does not reflect poorly on them. And therefore, both morally and conceptually, they cannot be ashamed of or guilty about it.

But there are other forms of shame and guilt which do not require culpability. For example, there is shame and guilt in regard to one's ancestors or to one's fellow citizens, colleagues, and others with whom one identifies. So too, there is shame and guilt over what one merely brings about—e.g., the shame and guilt even a careful driver might feel over the death of a child who suddenly darts in front of the car.[13]

Let us now turn to third-person judgements. There are various ways we regard other people who have done what merits shame or guilt. Some, of course, we blame in a fully retributive way, thinking they deserve condemnation and punishment. Some we only pity, and some we admire for how they bear their moral burdens, such as being immorally coerced to help implement another's evil project. Even, indeed especially, in this last case we can feel fortunate to have been spared their moral burden of guilt and shame and also, at least as importantly, their moral burden of having done what occasions and justifies their guilt and shame.

Thus, there need be no conceptual or moral error in thinking that even though agents of dirty hands are morally unable to avoid the dirty act, they can and should feel guilty and ashamed for doing it. Nor need there be any error in thinking that they can or should feel the need for atonement and cleansing, e.g. by punishment. Not all sorts of guilt and shame require culpability, and one and the same thing can be a punishment or a cure. Thus, we must reject those views which find shame and guilt over dirty hands conceptually or morally incoherent.

But even if they are recognized as coherent, it is asked why these emotions should be felt. The issues here are complex, but a brief reply should be useful. These emotions are important, and indeed morally important, for the reasons it is important for people to have the correct emotions: because they are central and essential constituents of human life.

As Aristotle stressed, a good life requires one to act well and also to have the right emotions. We can reinforce this by noting what so many ethicists now seem to have forgotten: a life without emotions would be at best a pathologically deficient life—perhaps the life of a severe schizophrenic, psychopath, or sociopath.[14] Emotions are not simply part of the phenomenology of morality, much less its epiphenomenology. They are at the heart of it.

We must, then, reject the charge that guilt and shame over dirty hands are incoherent or morally unimportant. But we should also question the contrary claim that dirty hands must evoke guilt and shame. For example, Walzer and others hold that those who act with dirty hands should suffer from guilt and shame, because their suffering shows that they are good people who know the gravity of what they do. It is said that those who do not regret their acts of dirty hands either do not see or do not care that they are bad.

We must, however, at the least take into account different forms of moral and emotional character. We should contrast the emotional warmth Aristotle requires for good people with Stoic and Buddhist coolness. So too, we should note that some good people are emotionally hotter and others cooler. Sometimes a strong emotion shows care for the forgone value, and coolness shows a lack of care. But sometimes heat is shallow and synthetic, show and bluster, while coolness goes along with a quiet, deep appreciation of the value. Thus, even though it is clear that some good people show their goodness by shame and guilt over dirty hands, it is unclear that all good people do.[15]

Dirty Hands and Acceptable Moral Theories

At the outset I claimed that double-counting and giving moral weight to impossible oughts and allowing for non-action-guiding act evaluations are what make dirty hands seem conceptually problematic. I have been concerned to argue that these are not restricted to the extreme and disquieting cases of dirty hands in particular and conflicts more generally. They are found across the board—in important and unimportant cases, in the centre and at the extremes, in political and private cases. They cannot, therefore, be passed off as aberrations found at the outer limits of ethical theory. Instead of being mysterious or objectionable, they are commonplace and unproblematic.

My point is not that we can show *prima facie* objectionable features to be unobjectionable by showing that they occur all over the place. The world can be generally objectionable. Rather it is, first, that those features are clearly not objectionable where they are not conflicting; and second, that I cannot see any relevant differences between those cases and those where they are conflicting.

My argument to show that dirty hands are conceptually un-problematic has focused on the similarities between them and other cases which present no conceptual problems. It will be useful to see that the same conclusion follows from focusing on three differences.

First, the loss of some values is not even regrettable. Suffering those losses is not regrettable in the circumstances, or perhaps at all, and we should not spend any time regretting them. But matters are different for some other losses, including those involved in dirty hands.

Second, the non-regrettable conflicts are often shown to be non-regrettable by showing that they really do not matter. From a moral perspective, they are really not important. Thus, we may have an outside and a higher standpoint from which to see that they are unimportant. But we cannot have this for the conflicts of dirty hands. They are important and they are moral.

Third, it does not seem possible for finite beings to live and act without having to choose between values and thus without having to suffer losses. But it does seem possible, even if humanly very unlikely, to live and act without having to suffer the losses of dirty hands. At the least, it does seem possible, even if humanly very unlikely, that we not create immoral situations which necessitate dirty hands.

These three differences, however, do not seem to me to show a conceptual incoherence. The first merely attests to the fact that dirty hands involve moral conflicts. The second fails to understand that no matter what level the *moral* judgement, it is nonetheless a moral *judgement*.

The third difference points, not to conceptual incoherence, but to the grounds for moral sadness or even outrage. Even good people may be unable to remain innocent or avoid shame, guilt, and emotional devastation—here caused by doing what is immoral.

We must not confuse this with the possibility that even good people, acting morally, may be unable to avoid acting evilly, in ways meriting full retributive shame, guilt, and punishment. Having avoided that confusion, we can recognize that even without any shame and guilt, much less dirty hands, good people can and do lose their innocence and wholeness and indeed suffer emotional devastation—e.g., by their family being killed by evil people or by a natural disaster.

The demand that it must be possible for us to be good and also innocent, and also to retain emotional wholeness, is not a demand for a conceptually or even a morally coherent morality. It is, rather, a demand for something else—a morally good world, or at least not an evil or bad world. But our world is not a morally good world. We therefore need to know more than simply what is to be done and how to avoid culpability. We need a moral theory that allows for and indeed gives prominence to dirty hands and thus double-counting, impossible oughts, and non-action-guiding act evaluations.

Notes

This is a slightly revised and abridged version of Michael Stocker, *Plural and Conflicting Values* (Oxford: Oxford University Press, 1990) Chapter 1.

1 For example: M. Merleau-Ponty, *Humanism and Terror* (Boston: Beacon Press, 1971); T. Nagel, "War and Massacre," *Philosophy and Public Affairs* 1 (1972): 123-44; M. Walzer, "Political Action: The Problem of Dirty Hands," *Philosophy and Public Affairs* 2:2 (1973): 160-80; R. Brandt, "Utilitarianism and the Rules of War," *Philosophy and Public Affairs* 1 (1972): 145-65; R. M. Hare, "Rules of War and Moral Reasoning," *Philosophy and Public Affairs* 1 (1972): 166-81; B. Williams, "Ethical Consistency" and "Consistency and Realism," *Problems of the Self* (Cambridge: Cambridge University Press, 1973); R. Marcus, "Moral Dilemmas and Ethical Consistency," *Journal of Philosophy* 77 (1980): 121-36; P. Greenspan, "Moral Dilemmas and Guilt," *Philosophical Studies* 43 (1983): 117-25; C. Korsgaard, "The Right to Lie: Kant on Dealing with Evil," *Philosophy and Public Affairs* 15 (1986): 325-49; I. Levi, *Hard Choices* (Cambridge: Cambridge University Press, 1986).

2 On the excessiveness of the concern, see my "Act and Agent Evaluations," *The Review of Metaphysics* 27 (1973): 42-61; "Rightness and Goodness: Is There a Difference?," *American Philosophical Quarterly* 10 (1973): 87-98, and "The Schizophrenia of Modern Ethical Theories," *Journal of Philosophy* 73 (1976): 453-66.

3 See my "'Ought' and 'Can,'" *Australasian Journal of Philosophy* 49 (l971): 303-16.

4 Williams, "Ethical Consistency" 179.

5 See e.g., F. Jackson, "Internal Conflicts in Desires and Morals," *American Philosophical Quarterly* 22 (l985): 105-14. See also Williams, "Ethical Consistency," 167ff.

6 Nonetheless, that account helps us see a foundational point about choice and action: acts have costs. Acts typically involve, and some acts simply are, means which are not also ends.

7 cf. W.D. Ross, *The Right and the Good* (Oxford: Oxford University Press, 1963).

8 My thanks are owed to Kimon Lycos for help here.

9 Walzer 164.

10 *Nicomachean Ethics* 3.1, 1110a6 ff.

11 On this, see e.g., John Rawls, *A Theory of Justice* (Oxford: Clarendon, 1971) on non-ideal theories. See also Korsgaard, 341 ff.

12 My thanks are owed to John Robertson for the first two of these cases, and to him and Emily Robertson for discussion of them and the general importance of immoral coercion. My thanks are owed to Patricia Greenspan for the final case.

13 See H. Morris, *On Guilt and Innocence* (Berkeley: University of California Press, 1976); R. M. Adams, "Involuntary Sins," *Philosophical Review* 94 (1985), 3-31.

14 See e.g., my "The Schizophrenia of Modern Ethical Theories," and "Psychic Feelings: Their Importance and Irreducibility," *Australasian Journal of Philosophy* 61 (1983): 5-26; my "Affectivity and Self-Concern: The Assumed Psychology in Aristotle's Ethics," *Pacific Philosophical Quarterly* 64 (1983): 211-29; and Michael Stocker and Elizabeth Hegeman, *Valuing Emotions* (Cambridge: Cambridge University Press, 1996).

15 My thanks are owed to David Armstrong here. See also my "Affectivity and Self-Concern."

Missionaries and Mercenaries

RONALD BEINER

I borrow my title from Chapter 9 of Conor Cruise O'Brien's book, *To Katanga and Back*. O'Brien's book relates his experiences as UN representative in Elisabethville, trying to defuse the crisis provoked by a successionist government in the southernmost province of what was formerly the Belgian Congo. His mission on behalf of the UN was to expel the European military and political advisors and European mercenaries who were crucial in sustaining the successionist regime. One of the stories that O'Brien tells concerns the relationship between missionaries, who are in the Congo to minister to the souls of Africans, and hired *gendarmerie*, who are in the Congo to protect the interests of Belgian capital.

> Months afterwards, after my resignation, I was asked to give a German television team, bound for the Congo, some briefing on the UN operation in Katanga. I told them that our main difficulty had been the mercenaries. I talked about the technical problems of apprehending and expelling mercenaries, how hard it was to track them down, how often they had come back through Rhodesia and had to be caught and expelled again, and so on. I noticed that my listeners were first startled, then increasingly horrified. I was puzzled by this apparently excessive reaction until I found that when I said "mercenaries" they thought I was saying "missionaries."
>
> It is probable that, to some missionaries, especially in Baluba territory, the confusion would not have seemed altogether ludicrous. For the missionaries had identified themselves to such an extent with the régime of which the mercenaries are the main prop, that in many regions of Katanga the missionaries cannot live in safety unless the mercenaries are at hand. In a very real sense, therefore, the UN *was* expelling the missionaries, at least from some areas and for a time, because it expelled the people who protected them. It is a hard fact for

the UN to face, and its implications are also hard for the missionaries themselves.[1]

Now, O'Brien makes clear that while he thinks better of these missionaries than he does of the mercenaries, his sympathy for the former group is by no means unqualified. He compares their typical cultural attitudes towards their African constituency to the racial attitudes of "a Dixie mob on one of its bad days."[2] But the point is not whether these missionaries are paragons of saintliness, but that they are in Africa (in certain respects) to serve the welfare of the black African population, and that they are dependent on the agents of a thuggish regime in order to carry on their work.

Exactly what does it mean to be dependent on the mercenaries of Katanga? O'Brien spells this out in very blunt detail.

> The reason why the gendarmerie, unlike the UN, could furnish effective protection was that the UN could not, and the *gendarmerie* could and did…employ *la manière forte* of collective punishment. If, in a given region, large elements of the local population, enjoying widespread sympathy, hate Europeans enough—for whatever reason—to want to kill them on sight, there is only one way in which a relatively small but well-equipped force can protect Europeans, and that is by terror. The Bishop of Kongolo must have known, and known better than I did, that the 'freedom of movement of the gendarmerie' meant freedom to burn villages, and to do certain other things of which some ex-gendarmerie officers have since boasted. He must have known also that these actions had a double effect: on the short term, they made the lives of missionaries and other Europeans more secure; in the longer run they were adding fuel to the flames of deadly hatred which similar actions in the past had kindled. The Bishop of Kongolo had, therefore, only too good reason for the anxiety which he felt on learning that the UN had, in effect, given a negative answer to a question which had hitherto, with his acquiescence, been answered positively. That question was: 'Is it permissible to burn villages in order to protect the lives of missionaries?'[3]

There would be no dirty hands problem if we were content to answer this last question in the negative and leave it at that. But O'Brien has another story to tell, and it indeed raises the dirty hands problem in all its force. It concerns an American missionary, a Seventh Day Adventist named Reverend Robinson who, unlike his Belgian Catholic counterparts, was not particularly concerned about the legitimacy or desirability of an independent State of Katanga. He was simply committed to feeding starving Africans.

> But at this time he could not go into the worst-affected parts of North Katanga without the co-operation of the gendarmerie: if he had tried, he would probably have been killed by the Baluba, in what had become their almost blind hostility to Europeans and especially missionaries. The result was that the aid was distributed under gendarmerie auspices, and within the framework, effectively, of Captain Labourdonnais's 'psychological warfare.' It is true, even so, that it is better that the people were fed than that they should have starved: 'warfare' by feeding people is better than 'warfare' by killing and burning. Yet the two kinds of warfare were systematically interconnected: the stick for those who refused to submit to the authority of the secessionist State, the carrot for those who submitted because they did not wish to starve.[4]

So: feeding starving people is a good thing; but one can only feed the starving if one is safe from the prospect of being murdered by European-hating Africans, and in this specific situation, such a guarantee is only available in practice from colonialist mercenaries who specialize in burning down huts and razing villages. What does one do in this situation? O'Brien himself, for all his horror at the village-razing tactics of the *gendarmerie*, concedes that the missionary had no choice: "For the life of me, I cannot see that the Reverend Robinson could have acted otherwise than he did."[5] A classic dirty hands situation!

Let me now confess that I have a theoretical point to pursue, albeit a modest one. O'Brien's story helps to highlight a deficiency or an imbalance in the most influential discussions of the morality of dirty hands. We commonly assume that dirty-hands is a problem that applies specifically to politicians or agents of the state. Politics is a dirty business, and so dirty hands is an entailment of the dirtiness of the political game. (You can't make omelettes without breaking a few eggs, etc.) According to the terms used by some philosophers, there is such a thing as "public morality" which is quite distinct in its character and in its ethical demands from "private morality," and—it is assumed—politicians and state officials are, paradigmatically, the agents of public morality, or the ones who must cope with its demands.[6] This way of thinking, of course, goes all the way back to Machiavelli, the arch-theorist of dirty-hands morality. The heart of Machiavelli's concerns is defined by the imperative deeds of the indispensable prince who knows he must forgo—and is willing to forgo—salvation of his own soul in order to save his fatherland; for instance, the iron-fisted policy of Cesare Borgia in the Romagna.[7] Machiavelli states his central doctrine in Chapter 15 of *The Prince*: "a man who wants to make a profession of good in all regards must come to ruin among so many who are not good. Hence it is necessary *to a prince*, if he wants to maintain himself, to learn to be able not to be good, and to use this and not use it according to necessity."[8] Acting according to conventional morality may be possible for private citizens; but it is an impossible luxury for those who dive into the pool of politics, and who therefore swim among barracudas. The same assumptions are shared by Max Weber in his classic discussion of the dirty-hands problem in "Politics as a Vocation." The context of his famous distinction between an "ethic of ultimate ends" and an "ethic of responsibility" is an analysis, throughout the text, of what it means to live the life of those he explicitly refers to as *professional* politicians, those who deliberately embrace politics and political responsibility as a "vocation" or a "calling," as opposed to the great majority of citizens who bear only a tangential or occasional relationship to political life.[9] In Weber's view it is specifically the political *professionals*—those who aspire to a position of leadership and, in making this commitment to a definite form of life, know that they have sold their soul to the devil—who are inexorably bound to the logic of the ethics of responsibility.[10] To cite another notable work in this *Realpolitik* tradition, Maurice Merleau-Ponty in *Humanism and Terror* also focuses on the moral bind faced by politicians: "since he is concerned to govern others, political man cannot complain of being judged for acts whose consequences others must bear.... In accepting the chance of glory in the role of politician, he accepts also the risk of infamy.... Political action is of its nature impure.... There is no politician who can flatter himself upon his innocence."[11]

As can be easily documented, more recent works in the dirty hands literature similarly presume that dirty hands is a problem that pertains to politicians and public officials. According to Bernard Williams, the problem of dirty hands involves "cases where the politician does something morally disagreeable."[12] For Michael Walzer, dirty hands refers to the problem of whether "those who govern us" can govern well—that is, "measure up to the duties of [their] office"—without losing their innocence: "the sort of actor I am considering ... acts in an official capacity."[13] Walzer's reflections on the problem are directed towards the "moral politician" whose *guilt* over the fact that his hands are dirty proves "that he is not too good for politics and that he is good enough."[14] Finally, Steven Lukes says that the problem pertains to "the character of *politicians* and the virtues they typically develop": "*they* [the politicians] must regularly confront this problem on behalf of the rest of us."[15] Hence it seems to be a deeply entrenched assumption throughout this literature that dirty hands is primarily a politician's problem—or at least that it is a citizen's problem only insofar as we non-politicians must worry about the moral implications of the fact that our politicians and public officials are, seemingly as a matter of occupational necessity, so morally contaminated.

I don't want to suggest that theorists in this tradition are completely oblivious to dirty hands problems in private life. After all, Machiavelli is the author not only of *The Prince* but also of *Mandragola*, and the protagonists in the latter work are no less crafty, deceitful, and manipulative than those in the former. It is not one of his princes, but instead his conniving Friar Timoteo in *Mandragola*, who utters the Machiavellian doctrine: "when confronted with a good that is certain and an evil that is uncertain, one must never renounce that good for fear of that evil."[16] There are some acknowledgments from recent theorists of dirty hands, as well, that dirty hands predicaments are not the exclusive property of politicians and actors in the expressly political arena. Walzer is clearly committed to a public morality/private morality split in the following passage: "Politicians often argue that they have no right to keep their hands clean, and that may well be true of them, but it is not so clearly true of the rest of us."[17] But he also writes: "I don't want to argue that it is only a political dilemma. No doubt we can get our hands dirty in private life also, and sometimes, no doubt, we should. But the issue is posed most dramatically in politics for…reasons that make political life the kind of life it is."[18] Lukes, too, offers qualifications: "The problem of dirty hands is, of course, a completely general and familiar one, arising in all spheres of life. It arises whenever, while doing the best thing in the circumstances, we know that we have done wrong. It tends, however, to be peculiarly stark in political cases."[19] I certainly don't wish to gainsay either Lukes's claim that the directly political manifestation of the dirty-hands problem is "peculiarly stark," or Walzer's claim that "the issue is posed most dramatically in politics." But I do think that closer attention to cases like that of O'Brien's missionaries, where the public morality/private morality dichotomy is subverted or transected, can help to highlight an imbalance in this literature, which unquestionably privileges the moral predicaments of professional political actors. It is at least worth asking whether dirty hands are as unique to "official" political actors as the tradition from Machiavelli and Weber to Walzer and Lukes suggests.

Again, what the *To Katanga and Back* stories nicely illustrate is the notion that dirty hands is in principle a universal human dilemma insofar as any ordinary citizen, occupying no special office and bearing no official public responsibilities, can find himself or herself in a situation where the dirty-hands problem is inescapable. The missionaries in O'Brien's story had no desire to involve themselves in politics or implicate themselves in the assumption of political responsibilities; on the contrary, they wished to divest themselves as much as possible from their political context and to keep their attention fixed on their missionary work. As O'Brien observes: "They did not think of themselves as having any political activities"[20]—even if this belief, as O'Brien points out, involved a large degree of self-delusion. And indeed, as *Christian* missionaries, they were committed to a religion of otherworldly salvation that, one would assume, exemplifies as much as any religion can the "ethic of ultimate ends" to which Weber opposes his "ethics of responsibility." Here's the lovely irony in this story: Who could be a less likely candidate for dirty-hands politics than a Christian missionary? And yet these people, no less than hardened statesmen and public officials, found themselves, in their peculiar circumstances, subject to the imperatives of "public morality"—and so, by extension, could any "private" citizen. That is to say, such ethical dilemmas are not unique to those who choose to enter the political arena, but can in principle descend upon *anyone* who tries to do something in the world.

My modest purpose in this essay has been to contest the presumed identification in the dirty-hands literature, both "classical" and more recent, between dirty-hands predicaments and professional agents of the state (or those who aspire to public office). In principle, *any* ordinary citizen who tries to do good in the public realm may find that their doing of good is inescapably implicated in or mediated by the doing of bad. The structure of the problem as we've seen it in O'Brien's narrative has a charming simplicity. In order to distribute food among starving Africans, one is obliged to rely upon a colonialist regime of terror that uses foreign mercenaries whose *modus operandi* consists of forcing Africans to flee their villages and burning their huts. To refuse to be involved in this whole business means leaving the Africans to starve. What is instructive about this particular example is that it concerns not politicians or agents of the state who have made a conscious choice to enter the realm of dirty hands, but rather Christian do-gooders who would like nothing better than to abstract themselves entirely from the unpleasant political context. Thus we seem to go beyond Machiavelli's teaching that it is specifically *the prince* who gets his hands dirty. In this instance, it is do-gooders who find themselves thoroughly implicated in the dirty handiwork of do-badders.

Notes

An earlier version of this essay was first presented to the Dirty Hands Workshop held at York University, December 1993.

1 Conor Cruise O'Brien, *To Katanga and Back: A UN Case History* (New York: Simon & Schuster, 1962) 162.

2 O'Brien 160.

3 O'Brien 163.

4 O'Brien 165.

5 O'Brien 166.

6 See Stuart Hampshire, ed., *Public and Private Morality* (Cambridge: Cambridge University Press, 1978).

7 Niccolò Machiavelli, *The Prince*, trans. Harvey C. Mansfield, Jr. (Chicago: University of Chicago Press, 1985) 65. For the famous statement about love of one's city vs. love of one's soul, see Machiavelli, *The Chief Works and Others*, vol. 2, trans. Allan Gilbert (Durham: Duke University Press, 1965) 1010 (letter to Francesco Vettori, 16 April 1527).

8 Machiavelli, *The Prince* 61 (my italics).

9 Max Weber, "Politics as a Vocation," *From Max Weber: Essays in Sociology*, ed. H.H. Gerth and C. Wright Mills (New York: Oxford University Press, 1973) 77-128; see esp. 83.

10 Weber 84, 117, 125-26.

11 Maurice Merleau-Ponty, *Humanism and Terror*, trans. John O'Neill (Boston: Beacon Press, 1969) xxxii-xxxiii.

12 Bernard Williams, "Politics and Moral Character," Hampshire 55; (my italics).

13 Michael Walzer, "Political Action: The Problem of Dirty Hands," *Philosophy & Public Affairs* 2:2 (Winter 1973): 161, 179.

14 Walzer 167-68.

15 Steven Lukes, "Marxism and Dirty Hands," *Moral Conflict and Politics* (Oxford: Clarendon Press, 1991) 196 (my italics).

16 Niccolò Machiavelli, *Mandragola*, trans. Anne and Henry Paolucci (New York: Liberal Arts Press, 1957) 36.

17 Walzer 165.

18 Walzer 174.

19 Lukes 193.

20 O'Brien 165

THREE

Bernard Shaw and Dirty–Hands Politics: A Comparison of Mrs *Warren's Profession* and *Major Barbara*

JOHN ALLETT

Introduction

Contemporary discussion of the politics of dirty hands remains largely indebted to Michael Walzer's 1972 article, "Political Action: The Problem of Dirty Hands."[1] This work was the first to establish a clear analytical distinction between dirty-hands politics and the politics of the ends justifying the means, with which it is easily confused. Further, Walzer identified three general perspectives—neoclassical, Protestant, and Catholic—in which the key problem of dirty-hands politics, namely the conflict that can arise between political necessity and private morality, is seen to strike ever more deeply (and properly) into the conscience of the political actor.

This essay further considers Walzer's argument by comparing two of Bernard Shaw's "conscience plays" (as C.B. Purdom describes them),[2] *Mrs Warren's Profession* (1894) and *Major Barbara* (1905). Shaw's position is especially interesting because in the first of these plays he utilized all three perspectives, as identified by Walzer, in order to explore the possibilities of a radical politics. In the second, he pushes the dilemma of dirty-hands politics to the point where it becomes transformed into an ends justifying the means position, much to the detriment of his problematic and to the merit of Walzer's analytic distinctions. In other of his works, *Spheres of Justice* (1983) for example, it is clear that Walzer himself is appreciative of Shaw's political insights, but he has not discussed the playwright specifically in the context of the analysis of dirty-hands politics. In so doing, this essay seeks not only to use Shaw to flesh out the concept and to illustrate its slipperiness, but also takes him seriously in his claim that his playwriting is inspired by important political themes. Finally, it is hoped that this focusing on the concept of dirty-hands politics also will prove useful in terms of an internal understanding of these two plays.

The Politics of Dirty Hands: Ancient Practice, Modern Precept

The politics of dirty hands is everywhere but is surprisingly little theorized. Perhaps it is too obvious for the telling, or, to the contrary, is too shameful a truth.[3] Whichever the reason, the making of a sharp distinction between political necessity and private morality, with the attendant claim that acts judged immoral on a private basis still may be considered legitimate in the service of political ends, is in fact of relatively modern origin. It is true, of course, that at the near beginnings of political and moral philosophy, Plato advocated that the ideal republic be founded upon "noble lies," but these were lies that supposedly deceived the rulers as well as the ruled and hence are not, strictly speaking, part of dirty-hands politics. Likewise, the seemingly related political claim that "might makes right" is also of ancient origin (it was key to Thrasymachus's challenge to Plato's ideal) but it, too, is of a different order of argumentation, since it seeks to escape moral confines in a way that dirty-hands politics does not. Those convinced of the necessity of dirty-hands politics are not moral relativists in the sense implied by the "might is right" doctrine. Rather, they accept that there exists a common moral universe, but recognize that exceptions to this moral law are also sometimes necessary. Here the essential moral dilemma is said to reside in "a situation, not where the end justified the means, but where the end dictated means of a type which rendered both the wholly good man and the wholly evil one superfluous."[4]

It is to Machiavelli and his decidedly this-worldly politics that we must first look to see the politics of dirty hands openly counselled. "The greatness of Machiavelli's thought," suggests Glenn Tinder, depends precisely on "the tension inherent in the idea that there is a moral law but rulers on occasion must break that law."[5] It is worth stressing that Machiavelli's advice was consistent for princely and republican rulers alike. Thus, while he notes his own originality in advising princes to "learn how not to be good and to use this knowledge ... according to the necessity of the case,"[6] he is being no less original in *The Discourses* when he advises republicans to take heed of the errors of Pietro Soderini, Gonfalonier of Florence, who, while recognizing the necessity of destroying the enemies of the republic, "had not the courage to do it":

> For he thought...that boldly to strike down his adversaries and all opposition would oblige him to assume extraordinary authority, and even legally destroy civil equality.... This respect for the laws was most praiseworthy and wise on the part of Soderini. Still one should never allow an evil to run out of respect for the law, especially when the law itself might easily be destroyed by the evil; and he should have borne

> in mind, that as his acts and motives would have to be judged by the result, in case he had been fortunate enough to succeed and live, everybody would have attested what he had done was for the good of his country.... But Soderini was the dupe of his opinions.... So that ... he lost at the same time his country, his state, and his reputation.[7]

In short, issues of personal integrity inappropriately encumber political decision-making: the betrayal of the self is a point of political principle.

There is much potential for pathos here. Machiavelli was sufficiently pleased with the shrewdness of his new politics, however, that his interest in the idea of a moral struggle between private conscience and public duty was not sustained. His moral sensitivity is suspect, Michael Walzer has suggested, "not because he tells political actors they must get their hands dirty, but because he does not specify the state of mind appropriate to a man with dirty hands." Walzer's guess is that a Machiavellian hero does not anguish greatly, though he must experience some pangs of conscience, otherwise it is "difficult to account for the strength of his original reluctance" to dirty his hands.[8]

"Here I stand: I can do no other."[9] With these words taken from Luther, the German sociologist, Max Weber, placed the inner moral struggle of the tragic hero at the forefront of an analysis of the dilemma of dirty hands. In so doing, he aligns himself with what Walzer identifies as an alternative Protestant perspective on politics and morality.[10]

Weber's essay, "Politics as a Vocation," in which he outlines a *realpolitik* of dirty hands, was written at the close of the First World War. Weber himself was near the end of a life that was dogged by deep inner struggle and debilitating nervous breakdown. He clearly viewed the tragedy of the war as a consequence of the failure of leadership and of the entanglement of politics in misplaced ideals and righteous causes. He thus sought to distinguish an ethics of (good) intentions from an ethics of responsibility, arguing that only the latter had a place in politics. The responsible leader was required to be relatively detached in his attitude towards things and people. He was to focus exclusively on the consequences of his actions, while recognizing that such actions often have unintended results and that this, too, was part of the burden of office. Above all, he was to be constantly mindful that "[e]verything that is striven for through political action operating with violent means and following an ethic of responsibility endangers the 'salvation of the soul.'"[11] To describe Weber's position as "Protestant," as does Walzer, is apt since the element of passion that remains in *realpolitik* is there to steel the politician against the softness of private morality, the temptation to do good as conventionally understood by the ordinary citizen. It is this that makes politics a vocation and the politician a tragic hero.

That the mood of Weber's work is very different from Machiavelli's is evident. That the result is qualitatively different is more questionable. Despite the emphasis on the tragic element in politics, Weber has no doubt how the struggle should be resolved. He thus overlooks, as Sissela Bok has commented,

> the dangerous seductiveness of seeing oneself as a tragic hero, forced to do the unspeakable for the sake of the community's good ... [T]he stark dichotomy that he sets up between what he calls the ethic of ultimate ends and that of responsibility leaves to one side a large part of that subtle process of moral deliberation about principles and practical cases that politics at its best requires.[12]

Much more ambivalent and therefore instructive in this regard is the third tradition of dirty-hands politics identified by Walzer as the Catholic tradition. (Walzer's latter-day literary representative of this preferred tradition is Albert Camus). Here the practitioners of dirty-hands politics are sufficiently wracked by self-doubt that they can take comfort neither in Machiavelli's fox-like cleverness nor in Weber's lion-like resolve. They continuously question the worthiness of what they do even as they do it. Furthermore, there is an expectation that those who engage in dirty-hands politics will do penance no matter how justified are their actions. In this tradition, dirty-hands politics is always and in each particular case, viewed as an exception to the rule which, in its turn, *must* be reaffirmed through some kind of openly expressed remorse.

It is not easy to imagine the kind of person who would willing undertake the burden of politics in such circumstances—to wear "a hair shirt beneath the motley," to use J. Percy Smith's phrase,[13] but for present purposes it suffices that such a "superman" would, at the least, do what is necessary and then seek not only understanding but also forgiveness. Otherwise, we should be wary that this superman is more a moralizer than he or she is moral. It is the contention of this essay that Shaw's character, Andrew Undershaft, is just this sort of moralizer, while his earlier counterpart, Kitty Warren, comes closer to the Catholic "ideal" identified by Walzer.

Before proceeding, however, I offer a word of explanation. The dilemma of dirty hands is usually, as above, thrown into high relief by strictly contrasting the public world of politics and the private world of personal relationships. This demarcation, however, though useful, is not an essential or even necessary one. Both Walzer and Bok allow that the problem of dirty hands is not only a political dilemma. Even more emphatic on this point is Virginia Held:

> We should not forget that ... the traditionally "private realm" is shot through with relations of power. Those acting within this realm seldom escape the "dirty hands" they associate with the traditionally "public" realm. This is clearly true of the economic activity imagined to be taking place in a 'private' sphere outside the "public" sphere of government.[14]

Held's point is, of course, directly relevant to the discussion of Shaw's plays. Both Mrs. Warren and Andrew Undershaft are the owners of profitable businesses and therefore use people in ways that likely would be considered immoral in more personal relationships. Moreover, in Undershaft's case, Shaw is explicit in placing him under the grip of the Life Force. Consequently, Undershaft's attacks on conventional morality are given a wider implication that ultimately rebounds, it is claimed, to the greater good. The operation of the Life Force renders the personal political: in this way Undershaft is made to serve the interests of others. The case of Mrs. Warren is less explicit. The play was written before Shaw had fully developed his philosophy of the Life Force. It is evident, however, that he wished Mrs. Warren's actions to carry a progressive socialist message of some sort. In both plays, Shaw seeks to promote the cause of those who refuse to be victimized by an inequitable social system and are willing to dirty their hands in order to survive and exercise their will.

Mrs Warren's Profession: *Realpolitik and Back Again*

The prostitution trade has long provided grist for the socialist mill. Here, it is argued, the hard slap of the market's invisible hand is felt especially by those women who are forced by economic circumstances to sell their sexual services as a commodity. Marx, for example, viewed prostitution "as a paradigm case of the sort of alienated relationships that are created by capitalism, where money substitutes for concrete human characteristics."[15] Shaw's play, *Mrs Warren's Profession*, written in 1893, follows in this tradition of analysis, although the courage to stage such a play is his alone. As the preface of the play announced: "*Mrs Warren's Profession* was written ... to draw attention to the truth that prostitution is caused, not by female depravity and male licentiousness, but simply by underpaying, undervaluing, and overworking women so shamefully that the poorest of them are forced to resort to prostitution to keep body and soul together."[16]

Given the degradation Shaw evidently felt was involved in the act of prostitution, his comment that prostitutes were nonetheless able to keep their "souls together" only indicates his altogether greater horror of poverty.

Poverty or prostitution? For Shaw this was a pernicious choice, but of the two, prostitution was the lesser evil.

It is Mrs. Warren's explanation of her choice to her daughter, Vivie (who, to that moment, has had no real knowledge of her mother's past or profession) that provides the climax to Act II of the play:

> MRS WARREN: My own opinions and my own way of life! Listen to her talking! Do you think I was brought up like you? able to pick and choose my own way of life? Do you think I did what I did because I liked it, or thought it right ...?

> VIVIE: Everyone has some choice, mother.... People are always blaming their circumstances for what they are. I dont believe in circumstances. The people who get on in this world are the people who get up and look for the circumstances they want, and if they cant find them, make them.

> MRS WARREN: Oh, it's easy to talk, very easy, isnt it? Here! would you like to know what my circumstances were?[17]

There follows a sufficiently harrowing account of Mrs. Warren's past as a child of London's slums and as a youthful drudge for other people's profit that, in reply to her demand, "How could you keep your self-respect in such starvation and slavery?"[18] Vivie sheds her priggishness and declares her mother "stronger than all England" for choosing prostitution above poverty.[19]

Mrs. Warren has dirtied her hands in order to survive and gain her independence: she pleads, in effect, that there were extenuating circumstances that drove her into prostitution and asks her eminently respectable daughter to suspend her judgment. What is especially important to appreciate is that Mrs. Warren does not reject society's moral codes as represented by her daughter. She does not wish to overturn middle-class morality, but simply seeks exemption. "It cant be right," she tells Vivie, "that there shouldnt be better opportunities for women. I stick to that: it's wrong. But it's so, right or wrong; and a girl must make the best of it. But of course it's not worth while for a lady. If you took it youd be a fool; but I should have been a fool if I'd taken to anything else."[20] Indeed, she takes pride in the fact that she "managed everything so respectably, and never had a word said against [her],"[21] and that her sister, who was her partner in prostitution, is now "living down at Winchester ... one of the most respectable ladies there."[22] It is evident, then, that Mrs. Warren's arguments are basically excuses, not transvaluations, and excuses are specific to the dirty-hands position.

Michael Walzer has emphasized this point by suggesting (along the lines first proposed by J.L. Austin) that although excuses and justifications (of which transvaluations are one important type) seem synonymous, they are in fact "conceptually distinct, differentiated in this crucial respect: an excuse is typically an admission of fault; a justification is typically a denial of fault and an assertion of innocence."[23] Mrs. Warren is not denying that prostitution is a dirty business. She is, however, excusing what she did because she believes she was forced into the trade by circumstances. Her moral code is not different from her daughter's, only her predicament. To have stayed conventionally moral in this environment would have denied Kitty Warren her independence—an appeal that Vivie, as an early representative of the "New Woman," finds especially compelling—but her moral reference is the same.

Furthermore, the tactical lesson for socialists to take from this is that they should not seek to bury liberal (bourgeois) values but to realize them by universalizing the conditions under which they apply. Liberalism, suggested Shaw elsewhere, is really "a post-Communist and not a pre-Communist doctrine and therefore has a great future before it when the world is full of Communists who will be at leisure for the greater part of their lives" and hence able to act freely beyond the limits of economic necessity.[24] In the meantime, socialists should resist the entrapment of a wrongly situated ethics, as did Mrs. Warren. For the Fabians this meant, among other things, the advocacy of a politics of permeation, a consorting with the enemy. It is noteworthy, for example, that in the same year *Mrs Warren's Profession* was produced, Shaw also wrote a position paper for the Fabian Society, *Plan of Campaign for Labour*, in which he recommended that the acceptance of "Tory gold" by Labour candidates was at bottom an issue of expediency, not morality.[25]

That Mrs. Warren has not rejected the moral code that she has nonetheless offended is also the source of her moral discomfort, or "inwardness," to repeat Walzer's description. Although she does not fully reach "Catholic" heights of self-conflict, nevertheless, she is "pitiably anxious"[26] to win Vivie's final approval and is obviously pained when that approval is not forthcoming. The reason for her daughter's change of mind is her discovery that her mother is still in the prostitution trade, indeed, is now a brothel owner, even though her economic circumstances have long since considerably improved. No longer able to claim that she was forced into prostitution, Mrs. Warren now seeks to excuse herself on the grounds that she has continued in the business at least partly to benefit others, most especially her daughter, and further, that no one who knew anything about the real world, of the pervasive and tentacular nature of immoral earnings, would blame Vivie for taking advantage of the situation. There are no rules where getting ahead is concerned. This has become Mrs. Warren's omnibus excuse:

> MRS WARREN: ... Vivie: the big people, the clever people, the managing people ... [t]hey know as I do, and think as I think. I know plenty of them. I know them to speak to, to introduce you to, to make friends of for you. I dont mean anything wrong: thats what you dont understand: your head is full of ignorant ideas about me. What do the people that taught you know about life or about people like me?...Would they ever have done anything for you if I hadnt paid them? Havnt I told you that I want you to be respectable? Havnt I brought you up respectable? And how can you keep it up without my money and my influence...? Cant you see that youre cutting your own throat as well as breaking my heart in turning your back on me?[27]

Vivie rejects these entreaties. While reaffirming that her mother's original predicament warranted her recourse to prostitution—"If I had been you, mother, I might have done as you did"[28]—the fact is, in the present situation, neither her mother's nor her own survival and independence are any longer at risk. It is, therefore, time to call a halt to dirty-hands tactics. Necessity no longer excuses. As Maurice Valency has observed:

> Shaw ... was a moralist. He wished to substitute for the rigid morality of the day a system which responded more elastically to the requirements of the individual situation, but he had no idea of doing away with morality altogether.... He therefore used Mrs. Warren to reproach society for its sins, then had recourse to Vivie to reproach Mrs. Warren for hers. In the end, having said some very shocking things about social morality, he concluded the play on an impeccably moral note.[29]

Mrs. Warren has become corrupt. Her excuses have degenerated into hypocrisy. Vivie now dismisses her as a "conventional woman."[30] This is not because Mrs. Warren professes to believe in conventional morality, however. Vivie is not the "New Woman" scolding "the Old," as is sometimes supposed. Rather, Mrs. Warren is rejected because she lacks the fortitude to live the conventional life she believes in, even when her circumstances enable her to do so. "I should not have lived one life and believed in another," Vivie tells her mother.[31] Even in her final moment of outrage, when it does seem that Mrs. Warren has moved altogether beyond the bounds of morality—"From this time forth," she cries, "so help me Heaven in my last hour, I'll do wrong and nothing but wrong. And I'll prosper on it."[32]—the point should not be missed that this is the overreaction of unexp(at)iated "Catholic" guilt, to use Walzer's term. Mrs. Warren is still aware that, in her own words, she is doing wrong.

Major Barbara: *Beyond Realpolitik to Religio-Politik*

Andrew Undershaft also seeks to escape conventional morality, but what was viewed as corrupting in Mrs. Warren is seen as a virtue in *Major Barbara*. The essential difference is the presence of the Life Force. Put simply, this is the contention that nature is filled with purpose and design. The Life Force has fashioned the human mind to reveal to itself its mysterious ways thereby to achieve its ends more consciously and efficiently. Likewise, it has fashioned human sexuality to provide itself with an endless line of minds upon which to experiment. In most other regards, the two plays are remarkably similar and invite comparison: as Shaw himself commented, he had originally entertained the idea of calling *Major Barbara*, "Andrew Undershaft's Profession."[33]

Shaw had become a convert to Creative Evolutionism shortly after writing *Mrs Warren's Profession*. J. Percy Smith suggests that 1884 marks the basic transition and *Candida* the first play fully to incorporate the idea.[34] Shaw's discovery of the Life Force undoubtedly had a profound effect on his own philosophical outlook and, in turn, reshaped his playwriting: " ... in the earlier plays the socialism, anti-romanticism, Ibsenism, and so on exist for themselves alone, are disparate and in a sense constricting. In *Candida* and after, these themes have come under the control of a vision that is large enough to contain them, and can see them from without even when it is presenting them from within."[35] But whatever the benefit accruing to his later plays from this metaphysical insight, in terms of Shaw's moral theory, the idea of the Life Force was a calamity. *Realpolitik* was transformed into a religio-politik, and his moral philosophy, as a consequence, lost its worldly mooring. Mrs. Warren was nothing if not down to earth. Indeed, Shaw was at pains to present her as coarsely so. Most particularly, she does not claim a different morality from the rest; only her circumstances differed. Hence came her excuse for dirtying her hands. But it must be allowed that Andrew Undershaft's private conscience is supernaturally inspired—he is in the grip of the Life Force—and that under this inspiration he claims the right to set a different moral course in which conventional morality is transvalued: "My sort of blood cleanses: my sort of fire purifies," he says of his cannons and grenades, and he takes as his motto the boast, "Unashamed."[36]

But what is it that gives the Life Force its authority? To rephrase Socrates's question in the *Euthyphro*: "Is conduct right because the Life Force commands it, or does the Life Force command it because it is right?"[37] Shaw's dilemma is that he cannot claim that the first is the case since this implies that the Life Force is arbitrary—a moral nominalist—yet he is convinced that there is purpose and design to its workings. On the other hand, to support the second case is to claim that what is moral is independent of the Life Force, so that Undershaft's being in its grip is not germane. Either way, the presence of the Life Force, it will be argued, does not afford a warrant comparable to that given by Mrs. Warren. To this extent it marks a decline in the level of Shaw's moral argument, his own opinion notwithstanding.

Like Mrs. Warren, Andrew Undershaft dirtied his hands early and for similar reasons. To survive London's notorious East End he had to deny himself "personal righteousness"[38] and become, as Shaw states in the preface, "spiritually as well as practically conscious of the irresistible truth which we all abhor and repudiate: to wit, that the greatest of our evils, and the worst of our crimes is poverty, and our first duty, to which every other consideration should be sacrificed, is not to be poor."[39] In the play itself, Undershaft gives an even more forceful presentation of the thesis:

> I was an east ender. I moralized and starved until one day I swore that I would be a full-fed free man at all costs; that nothing would stop me except a bullet, neither reason nor morals nor the lives of other men ... I had rather be a thief than a pauper. I had rather be a murderer than a slave.[40]

Ultimately Undershaft becomes involved in the armaments industry. This yields him enormous political power: "I am the government of your country," he declares to his priggish son, Stephen.[41] Thus daily and with disturbing delight, Undershaft wields those diabolical instruments of force which Weber associated with the dilemma of dirty hands.

It is with regard to Undershaft's latter-day wealth and power that the most obvious difference between the two plays becomes evident. Unlike Vivie Warren, Undershaft's daughter Barbara, who initially represents conventional morality, is converted, along with her fiancé, Adolphus Cusins, to a *realpolitik* of dirty hands that extends far beyond the issue of survival and the satisfaction of vital needs. Both agree, as Cusins puts it, to sell their souls not for "money nor position nor comfort, but for reality and for power."[42] Reality, for Barbara, is now the compromised world of her father, where good is mixed with evil: "There is no wicked side: life is all one," she declares and dismisses the contrary view, which was once her own, as "middle-class."[43] The Undershaft cannon factory both maims and nourishes, feeds the body and starves the soul. It is here that Barbara will do her missionary work. Power, for Cusins, is now the chance to "arm" the "common people" and "force the intellectual oligarchy to use its genius for the general good."[44]

All this may be regarded simply as the presentation of the politics of dirty hands with a vengeance. But it is more than that. The clue to the difference is given in the preface. Speaking of Undershaft's original decision to avoid poverty at any cost, Shaw allows that his actions would seem immoral "to what we call the honest poor man." Nonetheless, he goes on to maintain that Undershaft's "conduct stands the Kantian test."[45] Clearly, this is a reference to the test of universalizability: "If [the poor]," Shaw continues, "acted and believed as Undershaft acts and believes, the immediate result would be of incalculable beneficence."[46]

This is an attempt to turn the exception—which is how all theorists of dirty-hands politics, from Machiavelli forward, have conceived the problem—into the rule. Yet when everything is the exception there is no rule, a condition that Kant himself hardly would have endorsed as satisfactory. (Indeed, the main point he sought to make in his essay "Perpetual Peace" is that governments must resist the temptation to bully, deceive, or betray one another. This is a prerequisite for making "collective efforts to ensure survival." Otherwise, governments "face joint self-destruction.")[47] The fact is, Undershaft's actions do not pass the Kantian test. Where each takes as his or her maxim, "Thou shalt starve ere I starve,"[48] the result is anarchy not morality, a vicious circle rather than general beneficence. Shaw attempts to legitimatize such a beggar-thy-neighbour course of action under the rubric of the Life Force and in this way answer the question why one individual's gain at another's expense is justifiable (not merely excusable). Nature, he suggests, selects with its own higher purposes in mind. But this kind of "divine commandment," as noted earlier, merely renders morality arbitrary or redundant. As a true believer, however, Undershaft is self-righteous to the point where he lacks the moral ambivalence that Walzer seeks in those genuinely struggling with the dilemma of dirty hands. Undershaft refers to conventional morality only to deride it: "I wouldnt have your income, not for all your conscience," he tells Peter Shirley, the representative of ordinary working-class decency.[49] Certainly, there is in Undershaft no Weberian-like tragedy, only triumphalism, which at times reaches the heights of Dionysian ecstasy. His conscience is untroubled, except in his concern to see that the next stage of the Life Force goes forward by taking Barbara in its grip. And even here, unlike Mrs. Warren, he is never "pitiably anxious" to win his daughter's approval, let alone her forgiveness. If he is, as Cusins repeatedly calls him, a Machiavelli, then this, too, makes sense only if he is regarded as the (defamed) Machiavelli of Elizabethan repute, who was said not to possess even that minimum of moral ambivalence that is basic to his own analysis of the dilemma of dirty hands. Eric Bentley has written that Shaw's solution of the problem of power seems, perhaps, "too Machiavellian."[50] But from the perspective of a dirty-hands analysis, Shaw's solution is more accurately characterized as insufficiently Machiavellian, at the very least.

Conclusion

Writing on "Moral" in the *Fabian Essays in Socialism* (1889), Sydney Olivier had remarked that "there is on record a Greek proverb, that as soon as a man has ensured a livelihood, then he should begin to practise virtue."[51] The task for socialists, he continued, was to abolish the system of "private property in land and capital" which is "actively destructive of the conditions in which alone the common morality necessary for happy social life is possible."[52] Clearly, Shaw (who was the editor of the *Essays*) took this proverb and especially its caveat very seriously. This is evident in *Mrs Warren's Profession*, where he attempts to develop what might be considered a socialist strategy based on an appreciation that the present circumstances of the working class can deny them the opportunity to practise virtue. His version of dirty-hands politics is a credible response to, and utilization of, this predicament. Moreover, in examining the ultimate corruption of Mrs. Warren, Shaw not only gives flesh and blood to Olivier's essay but extends its analysis.

The moral and political lesson to be derived from *Mrs Warren's Profession* is appropriate to a democratic socialism that protests liberal-capitalism's exclusivity, its classism, precisely because it shares so much of its moral universe. As Shaw himself said of the Fabian Programme, only a few years prior to writing the play: "...there is not one new item in it. All are applications of principles already admitted and extensions of practices already in full activity."[53]

In *Major Barbara* these ideas are given an even more vigorous presentation but they are pushed to the point of hypertrophy. Believing that he has been saved from poverty by the operations of the Life Force, Undershaft emerges with a kind of survivor complex, convinced that he has a special mission. That mission is to facilitate the Life Force's dialectical evolution towards socialism, hence his recruitment of Barbara's spirit and Cusins's brains to complement his own genius for survival. The moral pathos that is at the root of the dirty-hands experience, however, is lost once Undershaft concludes that his own experience of poverty not only allows him his excuses for dirtying his hands in escaping that condition but also renders him guiltless. Instead of continuing to struggle with the dilemma of dirty hands, Shaw slid into the altogether more familiar (and disappointing) territory of the ends justifying the means. Thereafter, he found grounds for endorsing strong, even arrogant, leadership to a degree that raised questions as to his commitment to all but the most minimal definition of political democracy.[54]

Notes

This essay first appeared in the *Journal of Social Philosophy* 26:2 (Fall 1995) 32-45. It has been slightly revised by the author.

1 Michael Walzer, "Political Action: The Problem of Dirty Hands," *Philosophy and Public Affairs* 2:2 (1973) 160-180, reprinted in, Marshall Cohen, et al., *War and Moral Responsibility* (Princeton, New Jersey: Princeton University Press, 1974). All quotations are taken from this latter source.

2 C.B. Purdom, *A Guide to the Plays of Bernard Shaw* (London: Methuen, 1964) 102.

3 The latter is the suggestion of Glenn Tinder, *Political Thinking* (Boston: Little Brown, 1986) 111.

4 Sheldon S. Wolin, *Politics and Vision* (Boston: Little Brown, 1960) 208.

5 Tinder 110.

6 Niccolo Machiavelli, *The Prince and Discourses*, ed. Max Lerner (New York: Random House, 1950) 56.

7 Machiavelli 405-6.

8 Walzer 78.

9 Max Weber, "Politics as a Vocation," *From Max Weber*, H.H. Gerth and C. Wright Mills, ed. (New York: Oxford Univ. Press, 1958) 127.

10 Walzer 76.

11 Weber 126.

12 Sissela Bok, *A Strategy for Peace* (New York: Pantheon Books, 1989) 127.

13 J. Percy Smith, *The Unrepentant Pilgrim: A Study in the Development of Bernard Shaw* (Toronto: Macmillan, 1965) 201.

14 Virginia Held, *Rights as Goods* (Chicago: Univ. of Chicago Press, 1984) 26-27.

15 Alison M. Jagger, "Prostitution," *The Philosophy of Sex*, Alan Soble, ed. (New Jersey: Littlefield, Adams, 1980) 256-57.

16 Bernard Shaw, *Mrs Warren's Profession*, *Plays Unpleasant* (London: Penguin, 1982) 181.

17 Shaw *Mrs Warren's Profession* 246.

18 Shaw *Mrs Warren's Profession* 250.

19 Shaw *Mrs Warren's Profession* 251.

20 Shaw *Mrs Warren's Profession* 250

21 Shaw *Mrs Warren's Profession* 250.

22 Shaw *Mrs Warren's Profession* 248.

23 Walzer, 72. See also Sissela Bok, *Lying: Moral Choice in Public and Private Life* (New York: Vintage Books, 1979) chps. VI-VII.

24 Quoted in Eric Bentley, *Bernard Shaw* (New York: Limelight Editions, 1985) 20.

25 See Smith 115-16.

26 Shaw *Mrs Warren's Profession* 278.

27 Shaw *Mrs Warren's Profession* 282.

28 Shaw *Mrs Warren's Profession* 286. See also, 283.

29 Maurice Valency, *The Cart and the Trumpet: The Plays of George Bernard Shaw* (New York: Schocken Books, 1983) 98.

30 Shaw *Mrs Warren's Profession* 286.

31 Shaw *Mrs Warren's Profession* 286

32 Shaw *Mrs Warren's Profession* 285.

33 See Michael Holroyd, *Bernard Shaw: The Search for Love* (London: Chatto and Windus, 1988) 114.

34 See Smith 253.

35 Smith 254.

36 Smith 36 and 139.

37 Here I have followed the line of argument presented by James Rachels, *The Elements of Moral Philosophy* (New York: Random House, 1986) 41-44.

38 Bernard Shaw, *Major Barbara* (London: Penguin, 1974) 27.

39 Shaw *Major Barbara* 15.

40 Shaw *Major Barbara* 143.

41 Shaw *Major Barbara* 124.

42 Shaw *Major Barbara* 149.

43 Shaw *Major Barbara* 151.

44 Shaw *Major Barbara* 150.

45 Shaw *Major Barbara* 19.

46 Shaw *Major Barbara* 19.

47 Bok, 2, "Kant on Peace" 31.

48 Shaw *Major Barbara* 143.

49 Shaw *Major Barbara* 88.

50 Bentley 21.

51 Sydney Olivier, "Moral", in *Fabian Essays in Socialism* (London: George Allen and Unwin, 1962) 148.

52 Olivier 148-49.

53 Bernard Shaw, "Transition," *Fabian Essays* 235.

54 See, for example, Arthur Ganz, *George Bernard Shaw* (New York: Grove Press, 1983) 36-37.

FOUR

Politics, Power, and Partisanship

TOM SORELL

It is often claimed that those wielding political power are out of the reach of ordinary morality. Like businessmen, politicians sometimes regard moralising about what they do as naive and utopian, while the public, looking at the standards of MPs or Congressmen from the outside, no more expect upright behaviour from members of legislatures than from members of stock exchanges. There is an important disanalogy, however. Business, though it is conducted in public and though it often benefits the public, is not carried on for the sake of the public. Politics, on the other hand— democratic politics most conspicuously—*is* supposed to do the rest of us good, and not merely incidentally. Politicians are supposed to *aim* at the public good, with their own personal interests being served, if at all, only as a byproduct of serving the public interest. This means, at least in theory, that when things go wrong in politics, or when wrong is done by politicians, it can be in a good cause. A related point can be made about the *role* of politicians. Fulfilling this role can provide moral opportunities and reflect well on a person who is something of a moral failure in his private life. The careerist cabinet minister who never finds time for his wife and family and who is economical with the truth in his dealings with the tax authorities can for all that be an excellent representative, exerting influence skillfully on behalf of needy and helpless constituents. Or the politician can introduce legislation that helps a much wider public: not only all of the people of East Finchley or a certain congressional district in California, but all of the blind people in Britain, or all of the widows of military men in the United States.

The facts of political life raise at least two moral questions that are hard for moral theory to answer. First, how can it be morally right to represent the interests of a relatively small constituency or one's party when these are known to be narrower than, and sometimes in conflict with, the national interest or the interest of humanity? If politics is supposed to represent the public interest, doesn't the wider public interest always take precedence over the narrower? This is like asking how a genuine business *ethics* can permit a business interest to trump the public interest. Second, how far can reasons of state justify actions such as murder, torture, deception, misinformation, and the use of force that, in private life, would be prohibited by morality? Is there a special morality that governs the use of government power, so that the politician or the prince does something wrong if he allows reasons of ordinary morality to outweigh reasons of state, or is there only a single morality from which political power gives the illusion of immunity? This question is broadly analogous to asking whether in business, as opposed to private life, a ruthless gambler's morality can take the place of ordinary morality.

Moral theory does not easily justify the double standards that the segregation of political from ordinary morality suggests, any more than it easily justifies the segregation of morality in business practice from ordinary morality. As will emerge, the treatment of these questions about politics is prey to the same tensions as the treatment of questions in business. There is a strong temptation to reduce the gap between "ought" and "is" and abandon the normativity of morals—as when one attempts to use theory to rationalise well-intentioned political behaviour that would normally be wrong; there is a strong and contrary temptation to insist that wrong is wrong—so that even wrong that is done exceptionally and reluctantly and to protect the public shouldn't have been done. Despite the parallels, I shall suggest that the tensions of applying moral theory to politics are actually less strong than the tensions of applying theory to business.

Political Morality: The Moral Risks of Power for the Public Good

The idea that politics operates by different rules from those of ordinary morality is not put about only by cynics, but also by moralists impressed by the harshness of life at the top and the central place of power in politics. It has long been held that politicians in general and heads of state in particular need to be tough and able to use their power to the full when necessary; it may be too much to expect people to be tough *and* morally painstaking. In difficult times scrupulousness can look like indecision and generosity like weakness, and these unwanted appearances can reduce a political leader's authority and thus his effectiveness in carrying out any policy, even one that is morally admirable. In order to exercise their power without undercutting it, rulers are advised by writers like Hobbes and Machiavelli to show that they are willing to resort to force. Even democratic politicians are regularly urged by the newspapers to impose their will in the interest of demonstrating leadership. The common theme of these suggestions is that political power cannot quietly lie in reserve, but needs to be shown and exercised if it is not to ebb away. The need to keep using power, the moral risks of unleashing it at all, and of using it ineffectively—these things already stake out a distinctive territory for political morality.

The fact that the powers of those who govern are inflated far beyond their individual powers by the submission or compliance of the many, and the fact that these powers carry distinctive risks, suggest that the problems of political morality will differ from those of personal morality. Indeed, isn't political morality *so* distinctive that it stands apart entirely from personal morality? Might not political morality even involve a sort of inversion of the values of personal life, as Machiavelli claimed, so that in order to function effectively in public office the honourable private citizen has to *unlearn* his morality?

The Moral Demands of Public Emergencies

The idea that the norms of personal morality go into abeyance in politics has some justification. Whatever the form of government, events and the effects of public policy are often unpredictable, hard to reverse, and likely to occasion dispute even when they are benign. This means that in matters of collective life things can very easily go badly. All of this is anticipated institutionally. Government agencies exist to cope with types of public emergency that collective experience has shown to be severe and not entirely preventable. Thus there are established politically controlled bodies to deal with military invasion, with disease, with threats from the extremes of weather to food production and shelter, and with the breakdown of the financial system. Some of these calamities result from acts of God, others from large-scale imprudence or aggression. In the case of those that are humanly produced, institutions like armies and banking authorities often know where the threats are likely to come from, and take steps to discourage the relevant agents. But to deal with the actions of dangerous people across the board, other measures and institutions, perhaps less public and more questionable, may also have to be contemplated. Thus, if it is a moral requirement on governments that they be ready for terrorism or that they act to contain aggressive regimes abroad, it may also be a moral requirement that governments be ready to carry out assassinations or acts of sabotage, if there is reason to believe that the danger can be met in no other way. Action that might seem unthinkable to individual agents in danger may have to be considered seriously by the authorities if thousands are at risk.

The need in ordinary political life to prepare for or prevent emergency, or to respond to it when it has already occurred, seems to require those in government to be *ready* at all times to put scruples aside, even if circumstances never force them to act. But isn't this readiness itself a kind of unscrupulousness? If things do not go badly—for example, if there is no terrorist bombing to prevent by drastic means—isn't the general moral character of a government that is prepared to use those means already that of an agent who is ruthless and hard? And isn't such a government morally worse than a government that is unprepared just *because* it has scruples? No. If what faces a government is an emergency, and if pre-emptive violence, such as killing terrorists before they plant a powerful bomb in a city centre, is for protecting the public rather than getting away with armed robbery, surely what we have in the government is not ruthlessness in carrying out evil, but determination in preventing a worse evil by the only means that will be effective. It is unclear how readiness to carry out such action points to a defect of character. To say this is not to deny that when the policy is implemented people are killed, that it is better to prevent terrorism without loss of life than to do so by killing, and that the policy of taking pre-emptive action against terrorists is morally very risky, depending as it does on very accurate information about the identities and intentions of people who may not even have criminal records.[1]

If there is evil at all in acting pre-emptively to protect the public good, it may be a lesser evil than doing nothing, and it need not reflect badly on the character of the authorities who are responsible. In this respect, the excusing power of the public emergency in politics is far greater than the excusing power of hostile competition in business. Emergencies and competition each make life difficult for the relevant corporate agent—a government or a business—but only the emergency fully excuses taking action that is normally wrong—because the public good and probably many lives are at stake. And the fact that emergencies are exceptional events also matters. When competition is used as an excusing background condition for wrongdoing or as a condition that exempts business from the normal requirements of morality in the first place, one of the factors that makes the position hard to accept is that it affords such a sweeping exemption or excuse. If severe competition always allows corners to be cut morally, then it may license cutting corners all the time, since severe competition is intelligible as a pervasive background condition of business. In politics the only thing that is permissible all the time, according to the account so far sketched, is a readiness to do whatever is necessary to deal with an emergency. This is hardly an open-ended permission. On the contrary, it is compatible with glossing "doing whatever is necessary" as "doing the least evil that can reasonably be believed to be effective."

Dirty Hands

I have spoken of public emergencies as "excusing conditions" in politics. Does this terminology fit? Only wrongdoing can be excused, and perhaps killing to meet a public emergency is not wrong, even if killing normally is. Similarly for other things that are normally wrong and that might be done by governments in the belief that they are ways out of a public emergency. Part of what is in question here is whether the feeling of having dirty hands in politics is well grounded when the dirty deed is done in a good cause and careful deliberation fails to disclose a more acceptable alternative. When a political leader looks back and feels tainted by an act of public deception, or by a decision to have a terrorist assassinated, or by a campaign to put down an insurrection at the cost of many lives, does the fact that deception, assassination, and blood-letting are normally to be avoided show that the leader is *right* to feel tainted?

Different moral theories answer this question in different ways. Utilitarianism denies that there are any types of action that are intrinsically wrong—wrong regardless of their consequences—and so it leaves open the possibility that the consequences can make it right to break a moral rule. When this possibility is realized, utilitarianism says that no wrong is done and no real dirt is on anyone's hands. The hands may *feel* dirty—guilt may be experienced by those who break any moral rule, even one that there is utilitarian justification for breaking—but the guilt is baseless according to utilitarianism. Again according to utilitarianism, the guilt may be useful for guilt to be felt, for if it never were it would be psychologically easy to break moral rules—which would be a source of disutility. It may also be understandable: the loyalty to the rule one has broken may die hard. But there is not necessarily any moral ground for feeling guilt, and nothing wrong with someone who realizes as much and casts it off.

At first sight, utilitarianism looks cavalier in its treatment of dirty hands,[2] even when what has dirtied them is an action with the best consequences in the circumstances. Utilitarianism seems to deal counter-intuitively with the associated feelings of guilt, denying both that feelings of guilt are necessary for a good character and that guilt should attend the violation of mere rules of thumb. Intuitively, to feel one has dirty hands *is* evidence of good character—a character that shrinks from wrongdoing. Moral rules are more than rules of thumb, since their prohibitions are categorical and since feelings of guilt are in order when the rules are broken (because of their categorical content and not because of the good effects of feeling guilty). Moral character depends on the feelings one has about one's actions, and utilitarianism says that the consequences determine what feelings are appropriate, not the content of the rules. But someone who feels

71

guilt only on finding out the consequences of an act of torture or assassination—who does not react to the very idea of an act of his being an act of torture or assassination—is, again intuitively, either drained of moral character altogether or has a character inferior to that of the agent with automatic guilt feelings.

Nonutilitarian moral theories are able to accommodate intuitions about character, but they may do less well at accommodating intuitions about what is permissible in times of emergency. This is because they tend to represent moral requirements as exceptionless, and wrong or evil as unquantifiable. The idea of one evil being bigger than another, which utilitarianism captures by reference to the relative preferability of different states of affairs in the view of different numbers of rational choosers, is best reflected in arguments about certain prohibitions or precepts being ranked in order of priority. These rankings are sometimes implausible or controversial—as when truth-telling is supposed to trump life-saving—and they may imply that the more high-order the prohibition that appears to be threatened in an emergency, the more urgent it is to abide by the prohibition and take the consequences, even if the consequences are disastrous.

Here as elsewhere in moral philosophy, utilitarianism seems to capture part of the truth, and its competition seems to capture another part. Utilitarianism says that dirty hands are sometimes morally necessary, but falters in dealing with the fact that the associated guilt feelings always have a ground, even if acting in accordance with the guilt feelings is not justified overall. Nonutilitarian theories capture the truth that the feelings associated with dirty hands are often well-grounded, while denying that the actions that occasion those feelings are sometimes morally necessary. What is common ground between the two theories, however, is the recognition that (1) feelings of dirty hands exist; (2) the feelings are explicable; (3)they are associated with people who take the prohibitions and prescriptions of morality seriously; and (4) everyone *ought* to take the prohibitions and prescriptions of morality seriously. I am not sure that more than this common ground, more even than a suitable treatment of (2), is required to make moral sense of the feeling of dirty hands. Dirty hands need not be a theoretical blindspot, even for utilitarianism.

To see this, it important to notice that utilitarian and nonutilitarian theories alike can make sense of the feeling of dirty hands as a byproduct of practical deliberation that involves moral conflict. The conflict is between the dictates of welfare in the face of emergency and the dictates of morality in normal times. Welfare considerations in the face of emergency often require actions that moral rules normally prohibit or prohibit full stop. A Kantian theory does not deny that welfare considerations can make an unsavoury action *appear* necessary. Kant's own theory has elaborate claims about moral motivation to explain why happiness or welfare seems to determine what is right, namely that desire and inclination, not just self-regarding desire and inclination, but also sympathy and philanthropy, are important motivating factors in human action in general, and ineradicable even when one has limited their influence enough to let the messages of pure practical reason get through. When an agent decides on the basis of considerations about happiness that something prohibited by a categorical imperative must be done, that is not, then, inexplicable according to Kant. It is not even unusual, since it is part of what is radically wrong with human beings that they often subordinate what morality requires to other things. But it is also not right. So if the agent acts on welfare considerations in preference to a categorical imperative he *has* dirty hands, whether or not he feels he has.

Utilitarianism, for its part, can also make sense of a dirty or dirty-seeming action as the result of a moral conflict in the course of practical deliberation. But, and now contrary to Walzer, the utilitarian treatment can justify the feelings associated with dirty hands. Consider, for example, a decision to kill a couple of terrorists so that ten thousand lives can be saved. The consequences of killing or torturing are considered and found frightful; the consequences of letting an emergency take its course when it could be prevented by killing or torturing are found worse still; so the torture and killing are carried out. What justifies feelings of dirty hands after the unsavoury action has been carried out is exactly what justified keeping the rule against killing or torturing while deliberation was taking place. In short, feelings of dirty hands are justified by whatever justified keeping one's hands clean in the first place: the rule against killing, the rule against torturing, and the consequentialist justification for those rules in turn. So long as the action that occasions the feeling of dirty hands issues from moral conflict of this kind, there is always a ground for the feeling even if it is concluded that there is more utility in doing the dirty thing. A utilitarianism along these lines is not cavalier about feelings of dirty hands. It says that there is a piece of reasoning that counts against what was done, not just a baseless feeling that makes the action unpleasant in retrospect. But it also says that the force of that piece of reasoning can be outweighed.

Now it may be true that moral conflict is not registered in the conclusion of a piece of utilitarian practical deliberation. The conclusion may not be qualified by an "All things considered" or "One is reluctantly forced to concede that" or "Unfortunately." But that does not mean that it is arrived at in the same way as the conclusion of a piece of practical reasoning in which reasons against doing what is decided upon all along seem weak or far-fetched. An agent's conclusion may be unqualified and yet issue from heartsearching, from a long period of deliberation. Or it may come from a committee divided down the middle that reaches a judgement by a tie-break or the narrowest of majorities. The fact that the division is not alluded to in the conclusion reached by the committee does not mean that division does not affect the decision. Utilitarianism can reach the unqualified conclusion and yet do so with scruples. It is not clear to me that more than this is required to take the sting out of dirty hands.

Public Morality, Private Morality, and Moral Schizophrenia

I have said that dirty hands need not constitute a theoretical blindspot, since the feeling of dirty hands can stand to reason, even in utilitarianism. The feeling can be justified and the justification be outweighed by the justification for killing or torturing or deceiving in the face of an emergency. But a likely source of paradox is the following: as a ruler or member of a government, an individual must always be ready to authorise killing or torture if the threat to public safety is big enough; in private life, the very same person should be averse to doing anything of the kind and should probably show reluctance to take up public office if there is any likelihood of its involving dirty deeds. Yet public office should not—morally should not—be shirked by good people who are competent to carry it out: the reason is that the good that public office is supposed to promote or protect is bigger than the individual good. So the good private individual who is competent to manage public affairs should both avoid and not avoid political office. Yet the paradox is more apparent than real, because it is part of politics not only to carry out the duties of office, but to arrange things so that, in carrying them out, it is hard or harder to dirty one's hands. This may mean arranging for more and more political action to be done in public, or it may mean working for the adoption throughout public life of the rules of procedural justice, so that fewer of the people who become public dangers and against whom dirty-handed action is taken need to resort to clandestine or criminal or vigilante action themselves. In short, someone who has a horror of dirty hands in politics may have more of an obligation to adopt political means to eradicate underhand practice than to avoid politics.

Even if the demands of private and public morality do not have to pull against one another to the point of making the individual politician disintegrate, aren't the two spheres uncomfortably separate, so that the agent disappears into his role and becomes subject to its morality when carrying out the duties of office, and then becomes himself and takes on the different constraints of personal morality at other times? Yes and no. Occupying political office does require an individual agent to identify with the public interest, or at least the interest of a section of the public, but it can be a decision in private life to try to acquire political office with its responsibilities, and obtaining that office may depend on the further personal decisions of other people—often thousands of other people, when the way one obtains office is through election. If one acquires office after standing for it, one has a personal obligation to shoulder its obligations, and to face the tensions with other personal obligations that the duties of office may bring with them. The decisions of private individuals that result in an office being held, as well as the purposes of the office itself, create the split moral personality of politicians, but just because the acts that result in office often derive from the decisions made by a private individual *as* a private citizen, the appearance of split personality is all it is. Becoming subject to political morality is not a matter of dropping one's status as an individual or one's personality: it is more a matter of choosing to invest one's personality in a certain activity. So the responsibility of being a politician is often clearly personal.

The Problem of Specifying a Basis for Political Morality: Machiavelli and Hobbes

Even if an individual's political responsibilities are traceable to a decision governed by his personal morality, so that public and private morality do not entirely come apart, it is a non-trivial task of moral theory to rationalise the permissibility of dirty deeds done in political office beyond saying that they promote the public good. Machiavelli appears to hold that the rationale for these acts may lie in defining features of effective political office itself, which by definition requires power, including power in the form of popular support and submission. So the greatest misuse of office must be that which reduces power or threatens to eliminate power, as the political acts of the scrupulous can do. The political office defeats itself by co-operating in making itself redundant. On the other hand, ruthless deeds tend to preserve or increase power: so they are appropriate to political office. The problem with this position is that it does not offer a moral basis for the concentration of power in holders of political office. If the reason political officeholders ought to have power is that political power makes it easier to maximise the public happiness, then, since the costs of ruthlessness in human misery and fear may also be very high, perhaps power should be privatized and diffused—limited to the resources an individual can freely acquire and defend by individual effort.

Hobbes has an argument for this last possibility being the worst option of all. According to him, the state of affairs in which each person is free to acquire and keep what he can is a war in which no one can be blamed for being personally bloodthirsty or ruthlessly acquisitive if they sincerely think that otherwise they will risk death or loss of the means of secure life. For

Hobbes, the concentration of power in a sovereign authority is a better means of obtaining security and well-being than the pursuit by each of safety and well-being in conditions of perfect freedom. Like Machiavelli, Hobbes believes that the sovereign authority can properly act roughly both domestically and with respect to other governments in the interest of maintaining security and promoting well-being. The basis for this proper ruthlessness is the fact that with respect to both subjects and other governments the sovereign is a free agent and must remain so in order to do his job. His outward behaviour is for his own judgement to determine. It is different for inward acts of will, which are bound by morality. Morally, the sovereign is obliged, like every other free agent, to be willing to keep faith with everyone, to be forgiving, to keep his promises. But being willing is one thing; actually keeping faith in public, showing forgiveness, and keeping promises is something else—something that is obligatory only in conditions of general security, where acting morally does not confer an advantage on a competitor. The basis for being able to adjust one's will but not necessarily one's actions to moral requirements is the retention of what Hobbes calls the "right of nature"—the right of judging when an action conduces to one's safety and when it doesn't. Every private individual has this right; every *citizen*, on the other hand, can be understood to have transferred it to the government that is entrusted with the citizen's security. The sovereign is not a citizen. He *represents* citizens, according to Hobbes, and is *authorized* by citizens in whatever way will secure the peace; he *personifies* the union of citizens; but he does not contract with citizens to do this. On the contrary, he is an external beneficiary of a contract citizens made among themselves in a prepolitical state. He benefits by the agreement of the many to obey him, and in return for their submission he is expected to keep the peace through legal and other institutions.[3]

Hobbes's account of the relation between political morality and private morality is very rich, since it has the resources to connect political morality with far more than the idea of power. It connects political morality not just with ordinary personal moral requirements—what Hobbes calls "the laws of nature"—but also with collective and public acts of authorisation, and relations of representation and personification between the individual sovereign and the many or the sovereign council and the many. According to Hobbes, as according to any account that can cover the basis of political morality in a democracy, the prerogatives of political office that lead to dirty hands are justified partly by the responsibilities of office holders to those they represent. And the standpoint from which people who hold office or have authority are supposed to act is one of some sort of identification with the public—so that one's own interest is identified from the point of view of the many or the union of the many—rather than from the self-interest of the private person. Unfortunately, Hobbes's own distinctive variations on themes of authorisation and personification, and his distinctive organisation of the requirements of morality under a supreme requirement of seeking security, are all pretty disputable. Hobbesian representation is mainly a device for diverting responsibility for the sovereign's actions to the parties to the contract, so that they cannot complain of iniquity at another's hands. The idea of personification, though it captures the imagination, is none too clear. As for organizing the laws of nature, including the requirement of being just, under a supreme requirement of seeking peace—this has the effect of legislating away the question of whether there is any moral necessity to keeping a peace, when the peace looks unjust in a pretheoretical, non-Hobbesian sense.

Hampshire's Anti-Theory of Political Morality

A general account of political morality which, unlike Hobbes's, is initially attractive *and* faces up to the problem of dirty hands has been sketched by Stuart Hampshire. Hampshire's account concedes quite a lot to Machiavelli, for it agrees that innocence and a dedication to innocence can be a liability in a political role. Hampshire's account also allows for the possibility that in some conflicts in political deliberation, a sufficiently great gain in welfare may sometimes justify an injustice, if the injustice is not very big. On the other hand, Hampshire argues for the indispensability of what he calls "procedural justice"—the justice of hearing and adjudicating fairly between conflicting claims. He even identifies disrespect for procedural justice or a willingness to respond violently or by conquest to its judgements with evil. So the account both supports the idea that justice is the supreme virtue and concedes that in politics it is not always possible to do the virtuous thing.[4]

Hampshire is able to steer a middle course between absolutism and utilitarianism by putting at the centre of his account two theses: that the primary good can consist of the prevention of great evil, and that political choice can sometimes best be described, and in dirty-hands cases is naturally described, as choosing the lesser evil. These theses are made central in the (in my view correct) belief that it is easier to be definite and uncontroversial about evil than about the good.[5] Thus, as Hampshire points out, the aim of destroying life or pursuing a policy of domination is widely agreed to be evil; so is praise for violence and contempt for argument and persuasion; so is a ready tolerance for, or a willingness to glorify, misery and pain. People differ far more over the good. Hampshire also says that the Nazi tyranny and conquest in the 1930s and 1940s and the Russian Revolution are clear examples of great evils from the twentieth century that are important

77

to moral thought, and that they illustrate the indispensable guidance given to moral thought by history.[6]

The thesis about preventing great evils and choosing lesser ones is combined with certain theses about the claims that can be made on those in political power:

> What can reasonably be demanded of those who incur the responsibility of political power? The first demand is that they should recognise the weight of their particular responsibility in disposing of the lives of others. The second is that they should be clear-headed, and not divided in mind, about their obligations to protect the reasonable interests of their innocent fellow citizens; this is the Machiavellian thesis. The third demand is that they should at all times be prepared for the occurrence of an uncontrolled conflict in duties in situations which seem to preclude the possibility of a decent outcome, and in which all lines of action seem dishonourable and blameworthy. This is the point at which the contrast between innocence and experience becomes indispensable in ethics...A person of experience has come to expect that his usual choice will be the lesser of two or more evils.[7]

These demands are similar in effect to a requirement that the politically powerful identify with the interests of the public, and make best use of their experience in trying to serve the public. According to this passage, the fact that one is powerful, so that others are vulnerable to the effects of one's power, by itself obliges one to be careful in exercising one's power. Further conditions do not have to be met. So, for example, one has the obligation to be careful in using one's power even when the people who are vulnerable to uses of it have not elected one, even when the powerful person is not their chosen representative. Again, experience alone ought to make one expect that some of the choices one will face will be choices between evils. One fails in one's duty in a political role if the fact that one is going to be faced by such choices catches one by surprise.

Although Hampshire's is an attractive account that differs from more standard theories, it passes over an important question in silence: how can he acknowledge the separate claims of justice and utilitarianism without facing up to the conflicts those claims famously generate? To this he has both a normative ethical and a meta-ethical answer. The normative answer is that preventing great evils is one of the principal goods, and presumably is the special preserve of politics. The idea of a great evil is probably neutral between injustice and a great reduction of welfare, and is perhaps able to adjudicate between the demands of justice or the demands of utility where they conflict; but if so, there is still a legitimate theoretical task in making clear how evils are to be compared when they fall on either side of the divide between justice and utility. For example, is a small injustice always a worse evil than a small reduction in welfare? If, as it seems, the answer is "Yes," why doesn't justice always trump welfare? Another approach that Hampshire might be expected to develop is that of connecting the prevention of great evil with the vulnerability of those without political power. If politicians are always a danger to those with little power or those with less than the politicians, perhaps the avoiding-injury requirement of justice, such as has been proposed by O'Neill,[8] both particularly constrains political agents and partly justifies welfare-protecting dirty-handed acts.

These speculations about the directions in which Hampshire's theory might be developed sit uneasily, however, with his meta-ethical answer to the problem of adjudicating conflicts between justice and utility. He insists that one has to live with this conflict, and that living with this and other conflicts is characteristic of morality:

> ...there always will be, and always ought to be, conflicts arising from the universal requirements of utility and justice, and moral requirements that are based on specific loyalties and on conventions and customs of love and friendship and family loyalty, historically explicable conventions...[M]oral conflicts are of their nature ineliminable... there is no morally acceptable and overriding criterion, simple or double, to be appealed to, and no constant method of resolving conflicts. The worth and value of a person's life and character, and also of a social stricture, are always underdetermined by purely rational considerations.[9]

I call the theory that Hampshire endorses an "anti-theory" because once one believes that there is no small number of definite goods to guide deliberation and resolve conflict, it is hard to see what distinguishes theoretical from pretheoretical resources for resolving conflicts. Hampshire's anti-theory expresses a much deeper scepticism about moral theory than the willingness to live with conflict *faute de mieux*. Sometimes this scepticism is more or less explicit in Hampshire's writings as a set of claims about the limits of rationality in morals.[10] At any rate, the existence of moral conflict is not, in Hampshire's view, a problem for moral theory but a deep fact of life to which moral theory needs to reconcile itself. If it does not, it may be guilty of trying to model practical knowledge on scientific, and trying futilely to find a reality beyond the conflicts—such as an abstract human nature—from which to deduce its prescriptions, rather as physics tries to deduce the behaviour of particles of matter from the behavior of medium-sized physical objects.[11] I do not believe that the aspiration to a unitary moral theory has to be associated with failing to recognise the unscientific subject matter of ethics, and many writers who are working on the statement of such a theory are alive to the dangers of the scientific model. Nor is it clear that a very generous allowance for irremediable conflict is compatible with a *theoretical* enterprise in morals at all. Worse, Hampshire's account may invite the overrationalisation of ways of life that, from the supposedly wrongheaded rationalistic perspective of moral theory, are open to moral criticism. If we take to heart the idea that some practices are so embedded in a way of life that to attack the practice is to attack that which, according to Hampshire, people can be unreasoningly but still legitimately attached, then perhaps criticism of the practice has to be foregone on pain of moralising overreaching itself. This line of thought is not unfamiliar in discussions of the ethics of female circumcision, where its implications are also particularly worrying.

A more acceptable position, in view of the fact that Hampshire thinks that ways of life are not in principle closed off from moral criticism, is to say that all practices are *open* to moral criticism. This is compatible with the criticism being clumsy or insensitive, or turning out to be unjustified. But it is also compatible with the possibility that the critics of female circumcision are right. Still, for a practice to be *open* to criticism is for it to be within the scope of a rationalist technique and not part of its background. It is a big concession for someone as convinced as Hampshire of the unwelcomeness of reason in morals to make. I do not see, however, why the concession, combined with agnosticism about philosophers' abilities to find the relevant techniques, is not as reasonable as Hampshire's scepticism. If that is right, then Hampshire's account of political morality seems undermotivated as an anti-theory, while as a positive theory—i.e., in its preventing-greater-evil mode—it seems underspecified.

The Difference Democracy Makes

Since one can get dirt on one's hands even from choosing the lesser of two evils as an honourable politician, it may look as if it is a kind of moral bad luck to end up with political power. The chances of seeing out one's term of office with nothing to regret or of having an unblemished reign are probably small, and yet *someone* has to go into public life, and the better those people are, the better it is for everyone. If people repudiate public life, as they can sometimes repudiate certain types of private life, because they are too pure for it, that can be as morally suspect as what they are avoiding. Although no one seems to think it is a form of dirty hands, keeping out of politics in a democracy can also justify criticism, and perhaps more criticism than passive obedience under an unjust undemocratic regime.

That democracy makes a difference to dirty hands has been noticed before now. As Thompson has pointed out,[12] democracy spreads responsibility: not only politicians but also their electors are implicated. On the other hand, the justification for democracy also rubs off on dirty-handed acts committed under its auspices, especially when institutional measures have been taken to reduce the area in which dirty-handed acts can go undetected, unquestioned, and unpunished. At least in theory, democracy introduces controls on political activity and costs for political wrongdoing. The controls may not allow for the immediate control of ineffective or morally wrong policies, but they ensure at least the possibility of a decision to change course in relatively short order. Since democracy can also impose big standing obstacles to certain kinds of action against citizens or in the name of its citizens, it can act constitutionally against at least certain kinds of dirty hands. On the other hand, when democratically elected politicians do go in for dirty-handed acts, the moral arguments for democracy may lend legitimacy to those decisions, since, on one accepted understanding of democratic office-holding, people are supposed to have the latitude to use their judgement for the best within the law. It would be incredible if the allowable latitude were so limited that dirty-handed acts became unthinkable or unchoosable. Democracy does seem to provide a cleaner environment for political decisions than other forms of government. If politicians get their hands dirty in a democracy, it is not due to the dirty atmosphere they inhabit. Theoretically, too, democracy makes a difference: the prospects of clearing up what is paradoxical about dirty hands seem to improve when democracy is brought in. If a politician is in power quite independently of the choices of those ruled over, it does look as if there is something distinctively unfortunate about being a politician who acts for the public good by doing the least wrong thing. For, however justified by welfare a dirty-handed act is, the dirt in it can always be a reason for moral condemnation by a people who do not consent to it. The more democratic the regime is, the less justified the condemnation of citizens is, because their moral distance from the act shrinks. Democracy can even expose everyone—all citizens—to the same moral risks. Thus, some forms of democratic organisation require office to rotate among all those involved: it is sheer luck if one's term is up just as circumstances go sour, so that one's successor is left with dirty hands—and that can be generally acknowledged. Dirty hands in this setting can intelligibly prompt empathy rather than condemnation.

Thompson thinks that the biggest obstacle to reducing the politician's moral burden through democracy is secrecy: the government's need for secrecy in carrying out some of its legitimate functions, on the one hand, and, on the other, the politician's temptation to cover up or keep things secret where publicity would be personally or party-politically costly. Ordinary citizens, Thompson says, cannot be blamed for what they couldn't have known about, and yet it is out of the question for them to know everything, since this would render self-defeating some otherwise effective and legitimate measures; e.g., detecting and controlling crime and preventing and waging war. Where relevant knowledge is withheld from the voting public by politicians, on the other hand, something wrong is always done, and this wrong can compound the wrong in dirty hands.

I doubt that secrecy has the general moral significance that Thompson's account claims for it. For one thing, it is not always true that ignorance due to secrecy excuses. If a young child secretly commits arson but is known by his parents to be fascinated by matches, then more than ignorance of the act of arson due to the child's secrecy is required to absolve the parents of all responsibility: they need to have done their best to have dispelled the child's fascination with fire. In a democracy in which it is common knowledge that some political decisions are made in secret, and in which it is known that there is political advantage in keeping things secret, ignorance under conditions of vigilance rather than simple ignorance may be the minimum fully exculpating conclusion. If people cooperate in being kept in the dark by not wanting to know, or by not caring about politics, then that, as much as official or unofficial secrecy, can increase the moral burdens on those who do fill the political vacuum. Another and different reason why ignorance due to secrecy need not excuse people from responsibility for secret dirty-handed acts is that citizens can be consulted about the scope of secrecy and vote that it remain wider than even Thompson would recommend. If we agree that in a democracy partially blank checks of this kind can legitimately, even if wrongheadedly, be written, then secrecy is not in the permanent tension with democracy that Thompson seems to think it is.

Democracy and Partisanship

So far democracy has appeared as a framework that makes it harder to do wrong than other forms of political constitution, and that lightens the burden of responsibility when wrong is done by office-holders for the sake of the public. This morally improving character of democracy, however, may be counterbalanced by something else: the identification of different political agents with interests far narrower than the public interest. When a parliamentary representative of an extremely wealthy constituency argues for tax cuts that would make publicly funded schools worse or extend waiting times for publicly funded hospitals, he can be held to be arguing legitimately both for the interests of those he represents and the party he belongs to. Yet the tax cuts may be wrong from the standpoint of justice as well as utility. If they are wrong, is it really legitimate to argue for them? And since the already well-off can command the resources to promote their case outside legislatures, is it really as legitimate to give them access to legislators and influence over them as it is to open special channels of access and influence to those who find it hardest to make their reasonable interests visible or audible to politicians?

As things are, the democratic voters in the world do not expect their representatives to speak for other people's interests, even the interests of the much poorer. They vote for people who they believe will defend their own interests, whatever they are, morally good or morally bad, against the competing claims of other people.[13] Thus it is perfectly intelligible that the representative of one constituency should oppose the building of an indisputably necessary transportation link or prison or home for the mentally ill in his locality;[14] it may even be said that it is his moral duty to do so, though justice and utility both favour siting the link or the prison or home at exactly the place he refuses to countenance. A constituency of unselfish electors might elect a representative who had the freedom to vote for once from the point of view of the whole public and not just a section of it. But unselfishness is not a qualifying condition for being an elector, and the tiny impact of one's personal vote makes moral agonising over how it should be cast slightly ridiculous. The upshot of these considerations is that democracy at the grassroots level, the level of the many, the level which for Thompson helps to moralise dirty-handedness, includes elements of sectarianism that themselves need to be moralised. The point is that some elements of democracy may have to be acted *against* by morality, and that justice and self-interest may be independent and conflicting motivations in democratic life.

When the moral limits imposed on democracy by self-interest, sectional interest, and partisanship (in the broad sense of giving particular weight to the interests of those closest to one) are brought into the picture, do they reintroduce for political ethics a version of the dualism of practical reason that operates in business ethics? I am not sure. This is because cosmopolitanism—thought and action in which one identifies one's own interests with those of the widest possible community in which one is included—is intelligibly an ideal in politics, even in non-democratic politics, in a way nothing similar is in business. Again, one does not need to desert politics to deal with the competing demands of morals and politics. It takes political means to curtail the excesses of collective self-interest in business; but one does not need extra-political means of curtailing the excesses of self-interest. Politics is in that sense the more inclusive activity. And the ethical resources needed to think about how to regulate it never appear, as in business, to call into question the internal goals of the activity itself.

Utilitarianism as a Public Philosophy

Not only is politics not enough like business to reproduce as stark a dualism of narrow and wide interest as one finds in business; it seems to be better served by at least one moral theory than business is by any. Utilitarianism seems to be made for public life—or at least for the exercise of political power—in ways that disable it for the demands of personal morality.[15] Indeed, utilitarianism may come into its own only or primarily as a public philosophy, since its impersonal, strongly consequentialist, unashamedly calculating side very easily comes into conflict with the strong attachments to persons and projects and the emotions of private life,[16] even by the lights of utilitarians themselves. Goodin points out that it is only relatively recently that utilitarianism has been seen as anything other than a philosophy of public affairs.[17] And even anti-utilitarian or non-utilitarian philosophies of political life, Hampshire's for example, are consequentialist, often at the same time as they are talking about justice. Thus Hampshire speaks of the prevention of great evil as a requirement of justice, and characterises evil in ways that would certainly make evil morally necessary to oppose according to utilitarianism. In a way, this standpoint is unavoidable, once the morality of politics is made to hinge on how power can be used for good or ill and how the many in a society are vulnerable to the acts or omissions of those in power. And it is easy for utilitarianism to make sense of the idea that it is in the political sphere that great goods and evils are committed.

It is true, of course, that politics is not *all* about the exercise of political power. It is also about participation by individuals in civic life. Voting, membership in, and active support for political parties, participation in campaigning groups—all this is open to individuals with no particular influence on other people or events. The ethics of the politics that is open to such individuals is not the ethics of office-holding or power-wielding, but even politics at the level of the small cog in the wheel may engage utilitarianism. Utilitarianism may provide an argument for the relief of welfare through political participation as much as for the relief of poverty itself. So if one refuses to do anything about poverty, or to limit what one does to charitable contributions, avoiding political action of any kind, there may be a ground in utilitarianism for thinking one's omissions are morally wrong. If even political ethics for non-officeholders can be consequentialist up to a point, then anomaly in political ethics cannot come from the inapplicability of utilitarianism to politics. Strangely enough, it may come from the inapplicability of utilitarianism to private life. For if utilitarianism fits political life, and is perhaps the only one of the standard theories that can dispel what's paradoxical about dirty hands; if it is unsuitable for the conduct of private life (at least psychologically) while Kantian and virtue theories *are* suitable; then perhaps private life and public life are subject to two different types of morality. Admittedly, the two different moralities are not utter expediency on the one hand and reasonable scrupulousness on the other, as in Machiavelli's story. Utilitarianism does not endorse whatever maintains the government in power. But it may be that the divide between public and private life does coincide with the boundary between utilitarianism and non-utilitarian theories, even though some of the same agents are supposed to be governed by both. Separate spheres and double standards are troublesome for theory, and sometimes the stuff of anomaly.

Notes

A different version of this essay will be appearing in Tom Sorell, *Moral Theory and Anomaly* (Oxford: Blackwell, 1999).

1　There is still controversy about the killing in Gibraltar of three people believed to have been members of the IRA and believed to have been on the point of carrying out a terrorist act against the British military. After being shot, the three were found to be unarmed.

2　See Michael Walzer, "Political Action: the Problem of Dirty Hands," *Philosophy and Public Affairs* 2 (1973): 160-180.

3　For details, see my *Hobbes* (London: Routledge: 1986) ch. 9.

4　Stuart Hampshire, *Innocence and Experience* (Cambridge MA.: Harvard University Press, 1989) 140-177. See also "Public and Private Morality" and the title essay in Hampshire's *Morality and Conflict* (Oxford: Blackwell, 1983). Hampshire's 1996 Tanner Lectures return to the themes of these works.

5　Hampshire, *Innocence* 68, 170.

6　Hampshire, *Innocence* 66.

7　Hampshire, *Innocence* 170.

8　O. O'Neill, *Towards Justice and Virtue* (Cambridge: Cambridge University Press, 1996) ch. 6.

9　Hampshire, *Innocence* 165.

10　See the essays "Morality and Pessimism" and "Public and Private Morality," in *Morality and Conflict*.

11　Hampshire, "Morality and Conflict," *Morality and Conflict* 152.

12　See Dennis F. Thompson, *Political Ethics and Public Office* (Cambridge, MA.: Harvard University Press, 1987) ch. 1.

13　"Their own interests" in this formulation is admittedly vague, and ambiguous (but I believe excusably so) between each person voting in the interests of that person or each person voting in interests shared by other voters in a constituency. Both are natural interpretations of self-interest. Empirical studies of the influence of self-interest in voting preferences and opinions associated with these sometimes overdefine self-interest for the sake of testability, and then find that political opinions reflect self-interest less frequently and to a smaller degree than one might think. This may be what happens in the 1990 study by D. Sears and C. Funk, "Self Interest in Americans' Political Opinions," *Beyond Self Interest*, ed. J. Mansbridge (Chicago: University of Chicago Press, 1990) 147-70. Self-interest is measurable material short-term impact on the survey respondent or his/her family.

14　I think these issues come under Sears's and Funk's heading of "ambiguous severe threats" which do measurably mobilise self-interest in even their narrow sense. See Sears and Funk, "Self Interest" 160ff.

15　See the title essay in Robert Goodin, *Utilitarianism as a Public Philosophy* (Cambridge: Cambridge University Press, 1995).

16　See Bernard Williams's critique of utilitarianism in J.J.C. Smart and B. Williams, *Utilitarianism, For and Against* (Cambridge: Cambridge University Press, 1973). Similar themes resurface in Williams, *Moral Luck* (Cambridge: Cambridge University Press, 1981).

17　Robert Goodin, *Utilitarianism* 11-12.

FIVE

Principles and Politics

LEAH BRADSHAW

Among Hannah Arendt's most provocative claims is the assertion that lying is an intrinsic part of politics, that, indeed, it is the mark of political freedom. In her essay "Truth and Politics," she makes the sweeping statement that "no one has ever doubted that truth and politics are on rather bad terms with each other, and no one...has ever counted truthfulness among the political virtues."[1] Lying is a requisite skill not only for demagogues, but for statesmen in general, according to Arendt. Her most consistent argument is that the preservation of the world, and care for its sustenance and continuity, is the primary mandate of politics, so that should there exist a conflict between a matter of principle and the issue of sheer survival or continuity, the statesman ought to choose survival. If dirty hands in politics is defined as the willingness to use deception and fraud for supposedly good ends, then Arendt can certainly be counted among its defenders, but her argument for dirty hands is more complex than most.

Arendt is noted for her defense of the political realm, the spontaneity of action, and she always maintained that political integrity requires a measure of antipathy to truth and goodness. Politics, with its characteristic diversity and plurality, demands a different set of loyalties than the pull of truth. "Goodness," Arendt wrote in *The Human Condition*, "as a consistent way of life, is not only impossible within the confines of the public realm, it is even destructive of it...goodness that comes out of hiding and assumes a public role is no longer good, but corrupt in its own terms and will carry its own corruption wherever it goes."[2] Should a conflict arise between goodness in the absolute sense, or truth, and political loyalties, those who adhere to truth will justify their stand on the grounds of objectivity and duty. The problem for Arendt is that truth of this sort, even if it can be demonstrated, may violate other goods: those of friendship, for example.[3] One may be put in situations where one has to choose one set of goods over another. Jean Elshtain echoes this view in her Massey Lectures when she quotes Milan

Kundera as saying that "any man who was the same in both public and intimate life would be a monster." Kundera says that even if his friend has done something stupid and ought to be punished for it, it would be "indefensible" of Kundera to denounce his friend publicly.[4]

Arendt held that there simply are some goods that are incommensurable; a full human life has to take stock of these divergent goods, and the human condition is such that one constantly has to make choices that entail deliberative judgment. The notion that there are private and public 'selves,' a notion shared by Arendt and Elshtain, is not one that is upheld unanimously in the tradition of political and moral theory. The most vociferous opponent to this kind of split would be Kant. Although Arendt admired Kant's philosophy, and tried to recast his *Critique of Judgment* as a sort of forerunner to her own efforts to place practical judgment at the forefront of moral thinking, her efforts are strained.[5] In the end, Kant remains as the archetypical moral purist, the man who struggles for absolute consistency in all his thoughts and actions. Morality for Kant is a "collection of absolutely binding moral laws by which action ought to be governed." Kant claims that it is our duty to uphold the moral law in our actions, and that "there can be no conflict between politics, as an applied branch of right, and morality as a theoretical branch of right." Such a conflict could only occur, according to Kant, if we look at morality as nothing more than a kind of expediency that can be altered or breached when the conditions of expediency change. And for Kant, that would be tantamount to denying that there is any such thing as morality.[6]

Arendt's view, contrary to Kant's, is that action in the world, and particularly political action which requires the engagement with others and their particularities, requires a kind of practical and circumstantial judgment that cannot be derived directly from moral imperatives. Part of the glory of human action, for her, is the risk that is entailed in engaging with others. Promises are made and sometimes have to be broken. Bonds are forged on the basis of common projects, and sometimes our loyalties to those with whom we act outweigh our prior commitments to principles. This is why Arendt makes so much of the acts of punishment and forgiveness in *The Human Condition*. They have in common the potential to get beyond dirty hands and to restore moral coherence. Without the capacity to punish wrongful acts, or to forgive them, there would be no limit to the possibilities of human action and no moral judgment. The willingness to transgress and to forgive is a big part of the risk involved in entering into the political realm, and Arendt appears to have as much admiration for the *engagé* as she does for the philosophical or religious purist. She writes that "trespassing is an everyday occurrence which is in the nature of action's constant establishment of new relationships within a web of relations, and it needs forgiving, dismissing, in order to make it possible for life to go on by constantly releasing men from what they have done unknowingly."[7] To be political, one has to be willing to risk moral approbation.[8] To be morally responsible, one must be willing to accept the possibility of punishment for transgressions.

There is also the problem that truth, in its isolated context, poses problems for freedom because of its absolutist claims. It harbours within itself "frequently tyrannical tendencies;" and it is no accident, she continues, that professional truthtellers (by which she means philosophers) habitually live under a kind of compulsion.[9] People who are compelled by truth, whether that truth is apprehended by faith or reason, speak of being drawn to it by forces outside their own will; all the way back to the allegory of the cave in Plato's *Republic*, we have these accounts of the light of truth compelling individuals against their will. Arendt says that "our ability to lie—but not necessarily our ability to tell the truth—belongs among the few obvious, demonstrable data that confirm human freedom."[10] Lying, she seems to be saying, is the capacity to create meaning in defiance of truth, to spin a human story that has no reliable basis in reason or in fact. While lying may be deceitful, it nonetheless for Arendt is a high mark of the capacity for human freedom. One can fabricate a reality from lies or myths.[11]

Certainly, Arendt thought that the deliberate liar in politics is less of a moral danger than the person who is self-deceived. The cold-blooded liar, Arendt claimed, knows the difference between truth and artifice, and does not dissolve the distinction while lying. We may think immediately here of Machiavelli and his admonition to the prince that he must know how not to be good. In giving this sort of advice, Machiavelli implies that an astute prince knows the difference between truth (or goodness) and lies, and he deliberately chooses the lies. Arendt finds this sort of "Machiavellism" far less dangerous than self-deception, in which there is no possibility of a check on duplicity and fabrication. For Arendt, truth and politics each has its claims, both sets of claims are valid, and to be a complete human being—operating in the realm of truth and in the realm of politics—one needs to straddle both. Current moral prejudice, she ventures, tends to be harsh on the cold-blooded liar, and soft on the "art" of self-deception. But self-deception is far more dangerous, in Arendt's view, because in self-deception, truth is more than repressed: it is annihilated.

For the present discussion, what is significant in Hannah Arendt's argument about truth and politics is the distinction that she clearly makes between a reality that is apprehended through reason—the object of philosophical inquiry—and the worldly reality of politics, contingency, and plurality. Arendt is very much a traditional political philosopher in that she holds these arenas of activity as separate. For her, thinking about truth has moral implications, but only in an indirect way (if it is done properly). In an essay called "Thinking and Moral Considerations," Arendt wrote that thinking is a critical activity in moral life, and without the capacity to think we would have no notion of how to avoid evil; nonetheless, "the faculty of thought has a 'natural aversion' against accepting its own results as 'solid axioms' ... we cannot expect any moral propositions or commandments, no final code of conduct from the thinking activity, least of all a new and allegedly final decision of what is good and what is evil."[12] If we cannot expect solid axioms or principles of conduct to emerge from philosophical thought, we can expect practical judgement to come from it. In Arendt's profiles of actual people whom she admired, this is the quality that stands out: the capacity to move in the world, amid crises and unpredictable events, with a kind of measured and, ultimately, good judgment. What struck Arendt about her exemplary figures, whose lives are chronicled in *Men in Dark Times*, was not the consistency of their principles, but the weightiness of their persons.

What does all of this mean for the dirty hands question in political life? For Hannah Arendt, political engagement necessarily requires dirty hands, in the sense that lying and deceit are an intrinsic part of the world of opinions and the world of plurality. One gets the sense from her that the gap between truth and politics is never closed, by virtue of the fact that the two pursuits are distinct, and their loci are distinct as well. Truth resides in solitude and the life of the mind, politics dwells in plurality, community, and opinion, and while truth is always the final judge, its judgments—if they are to be useful and not tyrannical—are to be kept at a distant remove. The only way in which philosophy can become genuinely political is by example. Arendt points to Socrates's example of staking his life on the dictum that it is better to suffer an injustice than to commit one. While profoundly true, this statement does not lead to any political or social prescriptions, no moral codes that one can use to direct one's actions. Any philosopher who manages to garner widespread and enthusiastic support for such prescriptions, according to Arendt, should rest assured that this is just a happy coincidence, likely to dissolve with shifts in opinion and power. Truth is the anchor outside politics, for Arendt, the thing that grounds political judgments but, if held too tightly to political matters, destroys the freedom and novelty of political acts.

Lying is not necessarily immoral for Arendt, but it is anti-philosophical. Secrecy, or discretion as she designates the diplomatic rendition of it, is an intrinsic part of politics; the deliberate falsehood and the outright lie she regards as "legitimate means to achieve political ends." Arendt expresses surprise at how little attention has been devoted by political theorists to lying in politics.[13] The lie is not symptomatic of politics gone awry: it *is* politics for Arendt. Lying is easy, and it is even more likely to appeal than truth. "Lies are often much more plausible, more appealing to reason, than reality, since the liar has the great advantage of knowing beforehand what the audience wishes or expects to hear. He has prepared his story for public consumption with a careful eye to making it credible, whereas reality has the disconcerting habit of confronting us with the unexpected, for which we were not prepared."[14]

Arendt is careful to claim a final ascendency for truth, however. Single lies are often successful, even necessary, in politics, but lying on principle always fails. There always comes a point, she says, when "lying is counter-productive," and that point occurs when "the audience to which the lies are addressed is forced to disregard altogether the distinguishing line between truth and falsehood in order to be able to survive."[15] Again, we have to bear in mind that for Arendt, lies are conscious political tools, evidence of the human capacity for imagination, creativity and freedom, but lies are limited by the actuality of truth, however elusive the truth may be.

There are resonances of traditional political philosophy in Arendt's position on lying. One is reminded of the infamous Machiavellian confession that he loves his country more than he loves his soul. Arendt in fact cites Machiavelli in an accommodating manner: "Though it is true that by resisting evil, you are likely to be involved in evil, your care for the world takes precedence in politics over your care for your self—whether this self is your body or your soul. Machiavelli's 'I love my native city more than my soul' is only a variation of: I love the world and its future more than my life or my self."[16] For Arendt, and arguably for Machiavelli, the quality specific to the politician or the statesman is his civic responsibility, his allegiance to the community. Lying , if it can be said to have a positive cast, entails this kind of civic responsibility. One can imagine a politician lying, for example, about his position on an explosive moral issue if he thought that his honesty would destroy the cohesion of his community. Arendt does not see this sort of political "lying" as evil, or even as unethical. She sees it as necessary, and as proof of the insurmountable gap between truth and politics.

But Machiavelli does not stand isolated in the tradition as the one who defended an ethic for politics separate from philosophy. "Historically," Arendt writes, "the conflict between truth and politics came out of two diametrically opposed ways of life—the life of the philosopher, as interpreted first by Parmenides, and then by Plato, and the way of life of the citizen. For the citizen's ever-changing opinions about human affairs, which themselves were in a state of constant flux, the philosopher opposed the truth about those things which in their very nature were everlasting, and from which, therefore, principles could be derived to stabilize human affairs."[17]

Machiavelli is the political thinker who is most often associated with the dirty hands defense, but he may be only the most bold of those philosophers in the canon who have maintained the distance between truth and politics and who have sought ways of defending deception in politics. All students of Western thought are familiar with the myth of the metals in Plato's *Republic*, wherein Socrates tells a story about how people may come to associate their particular strata in the social hierarchy with particular metals: bronze, gold or silver. The implication is that it will be politically expedient if people understand that they occupy the position they do because of some natural order, or some cast of fate, rather than a matter of social and political determination.[18] The myth of the metals is called a "noble lie," a lie that is intended to serve the public good of social and political stability. The myth of the metals, whether or not one takes it literally as Socrates's political advice, is a powerful tale of truth and deception in politics. It informs Hannah Arendt's discussions of politics and morality in an all-pervasive way, for it is Socrates who initially sets up in the Western tradition the dualism between virtue, or truth, as something discoverable by reason, and politics as the realm of opinion and action. The myth of the metals would not be possible, not even conceptually, without the presupposed break between the human capacity to know something through reason, and the human capacity to act and live in the world among others. The myth is intended to cross the gap between what we can know by reason, and what we have to settle for in the world. We know, through reason, that justice demands that every human being perform according to his or her highest capacities. What we experience in the world is that people, for all sorts of reasons—some habitual, some inherited, some accidental, some economic, etc.—end up living lives that do not mirror their capabilities. The myth of the metals is meant to heal, in a way, the gap between the philosophical truth and the actual reality, by lying about the reality.

What would be the alternative to this noble lie? It would be the effort to change the world so that, as far as possible, it approximates the principles of justice that we know by reason are true. According to Arendt's logic, this effort would result in a much worse situation than that which is perpetuated by the noble lie, for we would be relying on human judgment to apprehend and execute a truth, and when people set out to implement truth they are ruthless and unbending. Much of Arendt's discussion in the last part of the *Origins of Totalitarianism* is about how it is that the "supersense" of ideological thinking wreaked such havoc in the twentieth century. What the ideologies that she calls totalitarian (she has in mind particularly the ideologies of Hitler's Naziism and Stalin's communism) have in common is their certainty regarding truth, and their willingness to implement it directly in the world without the mediation of politics. She writes there that: "No ideology which aims at the explanation of all historical events of the past and at mapping out the course of events of the future can bear the unpredictability which springs from the fact that men are creative, that they can bring forward something so new that nobody ever foresaw it."[19] The lie or the myth is much more flexible than the totalitarian ideology: since it is an act of free imagination, it can be changed at will.

Aristotle is not typically remembered in political science for his defense of dirty hands, yet a convincing case can be made that he did in fact understand, and justify, the gap between truth and politics that makes dirty hands an insurmountable problem in politics. Michael Stocker makes such a case in his discussion of Aristotle's analysis of "mixed acts" in the *Nicomachean Ethics*.[20] A mixed act, for Aristotle, is one in which the actions are good but the reasoning for the actions is base, or vice versa. Stocker's favourite example is drawn from the virtue of courage. There is no question that we identify courage as a virtue, but there is also no doubt that courage can be exhibited only under conditions that are unhappy: situations fraught with danger and risk, and frequently, the potential for great physical harm. The classic setting for the exhibition of courage, for Aristotle, was certainly the condition of war. Now one can argue that war in itself is not a good thing, even though we may look with pride upon certain virtuous, or courageous, actions that were performed because of it. Even from the standpoint of the individual, whose aim is happiness according to Aristotle, it would be hard to defend unqualifiedly the "good" of courage. Even for good people, says Stocker, the exercise of courage involves "a certain sort of pain and lack of pleasure—because important goods are threatened and there is the risk of suffering important bads."[21] Stocker makes the more general claim that for Aristotle, there certainly is a dirty hands problem, one that Aristotle regards as insurmountable because of the conflicts that people will necessarily experience between their desires and their values.[22]

The dirty hands problem in Aristotle is highlighted even more when we look at Aristotle's comparison, at the end of the *Nicomachean Ethics*, of the two ways of life: the contemplative and the active. Aristotle argues there that the most God-like activity is the one of study, and that is because the life of contemplation is the most self-sufficient, with no end outside itself.[23] The virtues connected with action, however, which we tend to associate with politics and war (according to Aristotle), require trouble, because they necessarily require immersion in the world of opinions, contest, power, and struggle. A life of action is tainted in the way that a contemplative life is not; on the other hand, if it were not for the possibility of corruption, one would not be able to exhibit virtues like bravery, moderation, and justice, which in fact require an element of deliberation and choice among goods.

Ironically, in Aristotle, the very possibility of dirty hands is really the condition for the exhibition of the moral virtues, or what Aristotle calls the *human* virtues.[24] A life of contemplation, dwelling upon truth in a quiet and virtuous way, is a life fitted for gods, Aristotle remarks, but not really for humans, although we ought as far as possible to live according to the divine principle in us.[25]

Aristotle's demarcation between the "divine" and "human" virtues I take to be very close to the distinction that Hannah Arendt makes between truth and action. The two ways of life are not identical; they require different aptitudes and even different virtues, up to a point. The point at which they converge is the juncture where final judgments are made. And so Arendt wrote at the end of her essay "On Humanity in Dark Times: Thoughts on Lessing" that the most profound thing that has been said about the relationship between truth and humanity is to be found in a sentence of Lessing's which seems to draw, from all his work, wisdom's last word: "Let each man say what he deems the truth, and let truth itself be commended unto God!"[26]

If there is a dirty hands problem for Hannah Arendt, it is not really the problem of having to engage in impure acts in order to participate in political life. Deception and manipulation is so intrinsically a part of politics for her that she does not regard engagement in them as immoral, provided that there is an apprehension of truth that lies at the base of our actions. Prudence, or practical judgment, is the crucial link between truth and politics, and for practical judgment to prevail, one has to maintain the theoretical distinction between the contemplative object of faith or reason, and the object of political action, which is building and maintaining a world. Dirty hands is not nearly so grave a problem for Arendt as the collapse of these two realms.

Far more alarming to her than the liar is the figure of someone like Adolph Eichmann, who, Arendt claimed, did not know the difference between truth and lying: here was someone for whom the critical distinction between the object of thought (truth) and the conditions of the world had been obliterated. When Eichmann stood up and quoted Kant as his moral guide, he was not lying to conceal the magnitude of his crimes; he thought he had got Kant right.[27] The infamous subtitle of Arendt's book on Eichmann—*A Report on the Banality of Evil*—is meant to convey the central finding from among her observations on Eichmann's trial: that possibly the greatest evils in the modern world are committed not out of deliberate contravention of truth and morality, but in ignorance of any standards of truth and morality. Arendt said that the greatest problem that emerged from the trials of war criminals was the question of judgment, and what it might mean for citizens of the twentieth century. What came to light for her was "a quite extraordinary confusion over elementary questions of morality."[28] Arendt attributes this confusion ultimately to the loss of the traditional hierarchy between philosophy and politics, between what Aristotle called the "divine" element and the "human" element. If there is no intimation of truth that is beyond the flux of politics, which can be appealed to as a final arbiter of right and wrong, then there is no capacity for punishment or forgiveness; indeed, there is nothing by which to measure transgressions.

There is really only a dirty hands problem in political life if one assumes that there are standards, or principles, outside or above the flux of politics that command our allegiance. These standards may be metaphysical reference points, such as philosophical truth or revelation, or they may be more secular, humanistic claims (such as the claim to universal human rights). In any case, the identification of dirty hands relies upon a comparison between practices and ideals. Lying is bad, because there is such a thing as truth. In conclusion, I would like to suggest that there are two currents of modern political thought that dispense with the moral difficulty of the dirty hands problem by collapsing the distinction between truth and politics. Postmodernism and certain kinds of feminism disallow the postulation of any reasoned criteria by which we can even measure dirty hands. Both these currents are grave challenges to the tradition of law and punishment that underscore Western liberal democracies.

There is a widespread inclination in political theory now to disavow any truth whatsoever. Broadly speaking, this is the postmodern movement, embodied in the work of people like Michel Foucault, Richard Rorty, and William Connolly. As Leslie Thiele, one contemporary commentator on postmodernism, describes this phenomenon: "Postmodernists challenge the very notion of a single, uniform human nature. What makes humans what they are, postmodernists claim, is not some metaphysical or even biological human essence, but a particular historical development, one that has been and remains grounded in social processes."[29] Postmodernism is a long way even from the dialectical understanding of someone like Marx, who thought that an ultimate meaning, or justice, for human beings revealed itself through the history of class struggle, resulting in a final full consciousness. For the postmodernist, everything is in constant motion; power structures are shifting and congealing all the time. Nothing definitive or true can be expected to emerge from these fluctuations. "The postmodern concern is that we have become the vehicles and chief effects of power, not simply the objects of repression and constraint."[30] If there is nothing but power, then how can there be any assessment of transgression? The postmodern diagnosis of contemporary democracy begins to look dangerously like Arendt's description of the nightmare state of the twentieth century.

What Arendt called the moral confusion of the darkest time of the twentieth century, postmodernists seem to be claiming as typical of the human
condition.

There is also an influential current in feminist theory that was initiated
by Carol Gilligan's formative study *In A Different Voice*.[31] Gilligan conducted surveys of male and female undergraduate students at Harvard,
analysing how these students deliberated about moral issues, and she came
to the conclusion that women appeared to have a distinctive moral voice.
The males seemed to conform to the classical pattern of moral deliberation,
which is to say they formed principles grounded in reason and applied them
to actions in the world. On the whole, this method of moral reasoning produced strong judgments about right and wrong, leading to clear prescriptions for punishment or exoneration. The females appeared to have a much
more diffuse moral sensibility, one embedded in relationships with others.
They did not have the "duality" of principle and practice that seemed to
characterize the males, but they had a greater tolerance for differences in
need among human beings that was accompanied by the abandonment of
absolutes.[32] Gilligan called this feminine moral voice one of care, and con-
trasted it to the predominantly male voice of justice.

The voice of care is less strident, less prohibitive, than the voice of justice. Gilligan finds it more compassionate, and more open to the frailties of
human life, but one should be cautious in embracing this new moral voice.
Gilligan looks at tough situations in which human beings have to make
choices that are bound to hurt someone. She does not want to call these
dirty-hands situations, where people are at a crossroads and must accept
moral responsibility for what they do. She wants us to understand, not to
judge. Nell Noddings is another contemporary feminist theorist who is
much moved by the ethic of care. She identifies a relational ethics that is
very close to Gilligan's notion of a different voice. She compares her relational ethics to the "ideology of individualism." Interestingly, one of the
virtues that Noddings castigates in the classical tradition is courage. The
courage to commit oneself to a cause or a set of beliefs, while admired by
people like Arendt, Aristotle, and Michael Stocker, is for Noddings an
intrinsic part of a competitive, adversarial form of life.[33] Standing resolute
on principle against the world is for Noddings a quintessentially male experience, "long synonymous with Western culture." Noddings would like to
see moral education restructured in our culture, so that we seek less for
heroes and villains, and try to understand more the tragic quality of human
judgment. To those who would claim that in any moral dilemma, one side
is more right than another, Noddings answers that we should stop thinking in terms of either/or. "We should stand by both parties. We should

stand sympathetically between the apparently good and the apparently evil and work toward reconciliation."[34]

What the postmodernists and "care feminists" have in common is their rejection of any measure of good or truth that can serve as a trustworthy yardstick against which to measure crimes and misdeeds. When Hannah Arendt wrote about truth and politics, she was concerned to show what happens when one tries to impose too categorically upon the world a version of truth: the consequence may be an ideological reign of terror, in which there is no room for the exercise of human freedom and the admission of error. Dirty hands in politics for Arendt is the price one pays for human freedom. One acts in the world in a creative way, one builds and destroys political bonds, but one is limited by the nagging voice of truth that puts a limit on what one can do.

In the postmodern context, we are faced with a different problem, however, and this is the problem that emerges not from the implementation of rigid truths in political practice, but the denial of any truths whatsoever. The dirty hands problem virtually disappears from this context, because we all have dirty hands. Judgments are necessarily relational, contextual, and particular. We return to Arendt's quotation from Lessing: "Let each man say what he deems the truth, and let truth itself be commended unto God." In a world in which each man and woman may say what he or she deems the truth, period, political responsibility is very difficult to assess. The problem of identifying and punishing offenders of moral principle is supplanted by the much graver problem of trying to figure out what, if any, our moral principles are.

Notes

An earlier version of this essay was first presented at the Dirty Hands Workshop held at York University, December, 1993.

1 Arendt, "Truth and Politics," *Between Past and Future* (New York: Viking Press, 1954) 227.

2 Arendt, *The Human Condition* (Chicago: University of Chicago Press, 1958) 77.

3 Arendt, "On Humanity in Dark Times: Thoughts on Lessing," *Men in Dark Times* (New York: Harcourt, Brace, Jovanovich, 1955) 28.

4 Jean Elshtain, *Democracy on Trial* (Toronto: Anansi Press, 1993).

5 Arendt really attempts to construct a political philosophy out of Kant's *Critique of Judgment*; she says so in her Kant Lectures, edited and published by Ronald Beiner: *Hannah Arendt: Lectures on Kant's Political Philosophy* (Chicago: University of Chicago Press, 1982) 61.

6 Kant, Appendix to "Perpetual Peace," *Kant's Political Writings*, ed. Hans Reiss (Cambridge: Cambridge University Press, 1970) 116.

7 Arendt, *Human Condition* 240.

8 Arendt's emphasis upon punishment and forgiveness for dirty hands trespasses puts her very close, in spirit, to Michael Walzer on the dirty hands problem. Walzer accepts that dirty hands are inevitable in political life. It is by his dirty hands that we know the moral politician, according to Walzer. If he were a moral man and nothing else, he would not have dirty hands; if he were a politician and nothing else, he would pretend that his hands were clean. But, according to Walzer, the moral politician still has to atone for his dirty hands. Walzer considers the tragic resolution of the dirty hands problem, exemplified for him in the Protestant stance of Max Weber, who nobly, and individually, bears the moral burden of his dirty hands. But Walzer rejects this highly individualistic response in favour of punishment as a social catharsis for dirty hands. What we really need to do, says Walzer, where someone has chosen a morally precarious course for some other good, is honour the man for the good he has done, and punish him for the bad he has done. Punishment has a cathartic effect, since it relieves the dirty hands perpetrator from guilt, and it also cautions against too cavalier an embracing of dirty hands. Walzer, interestingly, does not talk about forgiveness as the other side of punishment in the manner that Arendt does, but I think Arendt is right to put them together. Those who have the authority to punish also have the authority to forgive. Michael Walzer, "Political Action: The Problem of Dirty-hands," *Philosophy and Public Affairs* 2:2 (Winter 1973): 161-80; 174-80.

9 Arendt, "Truth and Politics" 239-40.

10 Arendt, "Truth and Politics" 250.

11 Arendt, it should be mentioned, was well aware of the dangers of lying. In *The Origins of Totalitarianism*, she spends a considerable amount of time demonstrating how the power of ideological thinking could construct a reign of terror out of a network of lies. Still, one sees in her work an uncomfortable closeness between the praise she gives to the artifice of human creation (and the role that lying may play in that process) and her condemnation of the excesses of ideological deception in totalitarian regimes. Arendt actually said that it is the "contempt for reality which makes possible changing the world, the erection of the human artifice," but there are cases in the 20th century that make us shudder at the

lengths to which human beings can go to try to transform themselves. For Arendt, the great excess of totalitarian regimes was that "in their effort to prove that everything is possible, [they] have discovered that there are crimes which men can neither punish nor forgive." *Origins of Totalitarianism* (New York: Harcourt, Brace, Jovanovich, 1951) 458-59.

12 Arendt, "Thinking and Moral Considerations," *Social Research* 38:3 (Fall): 425.

13 Arendt, "Lying in Politics," *Crises of the Republic* (New York: Harcourt, Brace, Jovanovich, 1969) 4-5.

14 Arendt, "Lying in Politics" 7.

15 Arendt, "Lying in Politics" 7.

16 Arendt, *Lectures on Kant's Political Philosophy* 50.

17 Arendt, "Truth and Politics" 235.

18 A very good discussion of Socrates' myth of the metals is found in Edward Andrew, "Equality of Opportunity as the Noble Lie," *History of Political Thought* x:4 (Winter 1989): 578-95. Andrew argues there that: "The reason Plato called the myth of the metals a falsehood is that he thought that there are no recognizable natural differences (golden, silver and bronze souls) between human beings which account for or justify their position in social hierarchy." 594.

19 Arendt, *Origins of Totalitarianism* 458.

20 Michael Stocker, "Dirty hands and Conflicts of Values and Desires in Aristotle's Ethics," *Plural and Conflicting Values* (Oxford: Clarendon Press, 1990). I thank David Shugarman for bringing Stocker's argument to my attention.

21 Stocker 83.

22 Stocker 84.

23 Aristotle, *Nicomachean Ethics*, trans. Terence Irwin, (Indianapolis: Hackett Publishing, 1985) 1177a25-1177b5.

24 Aristotle, *Nicomachean Ethics* 1178a5-10.

25 Aristotle, *Nichomachean Ethics* 1177b25-30.

26 Arendt, "On Humanity in Dark Times: Thoughts on Lessing" 31.

27 In *Eichmann in Jerusalem: A Report on the Banality of Evil* (Middlesex, England: Penguin, 1963), Arendt describes how Eichmann distorted Kant's categorical imperative from its original intent—that one ought to act as though the principle of one's will could become the principle for universal laws—to mean: "act as if the principle of your actions were the same as that of the legislator or the law of the land" (136) . By corrupting Kant's maxim in this way, Eichmann demonstrated that he had no notion of the gap between truth and politics, hence no gauge of the extent of his own self-deception.

28 Arendt, *Eichmann in Jerusalem* 295.

29 Leslie Paul Thiele, *Thinking Politics* (Chatham, New Jersey: Chatham House Publishers, 1997) 83.

30 Thiele, *Thinking Politics* 93.

31 Carol Gilligan, *In A Different Voice* (Cambridge, Massachusetts: Harvard University Press, 1982).

32 Gilligan, *Different Voice* 165.

33 Nell Noddings, *Women and Evil* (Berkeley: University of California Press, 1989) 189.

34 Noddings, *Women and Evil* 239.

SIX

Justice, Expediency, and Practices of Thinking

EVAN SIMPSON

Two Practices of Thinking

After examining Jesus of Nazareth, Pontius Pilate concluded, "I do not find this man guilty of any of your charges against him," but "when Pilate saw…that a riot was beginning, he took water and washed his hands before the crowd, saying, 'I am innocent of this man's blood'…Then he…delivered [Jesus] to be crucified."[1]

Pilate washed his hands, but did he cleanse them? Some would say he did, for he was able to transfer responsibility for harming an innocent person to the crowd, who willingly said, "His blood be on us and on our children!" Whether guilt can be transferred in this way is an interesting question, but it is not the question I wish mainly to address. I note only that it is a move favoured by one of the foremost rights thinkers of our period. Alan Gewirth suggests that if a band of terrorists tells a man that he must torture his mother to death or they will cause thousands to die, the man should refuse on the grounds that it is then the terrorists who are responsible for the many deaths, the unfortunate man for none.[2] A "principle of intervening action" provides an important part of the explanation why we properly honour such public figures as Martin Luther King, Jr. He was not responsible for the beatings and murders provoked by his non-violent demonstrations and marches, since it was his opponents who committed the injustices. This is less obvious, though, if we think of Gewirth's rule as the "Pontius Pilate Principle." Complicity is not avoided so easily, a burden King accepted.

The idea that people are admired because, or although, they are prepared to dirty their hands is a point I will return to in the end. However, my primary question is whether choices between justice and expediency can be conclusively justified or condemned in general. The simple answer I will offer rests upon a comparison of two ways of thinking. If one thinks solely in terms of rights, then expediency will be rejected. If one thinks only of the general welfare, then the governor of Judea and others like him may be seen as doing what is morally required. This is familiar philosophical ground, and it ranges far beyond the political arena. For example, business people frequently have to weigh the undesirability of engaging in corrupt practices against their responsibility to shareholders, employees, their local community, etc. Ordinary citizens sometimes face the mundane choice between breaking a promise and enabling a greater good.

This cluster of problems is usually described in terms of competing theories of justice and utility. My suggestion is that the broad controversy is more fundamental than this theoretical competition, but also more tractable. Issues of just versus useful action rest basically upon distinct practices of practical reasoning. These practices are defined by certain rules of inference and evidence. They are thus immune from effective attack from outside, as a game is immune from the criticism that it does not conform to the rules of other games. The rights thinker is not subject to refutation by the utilitarian thinker, or vice versa. Each may question the adequacy of the rules accepted by the other, but not decisively. Lest this suggestion be misinterpreted, a limiting condition should be clearly noted. It is rare for someone to think only in terms of individual rights, or only in terms of public utility. Judgments of each kind are normally circumscribed and balanced by considerations of the other kind, but for the purposes of this analysis it is useful to imagine rights thinking and utilitarian thinking as occurring without any such admixture. In this respect they function as tools of philosophical analysis rather than as theses of philosophical psychology or anthropology.

"To the contrary," one might object, "if your account does not extend beyond certain existing practices, then you are neglecting the philosophical task of trying to determine which practices of thinking are to be preferred. Simply to describe and distinguish between forms of mental behaviour falls far short of the more important task of determining which practices of thinking are correct or fundamental." Without insisting dogmatically that no such determination is possible, I do maintain that comparisons of practices are philosophically useful. One of the important virtues of this mode of analysis is that it more easily permits the combination of practices of thinking than does the attempt to reconcile theories of justice and utility. By avoiding the assumption that rights and utilitarian thinking express theories of which one, at most, can be true, one is not intellectually compelled to choose between them. Either practice is then available for use, as circumstances warrant. One implication is that dirty-hands problems are not best characterized as dilemmas in which an agent is in the unhappy situation of accepting contradictory principles of action. However, these are matters better taken up only after developing the point that it is also possible to adhere to a single practice in all circumstances.

Pure Rights Thinking and the Utilitarian Alternative

The pure rights thinking that occurs without admixture includes four distinctive features that are easily identified. First, respect, resentment, indignation, guilt, and the other passions of rectitude arise without the moderation provided by sympathetic concern for the general good. This is the uncompromising attitude expressed in the maxim *fiat justitia, ruat coelum*. Second, when claims of rights collide with consideration of benefits, rights systematically trump benefits. Rights thinkers are not impressed by assertions of concern presented to justify breaking a promise "for your own good," for example. Third, although rights entail obligations (for one to have a right is for another to be obliged to observe it), within pure rights thinking, responsibilities to others seem to extend no further. No duty of charity or of accommodation to terrorists exists, since one cannot help everyone who is in need of help. Hence, the fourth feature: as well as entailing moral protection for their holders and defining centres of independent agency, the perception of rights also promotes one's fundamental otherness. It takes the separation of persons very seriously.

Taking this rights thinking seriously as a feasible mode of practical reasoning leaves open the possibility of alternative forms of thinking. The rules of rights thinking are not adopted by utilitarian thinkers, who maintain that one does better to avoid this mode.[3] Suppose that you own a house with a private driveway, and a neighbour sometimes parks in it without permission, thus violating your rights. You may well resent this. Let us further suppose, though, that you are not actually inconvenienced by your neighbour's behaviour. A utilitarian thinker will find no good reason for resenting an act that does you no harm. To the contrary, such resentment may drive you to create situations that are worse rather than better, as you might if you refused use of your driveway. (The pain of your resentment does not figure in this calculation of better and worse because it is unreasonable by utilitarian standards.)

The characteristics of utilitarian thinking contrast with rights thinking in obvious ways. First, the operative passions are sympathy and compassion rather than resentment and respect. Second, the good overrides rights: doing the right thing, in utilitarian terms, is perfectly distinct from observing individual rights. Third, moral responsibilities extend to duties of benevolence that readily override the moral claims of particular individuals. Utilitarian thinking thus, as Rawls says, conflates all persons into one, as if through the imaginative act of an impartial sympathetic spectator.[4]

Construing these forms of thinking as alternatives has several interesting implications. First, their independence suggests that there is no general answer to the question of whether respect or compassion, rights or goods, duty or virtue, self or society should prevail in moral deliberation. It is intellectually futile to attempt to assign priority of place to one or the other in all circumstances. Second, theories of justice and utility therefore cannot successfully establish any such priority and must have some other role. They may serve to articulate and develop the salient points of the discrete practices of thinking. Third, by exploring rights thinking and utilitarian thinking independently of the theories that describe them, it should be possible to gain a clearer view of their place within practical reasoning generally, in particular in ostensible moral dilemmas of the dirty-hands type.

For pure thinkers of either kind these dilemmas do not arise. Rights thinkers like Gewirth recognize no justification for getting their hands dirty, for rights are absolute and must not be violated no matter what. There are, of course, cases in which rights conflict: dilemmas arise or can be imagined in which one must choose between saving one set of innocent lives or another, but these are internal problems for rights thinkers, rather than problems of the dirty-hands kind. Unless it is recognized that moral problems are not all of one kind, and dirty-hands conflicts between justice and expediency are distinguished from other problems, unnecessary confusions may frustrate analysis. As for utilitarian thinkers who accept harm to innocents, they identify no reasons for guilt, although they feel regret that some must suffer. Again, distinctions need to be drawn carefully. Regret connects with compassion and is perfectly rational when people suffer. Guilt is tied to one's violation of principles of right and is out of place for utilitarian agents, who act only on principles that express the greatest good.

Although rights and utilitarian thinking are the practices of moral thinking most obviously relevant to dirty-hands issues, they are not the only relevant ones. Others include those typical of the ethics of care and responsibility described by Carol Gilligan and developed in Sara Ruddick's conception of maternal thinking.[5] I will not pursue the suggestion here, but I believe that many points analogous to those stated above can be made in connection with conflicts between concern in relationships and justice or utility. Aeschylus's account of Agamemnon's bloody sacrifice of Iphigenia is not best rendered as a conflict between justice and utility. Clytemnestra's vengeful justice upon her husband does not simply express a problem internal to rights thinking, but it has little justification in utility. Both murders are committed by political agents whose deeds are worsened by violations of care and piety.[6] This third moral dimension makes a comprehensive definition of the problem or problems of dirty hands more difficult, but all appear to arise in collisions between forms of moral thinking. The structure of the issues may therefore be adequately represented by limiting discussion here to collisions of justice and expediency.

Hybrid Thinking and Theories

Dirty-hands problems appear, then, to arise only for hybrid thinkers who employ more than one set of rules. Such hybrid thinking is initially problematical. From each of the two pure perspectives on which I am focusing the other is incomprehensible, at least in the sense that utilitarian thinkers find it baffling that it might be seriously maintained that justice should be done though the heavens fall, while rights thinkers see it as morally absurd that seeking innocent scapegoats might be consistent with the overall good. Is it to be expected that mutual incomprehension between those who engage in different forms of thinking should suddenly disappear when these forms are present within a single person?

Ultimately I will answer in the affirmative, but there are good reasons to resist trying too readily to reconcile conflicts between forms of thinking. Suppose that appealing to rights is described as an indirect expression of utilitarian thinking, so that it becomes comprehensible how you might resent a person's using your driveway even when it does you no harm. In one standard account of this kind, utility justifies social practices and institutions, including those characteristic of owning and disposing of personal property together with the rights involved. As a good utilitarian who defends the institution on the grounds of its social usefulness, you can then press the right it gives you, even if it means inconveniencing your neighbour at no benefit to anyone. However, this assimilation of rights thinking to utilitarian thinking is unstable. It requires saying that rights that have a basis in their utility cannot be overridden by utility, contrary to the utilitarian style of thinking, according to which the basic objective of practical judgment is to make things better. Rights thinking remains a questionable practice from this point of view.

When utilitarian thinking is assimilated to rights thinking, similar instabilities occur. It is initially plausible to say both that one should make the consequences of one's actions as good as possible and that a fair distribution of rights is itself among the goods, possibly the most important of these goods. This grafts a principle of right onto the utilitarian perspective, creating the attractive possibility of representing utilitarian thinking as itself a version of the rights perspective.[7] The highest good is the protection of rights, which therefore cannot be overridden by other considerations of public benefit. However, diminishing the distinctiveness of the two forms of thinking in this way is easily subverted. Rights may indeed be goods, but if that is the rationale for observing them, competing goods may always make a more powerful claim. Of course, if the protection of rights is the highest good then no such claim should succeed, but because this identification of the highest good is extraneous to pure utilitarian thinking, it remains inherently questionable. The instability remains.

On the view I am developing, the practice of utilitarian thinking has no logical decisive justification, but it is a possible form of thinking. One might nevertheless favour rights thinking on the grounds that pure utilitarian thinkers are also subject to criticism as calculating individuals who are liable to a dubious elitism. This is not the charge embedded in the popular view of politicians as cynically using public office for their personal advantage. The politicians in the latter case are simply immoral; the agents in the former have a moral sense, but allow it to justify the supposition that they know best and are obliged on certain occasions to do better for the public by transgressing the laws that bind others.

It is an interesting feature of pure utilitarian thinking that legal rights lack moral force. For rights to have this force is for them to be able to resist direct utilitarian considerations, at least up to some threshold. But a clear-headed utilitarian thinker will reckon that if keeping a rule lowers welfare, then the rule should be broken at any level. There is no threshold. Hence, even if the law is generally justified, utilitarian thinking will not support a universal obligation to adhere to it.[8] This is a serious moral fault, however, only if it is supposed that the rule of rights always prevails against utility, and this simply would be to privilege one possible form of thinking over another.

A philosophically better alternative is to recognize that difficult choices will probably always arise in social life, and to conclude that the only evident way of coping with the grey areas of moral and political judgment is through hybrid thinking. I want, therefore, to suggest a way of freeing this hybrid thinking from the hybrid theories that try to assimilate one form of thinking to another or to place one above the other.

Thresholds of Appropriateness

Most people believe that there are cases in which it would be a great mistake to allow rights thinking to overrule considerations of the general good. Most also believe that in other cases, the general good is not sufficient to challenge individual rights. Most people thus recognize certain thresholds beyond which one or another form of thinking is not appropriate, and this recognition occurs without resort to theories. Theories of justice and utility seem required only because the alternative styles of thinking exist and must be adjudicated. As we noted earlier, the theories may be valuable in articulating and developing those styles, but they cannot replace them, bring them basically into question, or separate grey into black and white. Theories are particularly deficient in rules for determining when thresholds of concern are crossed, leaving it to preferred styles of thinking to fix these boundaries.

The difference between rights thinking and utilitarian thinking on the one hand and theoretical thinking on the other is evident from the fact that unlike theories of rights and utility, rights thinking and utilitarian thinking are not contradictory and can resist demands for demonstration. As a practice, rights thinking has constitutive rules of inference and relevance that distinguish it from thinking in terms of benefits or concern for others. Thinking in terms of rights and thinking in terms of benefits can, of course, produce conflicting outcomes, but not in the manner of utilitarianism and theories of rights, for the conflicts do not show that one of the practices is false. Rather they raise questions about the appropriateness of the practices in particular circumstances.

In order to state this point clearly, let me return to a familiar sort of objection to the utilitarian form of thinking. Utility does provide a reason for maintaining certain laws. Society is better off with these laws than without them. This gives a reason for conforming to the laws, since violating them with impunity jeopardizes a beneficial situation. The trouble is that this defense of a law-and-order view seems to be mistaken. Laws are broken all the time, but sufficient adherence to them survives that they retain their benefits. Hence, good utilitarians who have a reason to uphold certain laws may also have a reason to break them. Public officials sometimes do this and think that they are justified in doing it.

It is important for politicians (and others) to uphold valuable laws and rights, but it is also part of the job to break these laws when doing so is sufficiently useful to society. However, they cannot successfully uphold the laws, whether positive laws or moral laws, if they are seen to flout them. In such cases "it isn't the crime, it's the cover-up." Even if getting one's hands dirty is the preferred thing to do, one does not want to be caught red-handed if that will compromise one's ability to do good. However, the circumstances are significant here: there are also cases in which one can dirty one's hands in public without ceasing to be an effective administrator of the public interest. Pontius Pilate might serve as an example. Disguising one's deeds or acting deceitfully, therefore, is not a defining feature of such situations generally. Nonetheless, in contrast to civil disobedience, political effectiveness often depends upon not acting too publicly, since publicity would make it more difficult to provide this service to society in the future. Such attitudes are not cynical, perhaps, but only an uncomfortable part of the responsibilities of public officials.

To this point might be added the speculation that the vocation of philosophy makes one unfit for political service in a democratic society. Philosophical analysis shows that it may be justifiable to dirty one's hands, but to express this point publicly may undermine one's political usefulness. To be known as a person who is professionally prepared to advocate devious and dishonest behaviour when it is sufficiently useful is to invite suspicion. Practical philosophers may have to keep their opinions to themselves, disguise them, or hope for a theoretical resolution to the practical dilemma.

It is the condition of sufficient usefulness that shows the importance of sensitivity to thresholds. Utilitarian thinking is particularly appropriate in contexts in which serious good beckons or evil threatens. To a first approximation, these are contexts in which the seriousness of the good or the evil is demonstrable, making it easy to see that the agent had no moral choice but to act contrary to laws or rights. Where this demonstration is not possible, one remains below the evidentiary threshold—that is, within the region where rights thinking appropriately dominates. This is a formal point. In practice, thresholds are not always clearly identifiable. They are not distinguished by sharp lines but by diffuse shadows, which make the grey areas such interesting sites of moral difficulty and social controversy. Although there are clear cases, there are also those in which one must trust to discrimination rather than rules, and such perceptions may differ from person to person.

Dirty-Hands Problems, Practical and Philosophical

It is clear that the identification of thresholds depends powerfully upon social opinion. To assess a person as sufficiently discriminating, perceptive, or sensitive is to employ norms of judgment from which the social element cannot be abstracted. Such assessments are, of course, very complicated. They presuppose the kind of capacity for independent judgment that is demonstrated by imaginative extensions of norms to novel cases in contrast to slavish conformity to rule, but there must be a rough consensus from which to depart. The importance of imagination may be expressed in saying that in matters subject to judgment there is no objectively right answer, but for there even to be a question worth debating there must be the shared assumptions represented by conventional opinion. Leadership away from this opinion is recognized as a mitigating factor in public figures who, nonetheless, do remain connected to public opinion.

It follows that where social cohesion is so poor and shared assumptions so few that thresholds are impossible to discern, pure rights thinking may enjoy a great advantage. In authoritarian regimes whose rulers have a clear vision of the good society, utilitarian thinking may be dominant and rights may be abused, but elsewhere pure utilitarian thinking is hampered by the difficulty of agreeing about what constitutes a public good, promoting a culture in which political issues are routinely discussed in terms of rights.[9] Under these circumstances, rights claims may extend well beyond civil and political protections to economic entitlements, justice for the natural environment, or the advancement of any other political cause. However, the difficulty of identifying thresholds can also be developed in the following more modest way.

The inevitability of contention about the location of thresholds can be separated from the formal point that multi-dimensional moral and political discussion depends upon sensitivity to them: without recognizing thresholds, the hybrid thinking in which dirty-hands problems assume moral interest does not occur. We have noted that for pure rights and utilitarian thinkers, such moral problems fail to arise. However, they do not arise for hybrid thinkers either. As long as appropriate thresholds can be recognized, it is clear when rights or utility should prevail. In the grey areas in which the threshold cannot be located exactly, individuals will be uncertain and people will disagree, but these situations do not pose philosophical dilemmas. Rather, they are cases in which it is simply not possible to identify the right course of action. That is, there is no demonstrably correct judgment, so that one is faced with a practical quandary in which one must decide for oneself. This is not to say that one must simply depend upon personal opinion, but rather that one must do one's best to exercise responsible moral authority in the absence of clear guides.

It is in such situations that people may appreciate leadership in ambiguous circumstances and admire the ability to make painful choices that include acceptance of harm or injustice. Martin Luther King, Jr. is considered a leader because it is accepted that the harms to which his actions led were justified by the rights he sought to have recognized. Those rights are now so well established that their pursuit seems never to have pushed towards the threshold of harm where utilitarian thinking would have been preferred, although there was scope for doubt at the time. As for Pontius Pilate, while he receives little applause, he appears to have been a competent administrator. The Gospels criticize his weakness and vacillation, but they do not condemn him for injustice.

Notes

This essay is the ancestor of another, "Rights Thinking," which appeared in *Philosophy* 72 (1997): 29-58. This essay was also presented, in an earlier version, at the Dirty Hands Workshop held at York University, December, 1993.

1   Luke 23:14 and Matthew 27:24-26.

2   Alan Gewirth, "Are There Any Absolute Rights?," *Theories of Rights*, ed. J. Waldron (Oxford: Oxford University Press, 1984) 104.

3   Compare David Lyons, "Utility and Rights," *Theories of Rights* 127.

4   John Rawls, *A Theory of Justice* (Oxford: Clarendon Press, 1971) 27.

5   Carol Gilligan, *In a Different Voice* (Cambridge, MA.: Harvard University Press, 1982); Sara Ruddick, *Maternal Thinking* (New York: Ballentine Books, 1989).

6   The father's deed is related in lines 205-238 of Aeschylus's *Agamemnon*, the wife's justified by her in lines 1521-1529.

7   Thus, Jonathan Dancy, "Caring About Justice," *Philosophy* 67 (1992): 447-66; 454-55.

8   Cf. Lyons, "Utility and Rights," 133.

9   The tendency for rights talk to dominate is noted approvingly by L.W. Sumner in *The Moral Foundation of Rights* (Oxford: Clarendon Press, 1987) 1; and regretfully by Roger Scruton in *The Meaning of Conservatism* (Harmondsworth: Penguin, 1980) 50.

SEVEN

Democratic Legitimacy and Official Discretion

ARTHUR ISAK APPLBAUM

In the struggle to make and carry out public policy, the substantive views of government officials often are not, or are not yet, supported by their superiors, by most legislators, or by most citizens. May government officials create and exercise discretion to pursue their dissenting views of good policy (constrained only by political prudence and a reasonable interpretation of the law), or should officials faithfully serve the will or the interests of those who have formal authority over their actions or over the disputed policies?

The answer to such a broad question must be, it depends—but on what? Two considerations jump to mind: the substantive merits of the public official's views (right or wrong), and the job held by the public official (elected representative, appointed cabinet secretary, career administrator). Upon scrutiny, however, these two distinctions either do not do enough work or do too much.

If an account of justified discretion is to be of any critical use to a would-be political entrepreneur, it cannot turn on the rightness or wrongness of her substantive policy judgement: if she did not believe that she was right, she would not be dissenting. The question of justified discretion does not specify political appointees, bureaucrats, or generals, and it does not specify the executive branch, for a reason. An account of when a public official may legitimately act on her judgement of good policy in the face of the disagreement of superiors has much in common—at least, more than is commonly acknowledged—with accounts of when legislators may act on their judgements in the face of disagreement with their constituents, or when presidents can act on their judgements in the face of congressional disagreement. The ethics of official dissent, of legislative representation, and of executive authority under a separation of powers all appeal to a common consideration: if substantive *judgements* conflict, when should an actor subordinate her conduct to the *authority* of others?

I will restrict our attention to the moral point of view of the political actor who faces such a choice between judgement and authority, rather than to the standpoint of institutions or other observers of official entrepreneurship and dissent ... This, therefore, is an exercise in actor-centered moral reasoning in the face of nearly but not ideally just political institutions, rather than a contribution to the design of ideal political institutions.[1]

I also will restrict our attention to acts of discretion that are legal under a reasonable interpretation of existing law ... [because] questions of political obligation within the bounds of the law have not received the attention they deserve ... I will [also] wrestle with the doctrine that may be called *political* realism—the view that morally authoritative political mandates are simply whatever politics permits in fact, and nothing more pretentious.[2]

The argument about justified official dissent and discretion proceeds in three parts, and I have already hinted at each. First, although there is truth in political realism, the moral authority of a political mandate is at least partly independent of both the formal mandate on the books—laws, rules, policy declarations—and the effective mandate—what is politically possible and sustainable. Second, political actors can, and indeed ought to, make judgements about the moral authority of political mandates, and judgements about their moral authority to act on those judgements. Third, reasonable criteria to guide the exercise of such judgement can be formulated. To find our bearings in the relatively uncharted search for these criteria, we will triangulate from two well-trodden topics in political ethics. Theories of legislative choice in the face of the opposing will of constituents will be helpful in formulating an account of administrative choice in the face of the opposing will of legislators or superiors; and theories of civil disobedience in the face of legal mandates will be helpful in formulating an account of official discretion in the face of political mandates.

Two Examples[3]

For concreteness, consider [two] episodes in the exercise of official discretion taken from American government....

LEGAL AID IN RURAL CALIFORNIA

The [first] example is drawn from a now-forgotten skirmish in Lyndon Johnson's War on Poverty, David Goldman (a pseudonym), a young lawyer and community organizer, went to rural California in 1966 to start a federally funded legal services organization.[4] Cesar Chavez's new farm workers' union was then struggling to take root, despite the fierce opposition of growers and of then-Governor Ronald Reagan. Goldman took as his mission the use of legal action to organize and empower poor farm workers, in common cause with Chavez, thus rejecting tamer missions more acceptable to local interests.

Goldman's overseers in the White House Office of Economic Opportunity were in sympathy with the lawyer-organizer mission. When the California State Bar Association complained that the legal services organization proposed to advocate "the contentions of one side of an economic struggle now pending," an OEO official replied that that was the best one-line definition of the War on Poverty that he had heard.[5]

The formal, written mandate of Goldman's organization, however, reflected a political bargain between powerful and competing interests. The organization's lawyers were explicitly forbidden in its charter from representing any labor union, from organizing clients into collective bargaining units, and from moonlighting (to prevent any circumvention of the first two conditions).

For the most part, Goldman did not violate the letter of his mandate, although he devoted all his energy to the violation of its spirit, repeatedly reminding his staff, in their selection of cases and in decisions to settle or to go to court, that the union was the "real" client. On at least one occasion, however, Goldman clearly stepped over the line. Chavez asked a legal question about a contemplated boycott, and Goldman and staffers worked all night on the answer. When the press picked up a rumor that the poverty lawyers were advising Chavez directly, Goldman was called by a White House aide, who guardedly asked, "We don't have any problems with that, do we?" After Goldman answered "None," Washington asked no more questions.[6]

We, however, have many questions to ask David Goldman. Does he ... believe that the deals of democratic politics and the directives of political superiors have little or no moral authority if they fail the ... test of what "public policy should be in a pluralistic democracy"?[7] If so, who grades the test?

Does he reject the moral authority of merely *this* particular mandate, because it was forged in a bargain among competing interests in a smoke-filled room? Would his actions have been any different had his charter been deliberated openly on the floor of Congress and approved by a wide margin on principled reasons?

Does Goldman distinguish morally between the clear violation of the formal mandate (advising Chavez) and pursuing goals counter to the intent of, but that do not literally violate, those constraints—choosing cases and clients that advance the union's interests? And does he go so far as to claim that, in politics, there is no morally important formal mandate, apart from what the push and pull of political forces in fact permits or prevents?

COVERT MILITARY AID FOR THE NICARAGUAN CONTRAS

The [second] example is much better known: the Reagan administration's provision of covert military aid, without the knowledge or consent of Congress, to the Contras, opponents of the Sandinista regime in Nicaragua.[8] To stop U.S. military support for the Contras, Congress had added increasingly stringent and precise conditions, known as the Boland amendments, to defense appropriations bills.[9] The most strict read: "No appropriations or funds made available pursuant to this joint resolution to the Central Intelligence Agency, the Department of Defense, or any other agency or entity of the United States involved in intelligence activities may be obligated or expended for the purpose or which would have the effect of supporting, directly or indirectly, military or paramilitary operations in Nicaragua by any nation, group, organization, or individual."[10]

In the hope that Congress would eventually restore military aid, the administration sought ways to keep the Nicaraguan resistance intact. The general strategy was to transfer the management of covert operations in support of the Contras from the Central Intelligence Agency to the White House national security adviser, who was not *specifically* named in the amendment, and to seek third-party contributions to replace U.S. government funds. Oliver North, a marine colonel posted to the national security adviser's staff, took the main operational lead. North threw himself into the task with great energy and initiative.

North's activities were conducted on a compartmentalized, "need-to-know" basis, hidden from Congress and, for the most part, from the regular foreign policy apparatus. Secretary of State George Shultz opposed soliciting foreign governments, so Saudi Arabia and other countries were approached without his knowledge. Using the authority of the White House, North periodically called upon ambassadors, military officers, and intelligence officers to make things happen....

... As the administration had hoped, Congress eventually did reverse itself, and by October 1986 resumed military aid for the Contras. By year's end, however, the Iran-Contra story broke, leaving the administration's Central American policy in tatters.

Some of the activities of North and others did, of course, involve blatant violation of law, most notably episodes of straightforward lying under oath at congressional hearings. But the protagonists in the Contra affair exhibit a literalism that shows an odd deference to legal authority. They could have found more secure ways to get arms to the Contras that would have required undeniable violations of Boland. Instead, a strategy was adopted that was far more susceptible to exposure, but that allowed for a series of contorted legal claims: Boland does not cover the National Security

Council because it is not an intelligence agency, and Boland does not cover unappropriated money.

If some Ollie South, just like North but with a law degree, had managed never to cross the very thin line of legality, the strategies of evasion of and concealment from Congress would still have sparked a political crisis of the first order. The mandate of Congress, though fickle, was crystal clear, and the administration's actions, even when legal, repeatedly denied the *moral* authority of that mandate. The most important and interesting challenges of the Contra affair are not about statutory interpretation, but about legitimate political authority.

Reactions of liberal audiences to these two stories are fairly predictable: ... most condemn Oliver North in the strongest terms, but struggle to explain and justify David Goldman (in the end, splitting on whether, all things considered, he acted rightly).... [But] must we take our Oliver Norths with our David Goldmans?[11] Or can we find principled grounds to distinguish between them that do not turn—or do not turn merely—on our substantive views of good policy?

Mandates in Books or Mandates in Action?

Consider two extreme positions on this question ... [the] obedient servant ethic ... and the political realist ethic. On the obedient servant view, one's own beliefs about the good are never good reasons for action. Public roles are to be impersonal, public figures are to be interchangeable.... Discretion, though often necessary, is an evil.

Whatever one can say about the normative desirability of the obedient servant ethic, this accountant's version of public control and accountability is grossly inadequate as a description of political life. A public administrator who wants to do nothing but obey her superiors—or a governor who wants only to respond to the will of the people—faces a serious problem: the mandates of public officials to act are ambiguous, conflict-ridden, and forever changing, and are shaped in part by the very actions of these intendedly obedient public officials.[12]

Political realism takes this descriptive truth—that public officials have control over the conditions of their own discretion—and turns it into a normative claim. To the political realist, asking a public official to do only what she is mandated to do makes little sense. The mandate of a public official to act is precisely what is in play. The job of an official is to press a substantive agenda as forcefully and as skillfully as she can. She should heed prudence, of course—she cannot do a good job if she is stopped, undone, or ruined.... But in the end, her moral authority to act is nothing more or less than what in fact the political process allows her to get away with. To a public official who thinks like a political realist, any questions about the *legitimate* exercise of discretion, about moral authority, reduce to purely strategic predictions about the power, attention, and will of political opponents and supporters....

Who has the better part of the argument, the political realists or the obedient servants? There *is* a moral truth in political realism: ... there is a difference between formal mandates in books and legitimate mandates in action.[13] Democratic legitimacy—and not merely strategic opportunity, not merely the effective mandate—indeed is ambiguous, shifting, and in play, with government officials at all levels as players .... But what does *not* follow [... is] that there are no grounds independent of political prediction on which to make judgements about democratic legitimacy. The range of morally legitimate actions is not coextensive with the zone of possible agreement in the political bargain, and the reasons or considerations that count in a determination of legitimacy are different from those that determine the strength of a political coalition. Notions such as consent, representation, self-governance, publicity, transparency, reasonableness, and deliberativeness are quite separate from measures of political constraint and opportunity.

So there is more to democratic legitimacy than the intersection of rule books and political possibility. A public official may have both the formal mandate and the political support to act, yet lack the moral legitimacy to do so; and a public official may, in the face of both a formal mandate and political support for action, legitimately do otherwise. Public action demands independent judgement about the legitimacy of formal and effective mandates—which may very well turn on substantive, but not merely on substantive, grounds. To map those grounds is the task ahead.

Judgement or Authority: Who is to Decide?

When an official makes a judgement about what is good public policy, she has a substantive reason to act in accord with that judgement. But a public official also faces what Joseph Raz has called second-order reasons, which direct the official to not act on her first-order substantive reasons, but rather to defer to the strength of a different sort of reason, and act in accord with the judgement of an authority, or on the outcome of a procedure[14] .... Claims of democratic legitimacy, whether writ large as the moral authority of a regime or a form of government, or writ small as the moral authority of particular political actors to act or demand action, whether claims of authority over persons or claims of authority over actions,[15] are all varieties of second-order reasons....

A purely procedural view of justice, in which justice is nothing other than the outcome of a specified procedure, may collapse into a view of legitimacy, where the justice question of "what to decide"—given substantive conflict of interests, beliefs, or values—cannot be separated from the legitimacy question of "how to decide" or "who is to decide."[16] The result of a coin flip determining who kicks off in the Super Bowl is both just and legitimate. But when second-order reasons of justice have substantive content, they may conflict with second-order reasons of legitimacy. Solutions to democratic dirty-hands problems, say in times of war or civil unrest, may be both uncontroversially unjust and uncontroversially legitimate.[17]

One can interpret political legitimacy as yet a third order of reason: in the face of disagreement about conceptions of justice, seek agreement about conceptions of legitimacy in government that treat those who hold different views of justice fairly.[18] Lawmakers may disagree about whether or not justice demands the funding of legal services or medical care for the poor, but agree to enact the conception favored by majority vote....

At the risk of invoking the title of a spaghetti western, I have identified three orders of reason: the good, the just, and the legitimate.[19]... Within each order, moral actors form judgements, identify conflicts with one another, and engage in substantive deliberation about their reasons for those judgements. If conflicting judgements persist, the search for moral resolution moves to a new order of reasons.... Judgements of legitimacy include both judgements about others' actions and judgements about the judge's actions, given the legitimacy or illegitimacy of others. Someone else's lack of moral authority is not quite enough to justify your action or disobedience. And, as Raz pointedly notes, the (moral) right to (moral) authority is not the same as (moral) authority.[20] So judgements of legitimacy are of two sorts: the evaluative judgement about how to decide or who is to decide, given disagreement, and the prescriptive judgement about how to act, given one's evaluative judgement....

But do public officials also have the grounds on which to make judgements about whether or not they have the authority to *act* on their judgements and exercise discretion in defiance of a formal and effective mandate that they judge to be bad, unjust, or illegitimate? Perhaps public officials face very strong second-order reasons to not act on their judgements about defects in the goodness, justice, or legitimacy of the formal and effective mandates they face. On this view, the duties of office severely circumscribe the authority of officials to exercise judgement....

The logic of second-order reasons developed so far points to the reply. True, we do not have the authority to act on every justified judgement. We have no choice, however, at some level, to make judgements about our authority to act. An account of second-order reasons must allow for judgements about second-order reasons, for conflicts between second-order reasons, and for third-order reasons that exclude certain second-order reasons. We have nowhere else to stand but on our own two feet: moral agency requires making judgements that sometimes commit us to acting on our judgements. [Rawls stated—in response to the objection that his views on civil disobedience might be seen as an invitation to anarchy—that] "each person must indeed make his own decision. Even though men normally seek advice and counsel, and accept the injunctions of those in authority when these seem reasonable to them, they are always accountable for their deeds. We cannot divest ourselves of our responsibility and transfer the burden of blame to others. This is true on any theory of political duty and obligation that is compatible with the principles of a democratic constitution."[21]

Three Tensions in a Constitutional Democracy

... A satisfactory account of justified official discretion, in a world where legitimate mandates are not read straight from the books or the organizational charts, must attend to the substantive content of democracy, and therefore engage three tensions in constitutional democratic theory: democratic justice and liberal justice; legitimate jurisdiction and legitimate reasons; and democracy as method and democracy as value.

... Liberalism and democracy coexist uneasily.... Nonetheless, even those who are more deeply democratic than they are liberal agree that at least some democratic, or political, liberties are either logical or contingent preconditions of democracy. Some principles (such as freedom of political expression, or universal suffrage) ought to be excluded from the democratic agenda, some issues ought not to be decided by the will of the majority. This is the idea behind constitutionalism.... The moral authority of at least some political principles does not depend on their being recognized by majority rule. Liberals and democrats disagree about whether or not questions of liberal, or substantive, justice (such as freedom of religion, or the provision of basic medical care) also trump, or take priority over, the wishes of the majority. So an evaluation of ... Goldman and North may turn on whether their actions on behalf of ... disenfranchised migrants and legal representation, freedom fighters and presidential privilege, are in the service of democratic justice, liberal justice, or are not matters of justice at all....

How, or by whom, are these trumps to be played? Some indeed are matters of what might be called jurisdiction. Some actors—typically, legislators—are morally precluded from taking certain positions on some issues—such as a law that institutes slavery, or that establishes a state religion. A fuller account of democratic legitimacy would specify as well, or instead, the *reasons* upon which majorities may legitimately decide. On some questions of liberal and democratic justice, the trump attaches to the sorts of arguments that may legitimately support decisions, rather than to the sorts of issues that may legitimately be on the legislative agenda.... [22]

Therefore, a liberal like Ronald Dworkin and a democrat like Michael Walzer may disagree about whether or not majorities have legitimate jurisdiction over some issue of liberal justice, but still agree that the mandate in question is short on legitimacy—Dworkin on the familiar grounds of legitimate jurisdiction, Walzer on the grounds of legitimate reasons. Note that legitimacy does not collapse into substantive judgement: deciding on the right sort of reasons may still produce the wrong sort of answer. Some legitimate conceptions of justice are mistaken. A mandate that inflicts an injustice still meets the criterion of legitimate reasons if it was decided through a good faith effort at seeking justice....

A finding by a dissenter that a political mandate has not been decided in the legitimate jurisdiction or on legitimate reasons is, of course, still a judgement. But it is a judgement about legitimacy, not a judgement about the good or the just....

The notion that democracy is a formal decision-making method and the notion that democracy is a value, a practice that has intrinsic worth, stand in uneasy tension. [23] I have suggested throughout that the truth in the mandates-in-action view requires that we pay attention to the values realized in the actual practice of real democracies, rather than merely to the satisfaction of formal procedural requirements. In the construction of the political mandate in question, have citizens in fact participated in self-governance in meaningful and rewarding ways? Have their views been fairly noted? Have legislators and administrators opened their deliberations to public scrutiny and criticism? Are the reasons and motives behind the mandate sufficiently transparent? Are officials accountable for their decisions and actions? On the view presented here, these determinations about the value of the content of democratic practices count in an assessment of the legitimacy of a mandate, and the strength of a dissenter's allegiance to such mandates varies in part with this substantive evaluation....

Now that we have developed some analytic understanding of judgement and authority, and have taken a brief look at some of the enduring puzzles of constitutional democracy, we can embark on the search for criteria to guide the exercise of official discretion. The strategy: to triangulate between two well-understood topics in political ethics. A double analogy to legislative choice and civil disobedience will teach us about official discretion. First, the analogy to legislators.

Lessons From Legislative Ethics

... Appointed officials and civil servants face many of the same political, policy-making, and quasi-legislative challenges, opportunities, and responsibilities that legislators do. When we look to the actual circumstances of the jobs, and the degree of democratic responsiveness they require, rather than the mere formal criterion of standing for office, we find that important measures of actual democratic accountability are matters of degree.... The formal consensual link of elected officials to an electorate does not necessarily translate into the actual consent of the governed....

This question is as old as democratic representation itself. Should legislators be responsive to the express wishes of the electorate—that is, be delegates of the will of the people? Should legislators act in the interests, though not on the wishes, of the electorate, as trustees of the interests of the people? Or should legislators act independently and impartially, as principals for political-philosophical principles?[24]

Although this question is posed classically as a choice of role, the problem is understood more usefully as a contingent choice for particular issues and situations. In part, the choice should depend on the democratic tensions and conditions discussed above. What sort of issue is at stake? Do legislators and constituents disagree about the good, or do they disagree about the just? Are democratic freedoms or liberal freedoms at stake? Is legitimacy itself at issue? Does the legislature have legitimate jurisdiction over the issue, or is this a matter that individuals or the courts should decide? Are citizens and legislators invoking legitimate reasons for their positions? Has the political process been democratically valuable, or merely a formal method for decision?

A legislator faces a stronger second-order reason to defer to the wishes of constituents if citizens have engaged in an informed and valuable process of democratic deliberation over an issue that falls within the legitimate jurisdiction of majoritarian politics. As the quality of actual democratic discussion and participation degrades, legislators have more reason to assert trusteeship over citizens' interests. On questions of justice that fall within the jurisdiction of majoritarian politics, a legislator has more reason to defer to the views of constituents if those views are grounded in legitimate reasons, in some conception of justice. She has more reason to invoke her own principled reasons when the opposing view is not grounded in a principled reason. On questions of justice that should not be decided by majority rule, there is no second-order reason of authority to defer to constituents.

[Every step in a legislator's decision to oppose the will of constituents requires a judgement by the legislator] ... and some of these judgements will turn on substantive and contested questions of political philosophy—

the deeply democratic Walzer may answer differently than the deeply liberal Dworkin. But the answer does not turn immediately on the rights and wrongs of the [proposed legislation]: higher-order reasons have their due.

Lessons From Civil Disobedience

The exercise of official discretion need not, and usually does not, involve lawbreaking, and officials face duties that citizens do not. Still, we can usefully enlist the underlying logic of civil disobedience in our search for criteria of discretion. Ronald Dworkin offers one of the clearest accounts of civil disobedience and its justification, the main lines of which are easily put forward, I will follow the structure, but not always the content, of his argument.

Dworkin makes two important distinctions of interest to us: between justice-based and what I will call common good-based disobedience, and between persuasive and nonpersuasive strategies.[25] Justice-based disobedience counters what the actor believes is a violation of the rights of some minority by the majority. Common good-based disobedience counters what the actor believes is bad for all a mistake by the majority about what is in the public interest. Persuasive strategies are intended to work by changing the majority's mind about what justice demands or about what is in the common good. Nonpersuasive strategies are intended to work not by provoking any deliberation or reflection but by driving up the cost to the majority—in financial expense, inconvenience, or fear—of continuing the unjust or unwise course.

A justification of justice-based civil disobedience appeals to the notion, explored earlier, that some issues ought to be excluded from the democratic agenda and not decided by the will of the majority. Justice-based disobedience questions the jurisdiction of democracy over some issues. A justification of persuasive civil disobedience appeals to the notion of perfecting democracy, rather than finding the jurisdictional limits of democratic authority. Persuasive strategies defy formal democratic authority in the service of the ideal of democratic deliberation, in the service of the *value* of democracy. The persuasive disobedient aims to remind the majority that it is not living up to its own sense of the good or the just.

Civil disobedience may be grounded in the common good or in justice or both, and may adopt a persuasive or a nonpersuasive strategy or both. For example, Southern blacks who defied Jim Crow by sitting at segregated lunch counters were practicing persuasive, justice-based civil disobedience: persuasive, because their actions were symbolic and expressive in a way that provoked reflection in the majority; justice-based, because they were fighting for civil liberties that no majority may legitimately violate....

Dworkin argues that the type of civil disobedience most difficult to justify is nonpersuasive, common good-based disobedience because, over an issue that ought to be decided democratically, such disobedience both rejects the legitimate authority of democratic rule and does nothing to improve the quality of democratic deliberation.

In this theory of civil disobedience we can find the seeds of a more general account of judgement and authority that guides us in answering our questions about official dissent and discretion in a democracy. Dworkin points us in the right direction in matching the basis of the dissenter's disagreement (common good or justice) to the strategies of influence that such disagreement justifies (persuasive or nonpersuasive). We need not, however, subscribe to Dworkin's strict division of labor between legislatures and courts over matters of justice and the common good. We have already noted that majorities can have jurisdiction over at least some questions of justice if their answers are grounded in legitimate reasons.

To Play or Not to Play?
Four Conditions of Democratic Legitimacy

We are now ready to sketch out four conditions that morally matter to a dissenter deciding to exercise discretion in the face of or in the absence of a political mandate.

THE BASIS OF DISSENT

The first condition, the basis of dissent, identifies the type of disagreement between the dissenter and the source of the political mandate: Is the disagreement about the good—a common good-based dissent? Is the disagreement about how to proceed given irresolvable disagreements about the good—a justice-based dissent? Or is the disagreement about how to proceed given irresolvable disagreements about the just—a legitimacy-based dissent? We have distinguished two sorts of justice-based dissent: the claim that the political mandate involves a liberal or substantive injustice, [as might be seen concerning abortion, for example]; and the claim that the political mandate involves democratic, or political, injustice (disenfranchisement of migrant farm workers).

We have seen that, contrary to Dworkin's view, fixing upon the basis of dissent does not determine the question of democratic authority: basis does not settle the question of legitimate jurisdiction, or of legitimate reasons, or of democratic value. Having identified the grounds of one's substantive disagreement with a political mandate, one must still take the measure of the moral authority of the wrong-headed view.

LEGITIMATE JURISDICTION

Does the source of the political mandate have jurisdiction over the issue at hand?... Legitimate jurisdictions ... are fluid, overlapping, and demanding of moral interpretation. Whether the source of a political mandate has legitimate jurisdiction is a kind of higher-order moral question. If the answer is no, the dissenter has more reason to exercise discretion in opposition to the political mandate.

LEGITIMATE REASONS

Has the political mandate been decided on the relevant reasons? Have questions of the good been decided by appeal to conceptions of the good? Have questions of justice (in the face of irreconcilable disagreements about the good) been decided by appeal to conceptions of justice? Have questions of legitimacy (in the face of irreconcilable disagreements about the just) been decided by appeal to conceptions of legitimacy? Again, if the answer is no, the dissenter has more reason to exercise discretion in opposition to the political mandate.

DEMOCRATIC VALUE

Is the politics that created the mandate democratically valuable in the ways we have explored, or is the mandate a product of a politics that is democratic only in a formal sense? In judging the moral authority of mandates, public officials should attend to the actual conditions of the democratic process, and to the democratic values realized by it, not merely to the existence of formal democratic features. The more the values of democracy are realized, the more officials should defer to the authority claims of democracy's mandates; when democracy is merely a formal process, the case for observing merely the formal rules of law and politics is strengthened.

How to Play? The Strategies of Discretion

We saw that justification in the theory of civil disobedience turns in part on the strategies or means used to influence the actions of others. Similarly, a complete account of official discretion will match the strategies of dissent to the conditions of democratic legitimacy. Consider three classes of discretionary strategy that a public official might employ: persuasive strategies, incentive strategies, and deceptive strategies.

PERSUASIVE STRATEGIES: REASONS AND PUBLICITY

Persuasive strategies seek to change, in good faith, the beliefs, values, and interests of other political players through deliberation or symbolic action. Persuasive strategies are necessarily public, in the sense that they act openly on the rational faculties of some relevant audience. Secretary of State George Shultz attempted, in a limited way, to offer President Reagan reasons not to seek third-party funding for the Contras. One of David Goldman's intentions in publicizing the plight of the migrant farm workers through lawsuits widely covered in the press was to win the hearts and minds of Californians. But not every public strategy is a persuasive one: a political entrepreneur can publicly seek influence over mandates through honest political bargaining and coalition-building.

INCENTIVE STRATEGIES: OFFERS AND THREATS

Incentive strategies shift the location of the zone of possible agreement in the political bargain, either by improving one's alternative to agreement or by worsening the alternatives of those with formal mandates, and by making offers, trades, or threats to reach a favorable point in the zone.[26] The strategy works by altering the costs and benefits to political authorities of thwarting discretionary action. Had Secretary of State Shultz threatened to resign if the Contra affair proceeded (a threat he employed successfully before to halt the use of polygraph tests on State Department officials), he would have been pursuing an incentive strategy....

DECEPTIVE STRATEGIES: LIES, SECRETS, AND MANIPULATION

Deceptive strategies work by inducing beliefs about facts or values in the sources of political authority that the discretionary agent believes to be false. Lies and secrets are assaults on the autonomy of their intended public, and so are presumptively problematic in democratic politics. Oliver North and company clearly embarked on a deceptive strategy, seeking to hide from Congress the administration's continued military support of the Contras. David Goldman's covert direct aid to Cesar Chavez was also an example of a deceptive strategy of dissent (in contrast with his mandate-defying lawsuits, which were open to public scrutiny).

Matching Strategies to Conditions of Democracy

We are now prepared to offer some guidance to the entrepreneurial public official. Let us match, in a rough way, the three strategies of discretionary action to the four conditions of democratic legitimacy outlined earlier, and illustrate by returning to the [two] examples with which we began. These suggestions have the virtues of specificity and provocativeness, but the vice of probable error, I offer my reasons, but if you find them wanting, you are welcome to propose improvements, Obviously, there can be no knockdown proof for these tests. A sound suggestion will appropriately match discretionary strategies with the conditions the strategies seek to remedy (in the way that, on Dworkin's view of civil disobedience, persuasive strategies perfect democracy when dissent is common good-based), or exploit the weaknesses in a mandate's legitimacy (in the way that nonpersuasive strategies of civil disobedience are justified when majorities lack jurisdiction), and otherwise be fittingly proportional (so that the slightest defect in democratic legitimacy does not permit the gravest political fraud).

WHEN SHOULD A DISSENTER FORSAKE ALL ENTREPRENEURIAL ACTION AND CONFINE HER DISSENT TO FORMAL CHANNELS?

If the democratic process has done everything one can expect of it, short of producing a substantive outcome that matches one's view of good policy, to then deny the moral authority of such a mandate is to deny authority simply. Unless the most extreme catch-me-if-you-can political realism is true, there must be some conditions under which the substantive judgement of public officials gives way to authority. Consider one reasonable set of such conditions: when an official dissents on common-good grounds, not justice grounds, from a mandate decided on legitimate reasons, through a process rich in intrinsic democratic values, by authorities who have jurisdiction over the issue in question....

WHICH CONDITIONS OF DEMOCRATIC LEGITIMACY CALL FOR A PERSUASIVE STRATEGY?

Entrepreneurship that influences political mandates through deliberation and openness, that appeals to public reason, is always less problematic than nonpersuasive, coercive, secretive, or deceptive strategies. Honest persuasion seems particularly fitting in opposing mandates that rest on legitimate but mistaken reasons. Honest persuasion appears to be the only justifiable strategy for a common good-based dissenter when there are only minor defects in the conditions of legitimacy. Such justification appeals to the notion that public and persuasive entrepreneurship challenges democratic authority on behalf of democracy itself, to perfect democracy by improving the quality of deliberation and realizing democratic values.

On this logic of perfecting democracy, an official entrepreneur may exercise public, persuasive discretion even when matters of justice are not at stake. The legislator may vote her best judgement on trade bills and highway bills, as well as on the death penalty, so long as her dissenting performance is public and accountable in a way that contributes to the deliberation and political education of her constituents.

More controversial: on this view, even if justice is not implicated, the secretary of state may continue to protest a foreign policy initiative after a presidential decision has been reached, and may do so publicly, so long as the path of influence is largely persuasive, rather than coercive or threatening.

More controversial still: on this view Reagan and his national security apparatus may take public, persuasive dissenting action to convince the congressional majority that it erred in Boland, even if such action strains a good-faith interpretation of the amendment. For example, if the Contras required funds to document Sandinista support for other Latin American insurgencies, or some other evidence that might reasonably be expected to change congressional views, then the White House would be justified in engaging in an open, third-party fund-raiser to finance such documentation.

WHEN IS POLITICAL BARGAINING A JUSTIFIED STRATEGY FOR A DISSENTER?

The case for a nonpersuasive (but still nondeceptive) strategy of discretion, with its offers and threats, its coalitions and exchanges, is strongest when the source of the political mandate lacks legitimate jurisdictions or when the mandate has been decided for illegitimate reasons, or when the democratic value of the mandating process is low. Each of these conditions signals some serious weakness in the democratic legitimacy of the political mandate. The less legitimacy and value one finds in a particular episode of policymaking, the more one is justified in acting like a political realist. Here, proportionality is called for: the slightest defect in participation does not justify the most heavy-handed coercive threat, but one can treat such mandates as in play.

Now we can see why David Goldman's political entrepreneurship (although not necessarily his deception) is justified. The issue in question is one of democratic, political justice—the most egregious violations of which even deep democrats acknowledge no majority may legitimately inflict. Goldman need not go so far as to claim that legal aid for migrant farm workers is such a precondition of democracy, whose denial falls outside the jurisdiction of majorities. Though that is doubtful, the restricted political mandate of California legal aid was brokered for illegitimate reasons that do not appeal to some conception, right or wrong, of democratic justice. And clearly, the political process that produced Goldman's mandate scores low in the democratic values of deliberation and participation. Valuable, and not merely formal, democracy is particularly important to establish the legitimate authority of mandates about justice that fall within the jurisdiction of majority rule, because minorities and individuals must rely solely on their own political voices, not on the institutional protection of the courts. So, a valuable democracy both directly strengthens the authority of political mandates and improves the chances that majorities will decide on legitimate reasons.

In the face of a mandate democratic only in a formal sense, about an issue of democratic justice, decided on illegitimate reasons, Goldman justifiably took the role of a principal player, not a fiduciary agent, in the pull and tug of politics, and showed merely formal deference to a merely formal authority. If he used his entrepreneurial skills to raise the political costs of stopping him, he did not offend against any second-order reason of authority that comes from pluralist, interest group politics. Here, another truth in realism: realist politics in fact cannot generate mandates that have more legitimate authority than conceded by the ethic of political realism.

This should not be interpreted either as a tit-for-tat reciprocity argument (do unto others as others do unto you) or as a contingent obligation (do only if others do). Rather, the justification for a nonpersuasive strategy of discretion appeals to the nature of the political mandate's legitimate authority: if such a mandate has moral authority, it has it only by virtue of the satisfaction of some formal procedure, not because it is a substantive expression of reasoned principle or of some "general will," however that is understood. Therefore, second-order reasons of authority that arise out of some modus vivendi bargain are different reasons, with different force, than are second-order reasons of authority that arise out of a valuable, deliberative democratic process.

WHEN ARE MANIPULATIVE OR DECEPTIVE STRATEGIES JUSTIFIED?

Since manipulation, lies, and many sorts of secrets corrode the principle of publicity on which deliberative democracy depends, these strategies can be justified only when there is precious little, democratically speaking, to lose (when formal political mandates lack legitimate jurisdiction and legitimate reasoning and democratic value) or, perhaps, when there is much democratically to gain (when very important matters of democratic justice hang in the balance).

The most charitable tale we can tell about the deceptive discretion practiced by Oliver North in the Contra affair is that, far more than a common good-based dispute over the wisdom of military involvement in Latin America, it was a legitimacy-based dispute, a struggle between branches of government for moral authority over the making of foreign policy. On this view, the Reagan White House had made a judgement of legitimate jurisdiction and found Congress wanting. On the scheme developed so far, such a judgement (if made in good faith) would justify a public but nonpersuasive incentive strategy. One scenario: flout Boland's meaning through public appeals to foreign allies and domestic supporters to arm the Contras.

Under this charitable interpretation, can the case also be made for a secret and deceptive strategy? I think not. There was much, democratically, to lose. Congress, even if mistaken about its assertion of jurisdiction, was making a claim based on legitimate reasons, and the process of congressional decision-making—both about the substance of the Nicaraguan issue and, more generally, about authority over war powers—was moderately rich in the democratic values. And nothing, democratically, would be gained by the covert defiance of congressional authority, in contrast with public defiance. In any case, this charity is undeserved: the Contra affair, at bottom, was not a sincere claim of legitimate authority by the president, but a slinky evasion of the legitimate authority of Congress.

Objections and Refinements

In conclusion, consider three sorts of objection to this account of official discretion and democratic legitimacy .... [Firstly, it might be said that the] conditions of ideal democracy almost never hold in practice. The criteria for justified discretion would allow persuasive dissent in virtually all circumstances, and would allow nonpersuasive, open dissent in the normal circumstance of actual democratic decision-making, where presidents, cabinet secretaries, and legislators act on a mix of reasons, some legitimate and some not, in response to a mix of influences, some principled, some not, sometimes deliberating, sometimes trading and maneuvering, sometimes under public scrutiny, sometimes not. Political mandates will almost always suffer from some defect in democratic legitimacy or value, so the moral authority of those mandates will almost always be attenuated, commanding only a formal deference, thereby approving official entrepreneurship within merely formal constraints. The criteria of official discretion allow too much. Furthermore, this permissiveness sets in motion a spiral of democratic degradation. The more some dissenters exercise nonpersuasive discretion, the more other actors will respond in kind....

Here we return to theories of civil disobedience for instruction, this time from Rawls.[27] Rawls is concerned that excessive civil disobedience might undermine respect for the rule of law and a just constitution, so he adds to his account what amounts to an externality condition: those who would be civilly disobedient ought to consider whether or not their actions, justified on all other grounds, will damage the future capacity of democratic institutions to seek justice....

In this form, the externality condition can be readily endorsed as a criterion for official discretion as well: if the democratic consequences of your entrepreneurship are sufficiently bad, refrain. Whether or not the competitive dynamics of the collective action problem are such that no nonpersuasive discretion is ever justified requires further investigation. But note that the externality condition, for Rawls and for us, asks for a first-order, substantive judgement about consequences, and not deference to a second-order reason of legitimate authority....

[Secondly, it might be objected that this] account asks public officials to make judgements at every turn: judgements about the good, the just, and the legitimate; judgements about liberal justice and democratic justice; judgements about the legitimacy of jurisdiction and the legitimacy of reasons; judgements about the intrinsic value of a democratic process and, now, about future consequences for democratic processes. But reasonable people will disagree at each step about these judgements. Who is to say whose judgements are authoritative?

The answer given earlier still holds: if guidance is to be given to a political actor questioning the legitimate authority of her mandate, then there is nowhere else for her to stand but in her own shoes. She cannot, without judgement, defer to the very authority whose legitimacy she questions. We have tried to develop a sufficiently rich set of conditions sufficiently distant from the original substantive conflict so that the would-be entrepreneur must look beyond the initial disagreement for justification. But there can be no justification of authority without judgement about authoritative claims....

A would-be dissenter would be foolish and morally irresponsible to not seek out the best available help in making judgements about substance and legitimacy, and may judge that deferring to the judgement of an expert is more accurate than making all judgements herself. But this sort of deference is to expert, not to moral, authority.... Humility, a recognition of the fallibility of one's judgement, is a rare and noble virtue in public life. Democratic dissenters, because they act against the judgements of the many, must practice a special sort of humility, seek whatever wisdom is available, and safeguard against overconfidence or special pleading in their own judgements by taking cooler counsel.

[Thirdly, is this] a partisan view of democracy? No political theory can be neutral with respect to everything and still say something.... The scheme depends on commitment to a democracy that is both deliberative and liberal: deliberative, in that, to at least some degree, under some circumstances, the preferences and political views of citizens can and ought to change through reasonable discourse; liberal, in that the liberties of individuals are valuable, and that the value of at least some individual liberties does not depend on valuation by others—and in particular, does not depend on valuation by a majority of citizens. Because this version of democracy is liberal, the demands of justice and the will of democracy can conflict; because it is deliberative, under some conditions (perhaps difficult to specify and difficult to attain) the outcomes of democratic deliberation and the demands of justice converge. This conception of democracy is broadly consistent with the views of writers as diverse as Mill, Rawls, and Habermas.... [28]

[We may wonder about] whether we have to take ... our marine colonels with our poverty lawyers. The answer is no: we can find principled grounds to distinguish one act of official discretion from another, principled grounds that have gained some distance from our perhaps partial judgements about the rights and wrongs in the underlying political conflict. But we and dissenters may disagree in our judgements about legitimate authority as well, perhaps for the same political-philosophical reasons that give rise to the substantive dispute in the first instance. When it comes to legitimacy, it's judgement all the way down.

Notes

This is an abridgement of Arthur Isak Applbaum, *Ethics for Adversaries: The Morality of Roles in Public and Professional Life* (Princeton, NJ: Princeton University Press, 1999) 207-39; first published in *Philosophy and Public Affairs* 21:3 (Summer 1992): 240-74.

1 See John Rawls, *A Theory of Justice* (Cambridge, Mass.: Harvard University Press, 1971), for the distinction between ideal and nonideal theory (244-48) and for the book's only foray into nonideal theory, the account of civil disobedience (chap. 6).

2 I take [no] stand here on legal realism, the doctrine that law is simply the "prophecies of what the courts will do in fact, and nothing more pretentious." See Oliver Wendell Holmes, who anticipated the legal realist movement in "The Path of Law," *Harvard Law Review* 10 (1897): 461.

3 [The original discusses a third example: the case of Joseph Califano's conscience and abortion funding.]

4 This account relies on Stephen B. Hitchner, "California Legal Services, Inc.," Parts A-D, Kennedy School of Government Case #C94-75-9, -10, -11, -12; and Mark H. Moore and Malcolm K. Sparrow, "David Goldman and California Legal Services," *Ethics in Government: The Moral Challenge of Public Leadership* (Englewood Cliffs, N.J.: Prentice-Hall, 1990) 57-63.

5 Hitchner, Part A, 16.

6 Moore and Sparrow 63.

7 [For Father Richard McCormick there are three levels of judgement required for public officials to carry out the laws that the nation enacts.] See Joseph A. Califano, Jr., *Governing America*, excerpted in *Ethics and Politics*, ed. Amy Gutmann and Dennis F. Thompson (Chicago: Nelson-Hall, 1990) 260.

8 This account relies on Theodore Draper, *A Very Thin Line: The Iran-Contra Affairs* (New York: Farrar, Straus & Giroux, 1991) 3-119, 290-314, 332-51, 558-79.

9 After the chairman of the House Select Committee on Intelligence, Edward P. Boland, a Massachusetts Democrat.

10 Draper 24.

11 [This position was well argued, with different events in mind, by] Taylor Branch, "The Odd Couple," *Washington Monthly* (October 1971). Reprinted in Gutmann and Thompson 104-13.

12 See Richard E. Neustadt, *Presidential Power and the Modern Presidents* (1960; New York: Free Press, 1990); Mark H. Moore, *Creating Public Value* (Cambridge, Mass.: Harvard University Press, 1995); and Donald Warwick, "The Ethics of Administrative Discretion," in *Public Duties: The Moral Obligations of Government Officials*, ed. Joel L. Fleishman, Lance Liebman, and Mark H. Moore (Cambridge, Mass.: Harvard University Press, 1981).

13 To paraphrase Roscoe Pound, from "Law in Books and Law in Action," *American Law Review* 44 (1910): 12-36.

14 Joseph Raz, *Practical Reason and Norms* (London: Hutchinson Press, 1975), and *The Authority of the Law* (Oxford: Oxford University Press, 1979).

15 See Raz, *The Authority of Law*, 19, for the importance of this distinction.

16 For an elaboration of pure procedural justice, see Rawls 85-86.

17 For discussions of the dirty-hands problem, see Michael Walzer, "Political Action: The Problem of Dirty Hands," *Philosophy & Public Affairs* 2:2 (Winter 1973): 160-80; and Dennis F. Thompson, "Democratic Dirty Hands," *Political Ethics and Public Office* (Cambridge, Mass.; Harvard University Press, 1987).

18 This does not require denying that there are right and wrong conceptions of justice, and does not rule out the possibility that some conceptions of justice are incompatible with the demands of legitimacy in government.

19 Following Raz, I will continue to use "second-order" as a general term referring to all higher orders of reasons.

20 Raz, *The Authority of Law*, 9n. The modifier "moral" is mine.

21 Rawls 389.

22 For an account of democratic legitimacy that excludes fewer issues from the legislative agenda than does standard liberalism, in exchange for more principled restrictions on the way legislatures ought to talk about these issues, see Amy Gutmann and Dennis F. Thompson, "Moral Conflict and Political Consensus," *Ethics* 101 (1990): 64-68....

23 Cf Joseph A. Schumpeter, *Capitalism, Socialism, and Democracy* (London: Allen & Unwin, 1976); Walzer, "Philosophy and Democracy" *Political Theory* 9 (1981): 379-99; Gutmann, "How Liberal Is Democracy?" in *Liberalism Reconsidered*, ed. Douglas MacLean and Claudia Mills (Lanham, Md.: Rowman and Allanheld, 1993).

24 For extended treatments of legislative ethics, see Hannah Fenichel Pitkin, *The Concept of Representation* (Berkeley: University of California Press, 1967); and Dennis F. Thompson, "Legislative Ethics," *Political Ethics and Public Office.*

25 For clarity, I substitute the label "common good-based" for what Dworkin calls "policy-based." I do not include here what Dworkin calls integrity-based civil disobedience and what Rawls calls conscientious refusal. The liberal demand for public, political principles may prevent a public official—in contrast with a citizen—from disobeying on integrity grounds alone. But note that quiet, nonthreatening, nondisruptive resignation on integrity grounds alone is almost always justified....

26 See Howard Raiffa, *The Art and Science of Negotiation* (Cambridge, Mass.: Harvard University Press, 1982); and David A. Lax and James K. Sebenius, *The Manager as Negotiator* (New York: Free Press, 1986).

27 Rawls 373-75.

28 Much is made here of the contrast between legitimate political mandates and merely formal political mandates; for this distinction to do work, it requires an account of meaning and interpretation, which I have not begun to provide. But I do not believe it requires any particular account of meaning and interpretation....

Rejecting Dirty Hands

Introduction

In Part Two, our authors are concerned with what they see as flaws or dangers in classic dirty-hands defenses. Most of the essays caution against the troubling practical implications of the logic of dirty hands, though that is not the case with Kai Nielsen.

Nielsen comes to the issue of dirty hands from a philosophical position that is diametrically opposed to categorizing the defense of generally repugnant acts and decisions as dirty-hands dilemmas. This represents a sharp contrast to arguments set out in Part One by Michael Stocker, for example, since for Stocker dirty-hands cases naturally and appropriately produce emotional conflicts and perhaps guilt or shame. Both authors, however, take issue with much of Michael Walzer's now classic formulation. Remarkably, however, Nielsen does not differ substantially from dirty-hands defenders in the belief that the imperatives of politics will sometimes require cruel and deceptive *practices*. He objects to their approach on the basis of a *philosophical* disagreement, asserting that it is misleading to portray dirty-hands cases as tragic paradoxes and to say that politicians are doing wrong in order to do right. Instead, Nielsen argues that what he calls a "thoroughly contextualist" and "weak consequentialist" philosophical ethics fastened to a lesser-evils approach can better explain how to act morally in extreme circumstances. In a sense Nielsen puts forward his own defense of dirty hands, one that has resonances with Machiavelli, but because the grounds of his argument are so counter to all the major conceptualizations of dirty hands—as essentially involving philosophical paradox, contradiction, and tension between conflicting moral obligations—we have chosen to place him alongside objectors rather than defenders.

Michael Yeo, like Nielsen and a number of authors here, focuses much of his attention on Walzer's arguments and examples. For Yeo, Walzer's position is not merely conceptually problematic: both politicians and citizens, if they tried to act on his advice, would be likely to react to dirty-hands situations in a variety of ways not fully considered. Most importantly, defending dirty hands has the potential to create an inevitable circle of deception which poisons political morality. He concludes that even if Walzer has correctly captured the nature of political necessity, a just society will take meaningful moral and institutional steps to outlaw dirty tactics in its political affairs. This would prevent the tendency for dirty-hands reasoning to excuse unnecessary lying and would encourage those committed to honest politics to pursue power. Yeo therefore examines one of the central elements of the tension between dirty hands and democracy, a problem which is addressed further in the remaining papers.

Wes Cragg points to a number of parallels between political and business ethics which could lead theorists as well as business leaders to defend bribery in international business transactions in much the same fashion that dirty hands are defended in difficult political circumstances. He argues, however, that the same arguments that make dirty hands unacceptable in politics are also applicable in the world of business: we cannot base an ethics on the inconsistent notion that unethical practices are not just exceptional, but also obligatory. Unlike Tom Sorell, who held in Part One that implications for ethics in parallels between business and politics were ultimately unsustainable because of their divide in terms of private versus public morality considerations, Cragg holds that public and private interests are ultimately compatible and subject to the same ethical standards. He concludes that, since it is in corrupt circumstances that dirty-hands arguments seem persuasive, we need to devote considerable energy to reforming the conditions within which decisions are made in both politics and business. And, even in extreme circumstances where one is faced with nothing but unpalatable moral choices and when resulting moral censure may be unfair, it is inappropriate, says Cragg, to reward dirty-hands doers with moral praise.

A similar response to dirty-hands defenses is suggested by Michael McDonald. For McDonald the dirty-hands problem is pressing because "it is a general feature of life in organised communities." Drawing on work by Annette Baier, he argues that justifications of dirty-hands activity need to meet the criteria of a trust relationship between leaders and followers. The test of this fiduciary responsibility, he states, is whether an act or policy could survive publicity, which is precisely what dirty-hands perpetrators seek to avoid. He advocates a reciprocal tying of the hands of leaders in both politics and in the private sector: authority figures must pledge themselves to disclosure, transparency, and accountability and so to disavow dirty hands. Too often, McDonald argues, dirty-hands defenses over-simplify leader-follower relations and become rationalizations for actions which might have been avoidable. In some instances such excuses may even cover-up the bloody victimization of outsiders by leaders who abuse the trust given them. McDonald also notes that in cases of bloody hands that *do* have the support of citizens our worries should be even greater, for the fulfillment of trust in the cause of evil must never be regarded as morally justifiable.

Both Sharon Sutherland and David Shugarman draw attention to and criticize the role that heroic wisdom allegedly plays in dirty-hands deliberations: the image of the lone statesman tragically compromising himself to serve his country undermines democracy in a variety of ways. Both therefore elaborate on the complex implications which the dirty-hands problem has for the leader-citizen relationship, a theme also taken on by Sorell, Yeo, and McDonald. Sutherland emphasizes the importance of Dennis Thompson's work and the dependence of healthy democracy on the "retrospective-deliberative" processes which are integral to democratic accountability and constitutionalism. But it is these processes and principles which are threatened when dirty-hands defenses are employed, meaning that a just society will work vigilantly to ensure that the actions of leaders are disclosed, debated, and constrained. Sutherland also draws on a recent Canadian immigration case to drive home the point that dirty-hands policies betray public trust.

Bill Clinton's bungled attempt to use unjustifiable means—lying both to the public and under oath—to avoid public scrutiny of his sexual life appears at first glance to be a case of dirty hands. But Greene and Shugarman indicate why this is not so. They also argue that Clinton's lying simply does not constitute an abuse of public trust on the scale of, for example, Richard Nixon's cover-up of the Watergate break-in: Clinton lied about his sexual infidelities and not his activities as president. The lessons to be learned from his impeachment are that leaders must avoid public lying and that the boundaries separating the public and private must be respected. These are crucial requirements of mutual respect and public trust which must not be denied by recourse to dirty hands.

In the final essay, Shugarman argues that defenses of dirty hands err in generalizing from the extreme conditions of warfare to the everyday world of democratic politics. In opposition to Bradshaw, for example, he, like Sutherland, argues that if we allow an appreciation of exceptional circumstances to become our norm for the political realm then the moral breaches of leaders will be treated as normal and excusable. Against Walzer, Shugarman maintains that Albert Camus should not be read as an authority on dirty-hands sensibilities, especially insofar as Camus emphasizes that the morality of means and ends must be compatible. Shugarman accentuates the morally-constraining nature of a healthy democratic setting, holding that recent claims that dirty hands are democratic are only sensible in regard to a highly elitist, paternalistic understanding of democratic governance. Furthermore, to the extent that the dirty-hands rationale is seen as legitimate it will be nearly impossible to hold politicians to account and they will be tempted to believe that they need not be accountable at all.

EIGHT

There is No Dilemma of Dirty Hands

KAI NIELSEN

I

I will examine here the moral and political problem of dirty hands. In doing so, I will deploy and further characterize the method of ethics—with its appeal to considered judgements, and with its distinctive kind of consequentialism—that I have elucidated and defended elsewhere.[1] An acquaintance with those writings is not presupposed here, though of course it would be useful. It is often argued that politicians, and others as well, must sometimes take horrible (at least, normally unacceptable) measures to avoid even worse evils. They must, that is, sometimes dirty their hands to do what is right. When, if ever, are they justified in doing that? And in doing that are they guilty of committing moral crimes?

I shall take an austere line about the problem of dirty hands. Treating it as a moral problem for political leaders and for other political and moral agents as well, I shall argue that what should be done, in the horrifying circumstances in which problems of dirty hands arise with the greatest urgency, is to always seek to do the lesser evil where that is possible. The choice here—where there is a choice—is not between good and evil, right and wrong, but between evil and evil, between wrong and wrong. It is a truism that we should avoid evil altogether if we can. But often we cannot. Where we cannot, and yet when we still have some *lebensraum* to act, we should choose what we have the best reason to believe is the lesser evil.[2]

Anyone in such a circumstance with an ounce of humanity will feel anguish in so acting and very deep remorse for having so acted, or for condoning such acts. It is not that he should feel merely saddened. That is hardly an appropriate response. Indeed, someone who did not feel anguish and remorse in such situations would hardly count as a moral agent. But in so acting or in condoning such acts such an agent is not guilty of wrongdoing. He has (*pace* Michael Walzer) committed no moral crime, though, psychologically speaking, it is perhaps inevitable that he will feel guilty.[3] But to *feel* guilty is not necessarily to *be* guilty. Plenty of people feel guilty without being guilty, and plenty of others are guilty without feeling guilty. The connection is a contingent one. Where our choice is inescapably a choice between evils—where there is no third possibility—we should, as responsible moral and political agents, batten down the hatches and try to do the lesser evil. Jean-Paul Sartre's character Hoederer, in the play *Dirty Hands*, is exemplary: a paradigm of what a morally committed political agent should be in the world in which he finds himself. To try to wash one's hands, Pontius Pilate-like, of a dirty-hands situation—to say, "It is none of my business, my hands are clean," where some choice on our part might make a difference—is impossible. We do not escape responsibility by so acting. Failing to act in such a circumstance is itself an action. By so refraining, we dirty our hands just as much, and perhaps more, than does a person who acts resolutely to achieve the lesser evil, though in doing so he does horrible things. It is a conceptual confusion with unfortunate moral residues to describe the problem of dirty hands as Thomas Nagel, Michael Walzer, and Bernard Williams do.[4] They start out on what seems to me to be the right track by contending that even when our political ends are the noblest of ends, it is sometimes true that, to succeed in politics, political leaders, and frequently others as well, must get their hands dirty. That is, they will have to do things or condone the doing of things which, in normal circumstances, would be utterly morally impermissible. Moreover, it is sometimes right to try to succeed even in those circumstances and thus it must be right in those circumstances to get our hands dirty. To not do so would be irresponsible and immoral, or at least a not inconsiderable moral failing, on the part of those political actors. Walzer *et al* get off track, I shall argue, when they maintain that we are caught in a paradox here. This very paradox, they take it, is the problem of dirty hands. Walzer puts it thus:

> sometimes it is right to try to succeed, and then it must be right to get one's hands dirty. But one's hands get dirty from doing what it is wrong to do. And how can it be wrong to do what is right? Or, how can we get our hands dirty by doing what we ought to do?[5]

In certain circumstances—Hoederer-like circumstances—political agents, Walzer has it, *must do wrong to do right*. But that is, if not a contradiction, at least a paradox. It would seem that *one cannot logically do what is right by doing what is wrong*. However, I shall argue that this is a mistaken way to conceptualize things. Where *whatever we do or fail to do leads to the occurrence of evil or sustains it, we do not do wrong by doing the lesser evil. Indeed, we do what, everything considered, is the right thing to do: the thing we ought—*

through and through ought—in this circumstance, to do. In doing what we ought to do, we cannot (*pace* Walzer *et al*) do wrong. We may do things that in normal circumstances would be horribly wrong, but in these circumstances of dirty hands, they are not, *everything considered*, wrong. It is difficult enough in such situations to ascertain what the lesser evil is and to steel ourselves to do it, without adding insult to injury by making, artificially and confusedly, a conceptual and moral dilemma out of it as well.

II

It is a mistake to say that this is just the same old utilitarianism all over again and that, as we all know very well by now, utilitarianism is mistaken: a thoroughly inadequate moral and normative political theory. We cannot use that to dismiss the way I am arguing about dirty hands. In the contexts described, the above conception of always doing the lesser evil is, of course, *compatible* with utilitarianism, but does not *require* it. However, it may require, or at least its clear articulation will be facilitated by, what I have (following Brian Barry) characterized as *weak consequentialism.*[6] But this view is compatible with accepting, as I do and as Barry does as well, a *roughly* Rawlsian conception of justice as fairness, where in addition to Pareto-optimality an independent principle of just distribution is required for the structuring of our institutions, if they are to be morally acceptable institutions. Unlike Rawls, I am not saying that, morally speaking, considerations of justice always override considerations of utility.[7] Normally they do, but again in certain extreme situations they do not. We should not—morally should not—do justice though the heavens fall, Michael Kohlhaas-style.[8]

However, what I am committed to denying, with such a conception, is that there are any absolute side-constraints that, where they apply, must always determine what we are to do no matter what the consequences. The serious moral and political problem over dirty hands is not over some trumped-up moral dilemma rooted in conceptual confusion, and perhaps even in moral evasiveness as well. It is over whether moral agents acting in the political sphere, including sensitive and aware moral agents, who have taken Machiavelli's lessons to heart, should always try to do the lesser evil in inescapably dirty-hands situations, or whether instead they should follow Leszek Kolakowski, and a host of others, in believing that we must always stick with putatively absolute side-constraints, no matter what.[9] I shall argue, against Kolakowskian Absolutism, that that is not the way to have clean hands. It is, rather, a way of evasively and irresponsibly dirtying our hands even more than we would by resolutely and intelligently seeking, in such circumstances, to do or assent to the lesser evil.

In many, perhaps most, circumstances, we cannot ascertain what the lesser evil is and, in such circumstances, we should be *morally conservative*. This is particularly evident where it is possible not to act in such a circumstance: where inaction is not itself a form of action. There, we should not do things which in normal circumstances would plainly be horrendous. Where doing nothing is possible (and not, in effect, a taking of a side on the issue in question), and where doing what we only have a hunch is the lesser evil would mean doing something horrendous, then we should do nothing. In such a circumstance, we should not risk doing something that normally is an unquestionably evil thing to do. In that respect, and in that context, moral conservatism is a good thing.

Similarly, where the foreseen consequences of our proposed actions or policies are opaque, and careful reasoning and investigation will not make them tolerably clear, then we should, in most circumstances, stick with the normal moral verities, that is, our firmest considered convictions. But the probable consequences are not always that opaque. More crucially, even where they are, if it is also evident enough that we will do considerable evil *no matter what we do or fail to do*, then we should act on our best hunches about where the lesser evil lies, even when our best hunches are not very good. Where so acting is a moral necessity, moral action is traumatic. There is no escaping anxiety and anguish here. This, in some circumstances, is just what the moral life is like. But to try to do nothing—as understandable as it is—is, in most circumstances of this sort, deeply morally evasive. There is the problem of how much we can expect from human beings: it is not reasonable to expect people to be saints or heroes or to try to make this a requirement for the status of moral agency. But people who can and do so act are morally admirable. Their actions are often so supererogatory that we can hardly say of others that they *ought* to so act, let alone that they *must* so act. That is both morally sanctimonious and unreasonable. But that does not gainsay the fact that each of us, when we reflect on what we as individuals should do in such situations, will, if we are reasonably clear-headed, hold that this is what we should ideally do, if only we can summon up enough courage to so act. Some of Jean-Paul Sartre's and Bertolt Brecht's moral heroes are persons who, though not without anguish and remorse, act resolutely in dirty-hands circumstances. I think, if we carefully reflect on what morality is, they will be our heroes and our exemplars too, even where we do not share their background politics.

III

It might be thought that I am begging questions and sweeping things under the rug with my conception of the lesser evil. I am assuming implicitly, it might be argued, that the lesser evil is what results in the least harm (the fewer deaths, the lesser misery or pain, the lesser undermining of self-respect, autonomy, security, and the like). But, the objection will continue, the "lesser evil" may not be that, but the not-doing of such plain moral evils as, for example, not violating someone's rights, not administering unjust laws, not taking (let alone shooting) hostages, not refusing to take prisoners, not lying, and the like. Where any of the rights violations that go with the doing of these forbidden things occur, we have a greater evil than if they do not. Suffering and misery are bad, but rights violations are even worse.

It seems to me that this is an implausible response. Sometimes violating someone's rights may avert a catastrophe. In this case, it seems to me, these rights should be violated. There are other sorts of examples that drive home my point as well. Even when, under the Nazis, it became apparent that he would be required to administer abhorrent racial laws, a German judge, appointed during the Weimar Republic, might rightly have not resigned. He might have stayed because he realized that, by applying these vile laws in a discriminatory way, he might very well be able to save lives that would not have been saved if he had been replaced by a Nazi hack. To move to a different example, shooting a hostage and threatening to shoot some others might prevent the sacking and shooting of a whole village, or at least give the villagers time to flee. (Remember the comments of Bertolt Brecht, as well as Karl Marx, on the Paris Commune.) It seems to me that there is no serious question where the lesser evil lies in situations where one might violate someone's rights to prevent a massacre. The violating of one person's rights here is plainly a lesser evil. It is blind rights worship or rule worship not to see that.

IV

The view I take here, as I remarked, is compatible with utilitarianism but does not require it, for it is also compatible with a pluralistic deontological view of the familiar and sophisticated sort set forth by W.D. Ross and C.D. Broad. For these thinkers we start with a collection of familiar *prima facie* duties. These duties are just that: *prima facie*. They not infrequently conflict with each other, and we must determine in the particular situation in question which of these conflicting *prima facie* duties is our *actual* duty. There is, for such deontologists, no overriding moral rule or moral principle—no categorical imperative, no lexical ordering of *prima facie* duties—which will tell us in any situation what we must do. They, like utilitarians, do not appeal to any absolute moral prohibitions that we must always act in accordance with come what may. My account, however, is incompatible with Kant's Absolutism about particular moral principles, or Elizabeth

Anscombe's and Alan Donagan's Christian Absolutism, which maintains that there are some particular things that must never be done, no matter how much evil results from our not doing them.[10] In rejecting such Absolutism, I am not saying anything that now, for us, is at all iconoclastic or even unusual. Williams, Walzer, and Nagel no more accept such an Absolutism than do I. But I am trying to think through such a non-Absolutism consistently, while still starting, as they do, with our considered convictions, and continuing to take them seriously—realizing that they are as close as we can get to a rock-bottom court of appeal in moral deliberation.

V

In so reasoning, I utilize the justificatory method of an appeal to our considered judgements in wide reflective equilibrium (a thoroughly holistic form of coherentism), and I appeal consistently with that coherentism to consequences.[11] But my consequentialism is, as I remarked, a weak consequentialism; it does not commit me to utilitarianism. I shall now, expanding a bit on what I have said elsewhere, briefly explain my consequentialism.

As we have seen, Absolutism has it that there are certain things that we must never do no matter what the consequences of not doing these things are. It will forbid certain kinds of actions, even if they will produce lesser overall harm than the other alternatives. Torturing someone, for example, can never be justified on such an account. My *weak* consequentialism, by contrast, neither affirms nor denies that sometimes an individual may rightly refrain from doing that which will have, or may be reasonably expected to have, the *best* overall consequences, everything considered. I do not (*pace* G.E. Moore) argue that we have a duty to try to produce or secure the greatest overall good; I do not argue that we have a duty or an obligation to do our best to achieve either the greatest average utility in the world or the greatest total utility. I refrain, as contemporary utilitarians do not, from making such strong claims. Weak consequentialism is most usefully seen as a negative doctrine that denies (*pace* Elizabeth Anscombe and Alan Donagan) that it is possible to specify a list of act-descriptions which, in terms of their very nature, can be recognized in all circumstances to be the wrong thing to do, where the wrong in question is an everything-considered wrong. My *weak* consequentialism rejects such Absolutism and asserts, rather, that it all depends. Acts of a kind which we are inclined to believe would always be wrong (wrong everything considered) might very well not be if the circumstances were altered and the consequences were very different than they usually are. *There are no acts, such as consequentialism avows, that we can rightly say never should be done without taking into consideration their circumstances and consequences.* And with such consideration of circumstances and consequences, our judgements concerning whether they can be rightly be done in some particular circumstances may shift.

"Weak consequentialists," as Brian Barry puts it, "hold that there is no class of cases, definable in advance, such that the consequences are never relevant to the question of what is the right thing to do."[12] By contrast, strong consequentialism holds that there is at all times a duty to act so as to maximize the amount of good in the world. More generally, consequentialism, both weak and strong, should be conceptualized as follows: the morality of any action is to be judged by its consequences, or in part by its consequences, and not just, or perhaps not even at all, by what the action is apart from its consequences.

Weak consequentialism takes the two weaker alternatives in the above characterization; strong consequentialism the stronger alternatives. Both deny that there are any actions that, simply by virtue of what they are, regardless of their consequences, their circumstances, and their relations to other actions, must be done or avoided *sans phrase*.

Pace Absolutism, there can be no justified *categorical denials of permission to act to avoid the lesser evil.* There are no such *categorical prescriptivities* which are justified. My defense of doing the lesser evil in dirty-hands situations even when that evil is very considerable indeed cannot be defeated by arguing that my consequentialism commits me to utilitarianism, as, it is argued, any consistent consequentialism does. There can be forms of consistent non-utilitarian consequentialism.[13] We can reject the inflexibility of moral Absolutism without ending up in the strait-jacket of utilitarianism. Still, with the type of appeal to consequences that I have defended, we can attend to important factors of context, circumstance and situation without committing ourselves to utilitarianism. We need not go from one inflexibility to another.

VI

Even where (if ever that obtains) the government truly represents the people, there still may be dirty work for it to do, and in such a circumstance the dirty work is ours.[14] When, if ever, is it morally justified, everything considered? My answer is that it is justified where the dirty work cannot be avoided without there remaining or resulting still greater evil, everything considered, than would obtain without the government so acting. In such circumstances its "dirty work" is morally justified, and so we have the scare quotes. If that situation does not obtain, then the dirty work is not justified and should not be morally condoned.

This doctrine is generally thought to be both too simple and too morally insensitive to be right. It is believed to smack too much of the spirit of utilitarian calculation even if it is not strictly utilitarian. In the gloss I have given it in the previous sections, I have tried to show that it is neither too simple, nor morally insensitive, nor committed to utilitarianism or to simple reliance on utilitarian calculation. In so arguing I am running against a rather persistent orthodoxy over the problem of dirty hands articulated in sophisticated forms in some of the writings of Thomas Nagel, Michael Walzer, and Bernard Williams, previously cited. Michael Walzer's "Political action: the problem of dirty hands" is a particularly developed and reflective statement of such a view. I want to argue in this final part of this essay that we are not caught in the dilemma in which Walzer and others think we are caught and that he has misconceptualized the problem.

Walzer believes, as does Nagel, that sometimes we must choose between two courses of action, both of which it would be wrong for us to undertake. This obtains wherever we must choose between acting in accordance with some important moral principle and avoiding some looming disaster. Here we have the stuff of moral tragedy. Walzer remarks that:

> a particular act of government...may be exactly the right thing to do in utilitarian terms and yet leave the man who does it guilty of a moral wrong'.[15]

But it becomes clear from what he says later that, Walzer, like Nagel, in effect drops the above "in utilitarian terms" and claims, more generally, that a particular act or policy of a government could be exactly the right thing for it to do *full stop* and yet leave the people who carry out the act or policy guilty of a grave moral wrong. It is this claim that I am resisting. For me the dirty-hands *dilemma*, psychological anguish notwithstanding, is unreal. There are indeed problems about when to take normally unacceptable means, but there is no resulting moral or conceptual dilemma. For Walzer, Nagel, and Williams, the alleged dilemma is very real. As Walzer puts it, the very "notion of dirty hands derives from an effort to refuse 'absolutism' without denying the reality of the moral dilemma." I want to argue that this position, psychologically attractive as it is, is incoherent. It can only, in Walzer's phrase, "pile confusion upon confusion."[16]

To act politically, particularly if you are a political leader, is to put yourself into a position where you might be required to do terrible things.[17] Walzer works carefully with a key example—indeed a realistic and not a desert-island example—that he believes will strikingly confirm his account of how a morally committed politician can be caught in a moral dilemma in which *he must do wrong to do right*. I think it is a key, indeed a perfect, example for the discussion of such issues, though I shall argue that his moral-dilemma account of it is wrong and that, in his commentary, he misdescribes and misconceptualizes what is involved.

I shall first quote his own statement of his paradigm case in full, then describe his discussion, and finally try to make good my claim that he misconceptualizes the matter.

> ...[C]onsider a politician who has seized upon a national crisis—a prolonged colonial war—to reach power. He and his friends win office pledged to decolonization and peace; they are honestly committed to both, though not without some sense of the advantages of the commitment. In any case, they have no responsibility for the war; they have steadfastly opposed it. Immediately the politician goes off to the colonial capital to open negotiations with the rebels. But the capital is in the grip of a terrorist campaign, and the first decision the leader faces is this: he is asked to authorize the torture of a captured rebel leader who knows or probably knows the location of a number of bombs hidden in apartment buildings around the city, set to go off within the next twenty four hours. He orders the man tortured, convinced that he must do so for the sake of the people who might otherwise die in the explosions—even though he believes that torture is wrong, indeed abominable, not just sometimes but always. He had expressed this belief often and angrily during his own campaign; the rest of us took it as a sign of his goodness. How should we regard him now? (How should he regard himself?).[18]

Let us assume, as I assume Walzer assumes, that there was no other way of defusing the bombs or otherwise effectively canceling their effects, that there was no other way of extracting the information from the rebel leader in time or otherwise gaining the relevant information, that the torture ordered was no more severe or prolonged than was necessary to get the information in time, and that afterwards the rebel leader was promptly and humanely cared for. Given all this, and the case as described, both Walzer and I believe that the politician should order the torture. But Walzer believes that the politician does wrong, indeed commits a moral crime, in order to do right, while I do not. Walzer remarks:

> When he ordered the prisoner tortured, he committed a moral crime and he accepted a moral burden. Now he is a guilty man. His willingness to acknowledge and bear (and perhaps repent and do penance for) his guilt is evidence, and it is the only evidence he can offer us, both that he is not too good for politics and that he is good enough. Here

is the moral politician: it is by his dirty hands that we know him. If he were a moral man and nothing else, his hands would not be dirty: if he were a politician and nothing else, he would pretend that they were clean.[19]

This seems to me the wrong way to think about the case and about the morally committed politician forced by circumstances to do such a terrible thing. Walzer will have it that our conscientious and morally committed politician, in ordering torture, has committed a moral crime. This politician, if he is morally serious, will know that, and "he will not merely feel, he will know that he is guilty (and we will know it too), though he may also believe (and we may agree) that he has good reasons" for so acting.[20]

Let me first clear the decks by pointing where there are important areas of agreement between Walzer and myself. The belief that torture is wrong and *always* wrong is something we both share. I view that belief as one of our firmest and most deeply embedded considered moral convictions. It is not a conviction we are about to, or even can, abandon, if we are moral agents. And we also agree that that considered conviction, and indeed any considered conviction—any deeply embedded moral principle—can be rightly overridden "to avoid consequences that are both imminent and almost certainly disastrous."[21] The torturing case is a good example of where that condition obtains. In addition, we both believe that where the rules or principles articulating these considered convictions are rightly overridden, that overriding should be a painful process. When, in the case in question, the conscientious politician, after soul searching, orders the torture to avoid the loss of many lives, including the innocent lives of children, his decision to do so will still leave "pain behind, and should do so, even after the decision has been made."[22] He will, if he is a decent human being, feel that acutely.

About all these things we agree. Where we disagree is over his claim that the man knows he has done something wrong, that he has committed a moral crime, that he is guilty, and that perhaps he should repent and do penance, fully acknowledging his guilt. He should, I agree, feel pain, anguish, and remorse. He should do what he can to compensate the torture victim for the dreadful harm done to him (incommensurable as it must be), show that it is something he did not want to do, and if possible give a clear accounting of his own actions so that the victim, if he can be clearheaded about it, will recognize that he would have done the same if their roles had been reversed. If the politician is morally sensitive, his pain over this should be a pain that will be with him the rest of his life. It is not something that he will just set aside as he might set aside a bad dream. But guilty he is not; a moral or any other kind of criminal he is not; a person who has departed from the bounds of morality or failed to reason in accordance with the moral point of view he is not. It is, in fine, a mistake to say, as Walzer does, that he has done something that is wrong. He was not doing something which was both right and wrong; he did something which, *everything considered*, was the right thing to do in that circumstance. What he did would in almost all circumstances be an utterly impermissible, indeed a heinous and vile thing to do, but in this circumstance, as Walzer himself acknowledges, it was the right thing to do. So, *contra* Walzer, he could not have done wrong in doing it. The best succinct way of describing the situation is to say that the politician, in ordering the torture, did something which in almost all circumstances would plainly be a very wrong thing to do indeed, but that in that circumstance, which was very extraordinary but still generalizable (*universalizable*), it was not wrong to do it but right.[23] (It is, of course, always at least *prima facie* wrong, but it may not always be *actually* the wrong thing to do. And thus when that obtains, it is not the wrong thing to do, full stop.)

Where the only choice is between evil and evil, it can never be wrong, and it will always be right, to choose the lesser evil. The politician in the situation described, if he is clearheaded as well as morally sensitive, will not *excuse* his behaviour, either implicitly or explicitly acknowledging guilt, but will be prepared to publicly *justify* it. Whether it is *politically expedient* to do so at a given time is a *tactical* matter and, as such, is another thing altogether. But it can be publicly justified and, at least in the fullness of time, it must be publicly justified. (Remember that if something cannot be *publicly justified* it cannot be justified, period.) Since the choice is such a revolting, morally enervating choice between evils, he will not be proud of it, but if he is clearheaded, he will be able to accept himself, recognizing that he has soldiered on and has done what, morally speaking, was the best thing to do under the circumstances. Doing it, and the memory of doing it, will not make him happy, will not give him a sense of satisfaction, and certainly will not make him proud; but he will be able to hold his head up, realizing that he did what he had to do and that others in similar situations should do so as well if they are able to act on the most compelling moral considerations. With such an understanding, he can accept himself. He did not, when he made his choice, depart from the moral point of view; quite to the contrary, he steadfastly stuck with his decision in spite of its difficulty.

VII

Walzer is aware that a response like the above could be made. But he thinks he can set it aside because he takes it to be tied up with the acceptance of utilitarianism. He argues, not implausibly, that utilitarianism has certain evident defects which make it a problematical morality. We have already seen that the lesser-evil argument, while compatible with utilitarianism, is also compatible with a Russian-type pluralist deontology, with a weak consequentialism that makes no commitment to utilitarianism, and with my own, largely coherentist account of morality, which is similar to the justice-as-fairness conception of Rawls. (The latter conception is also compatible with weak consequentialism and, on my account, they work together like hand and glove.[24])

It seems to me that any coherent morality will be consequence-sensitive (something I do not think Walzer would deny) and in morality we can, in some contexts, use utilitarian calculations without being utilitarians. Moreover, sometimes we not only can do it, but we should.

However, while I think that it is important (perhaps even unavoidable) to appeal to consequences in the way I specified, the core of my account about dirty hands does not even require that, *unless* all moral reasoning requires it in some contexts. But I can leave that open here. In deciding what is the lesser evil, we could perhaps treat rules such as "Torture is wrong," "Suffering is bad," "Life should be protected," and "Security should be maintained" as being rules that hold *prima facie*. Moreover, they are rules which *always* hold, *prima facie*. But any one of the things they say should always *prima facie* obtain, be done or be avoided, should also *actually* be done (or obtain, or be avoided) if, on reflection, we come to appreciate that of all the various principles or rules holding *prima facie* and applicable in the circumstances at hand, this is the rule or principle which has the most stringent claim on us. All of them always hold *prima facie* (not doing them, or avoiding them, is always *prima facie* wrong), but they sometimes conflict. When they do, we must simply try to "see" (appreciate, apprehend, intuit) which moral rule or principle has, in that situation, the strongest claim. There is, on such a Russian account, no higher rule or principle we can appeal to and there is no lexical ordering of rules; we must just reflect and come to appreciate which claim in that particular situation is the most stringent.

Thus the Russian deontologist, in acknowledging that torture is always wrong, does not say that torture is *never* permissible as a necessary evil to avoid a still greater evil. We have a duty (*prima facie*) not to torture, but we also have a duty (*prima facie*) to prevent harm to others. The person saying that torture is not wrong in that situation, *everything considered*, need not be a utilitarian; he could be as thoroughly deontological as Ross and Broad. My account here does not have to choose between utilitarianism or other teleological views, on the one hand, and deontological views on the other. What my account is incompatible with, as I have already remarked, is an Absolutism such as Kolakowski's, Anscombe's or Donagan's which claims that there are some specific laws or rules principles, such as "Torture is always impermissible," which must be acted in accordance with no matter what the circumstances, no matter what the consequences, no matter what human catastrophes follow. To be consistent, such an Absolutism would have to say that the politician in Walzer's example should have never ordered or condoned torture. Let the bombs go off, if they have to, and let many people be killed, if there is no other way to prevent the bombs going off except by recourse to torture. That fierce Absolutism is not Walzer's, William's or Nagel's position any more than it is mine. But it would take the establishment of such an Absolutism to undermine my argument that in this situation—and it is a good paradigm for the dirty-hands problem— it is a mistake to say that our politician has done something wrong, committed a moral crime, in ordering torture to achieve what is plainly right. According to such an Absolutism, his ordering torture is *absolutely* morally impermissible, and is thus a moral crime. Such a moralist might even describe it as morally monstrous. However, such an Absolutist, to be consistent, must agree with me that there is no moral dilemma of dirty hands, for, unlike Walzer, he will not accept that we can do right by using such an absolutely and categorically forbidden means. The politician, on this view, cannot rightly so act. But there is nothing for him to be in a *dilemma* about, though he will not infrequently be anguished by the consequences of his Absolutism. Indeed, to the extent that he has much in the way of moral awareness, he will have to be anguished. Such Absolutists are often Christians and, as Kierkegaard stressed, it is not easy to be a Christian. There were very few Christians of this type in what was then Christian Denmark.

VIII

Let me return to Walzer's argument from a somewhat different perspective. Whatever may be true for utilitarians, I do not take moral rules or moral principles as mere rules of thumb or guidelines to be used in trying to calculate what we should do. Moral rules are very often, as Walzer observes and as we both believe, prohibitions on our acting which nonetheless may be overridden in the ways we have discussed. But we also agree that in their being overridden "we do not talk or act as if they had been set aside, canceled, or annulled. They still stand…"[25] However, in certain circumstances they can still be overridden by another rule or principle which takes precedent over them in that situation, or by the fact that the consequences of following the rule in that situation would be disastrous.

However, this does not make moral rules *mere guidelines*, and some of the more deeply embedded ones in our moral life, such as prohibitions against killing or torture, are not annulled or canceled even when they are rightly overridden. "Moral life," as Walzer well says,

> is a social phenomenon and it is constituted at least in part by rules, the knowing of which (and perhaps the making of which) we share with our fellows. The experience of coming up against these rules, challenging their prohibitions, and then explaining ourselves to other men and women is so common and so obviously important that no account of moral decision-making can possibly fail to come to grips with it.[26]

We have these moral rules; they are social prohibitions which partially constitute our morality. There would be no morality without them. They are just part of what it is for something to be a morality. Still, there are good reasons not to treat these rules as absolute, exceptionless prohibitions. And when we do not, we can also see how, without paradox or inconsistency, they can be rightly overridden *without* being annulled or set aside. When a rule in a certain circumstance is rightly overridden, it is overridden by what, in those circumstances, are more demanding moral considerations. When this obtains, the moral-political agent does not do wrong to do right. Such paradox-mongering is confused. Rather he rightly and justifiably does what, but for these special circumstances, would be the wrong (indeed in the cases we have been discussing, monstrously wrong) thing to do. This is not relativism, subjectivism or even historicism (though it is compatible with the latter), but a thorough contextualism.[27] It all depends on the circumstances, and these will vary. But to say that is no more relativist, subjectivist or attitudanalist than it would be to say that in the Yukon people ought to have very warm clothes, but there is no good reason for people to have them in the Amazon. What determines the shift in judgement about what is appropriate or inappropriate or about what is right and wrong in these cases is *the objective situation itself* and not the feelings, attitudes, cultural set or perspective of the people involved. "It all depends" and "*Alles ist relativ*" are very different things. The importance of circumstance and context is vital. We are not likely to have very useful general rules for determining what is the lesser evil in any complicated case where there is a live moral issue. Philosophical generalizations are more or less useless here. But careful concrete attention to the situation will sometimes give us a good understanding of what is the lesser evil in particular cases, though at other times we simply have to act in the dark. Sometimes we should take hard means (including means that are normally morally impermissible) to achieve morally imperative ends, but we will have very little in the way of general formula telling us when this is so. The formula "Always do or support the lesser evil, when it is necessary to choose between evils" does not tell us very much. It is important not to lose sight of the maxim "It all depends," while also keeping in mind that there are repetitive patterns in the problems of human life. When we know that there are several evils, not all of which can be avoided, we should always go for the lesser evil, but *what* the lesser evil is can only be determined on the scene and contextually.[28]

IX

What, in its most morally demanding form, is the problem of dirty hands? Dirty work aplenty goes on in the world (and not only in politics), and the "foundations of kindliness," to use Brecht's phrase, do not seem to be anywhere in sight. Maybe such a notion is like "pie in the sky, by and by." The problem of dirty hands in its most pressing form is this: when, if ever, are we justified in using what would in normal circumstances clearly be a morally impermissible means to achieve what is clearly a morally demanding end? The answer is that we are justified when (1) evil (e.g., killing, destruction, misery, oppression, suffering, and the like) is inescapable and (2) we have good grounds for believing that in such circumstances using what are normally morally impermissible means will make for less evil in the world—and *not* taking those means would, most likely, plainly and immediately lead to greater evil (e.g., more deaths, destruction, misery, etc.) than would obtain from taking them. When these conditions obtain (something which is sometimes very difficult to ascertain) we should use the otherwise impermissible means. It is in such circumstances that morality enjoins seizing the day and taking measures that otherwise would be totally unacceptable. This is not romanticism but moral non-evasiveness. There are no categorical prescriptions built into nature, including human nature, or substantive ones built into our choosing souls, whether our choices are rational, non-rational or irrational. In morality, it all depends.

Notes

This essay first appeared in the *South African Journal of Philosophy* 15:1 (1996), and an earlier version was presented to the Dirty Hands Workshop held at York University, December, 1993.

1 See Kai Nielsen, "Rights and Consequences: It All Depends," *Canadian Journal of Law and Society* 1:1 (1992); and Kai Nielsen, "Philosophy Within the Limits of Wide Reflective Equilibrium Alone," *Iyyun* 43 (1994): 3-41.

2 See Nielsen, "Rights and Consequences."

3 Michael Walzer, "Political Action: The Problem of Dirty Hands," *Philosophy and Public Affairs* 2:2 (1973): 160-80; 169-80.

4 Bernard Williams, "A Critique of Utilitarianism," *Utilitarianism: For and Against*, ed. J.J.C. Smart and B. Williams (Cambridge: Cambridge University Press, 1973) 98-118; Walzer; and Thomas Nagel, *Mortal Questions* (New York: Cambridge University Press, 1979) 53-90; 128-41.

5 Walzer 164.

6 Brian Barry, *Liberty and Justice* (Oxford: Claredon Press, 1991) 40-77.

7 Kai Nielsen, *Equality and Liberty: A Defense of Radical Egalitarianism* (Totowa, N.J: Rowman and Allanheld Press, 1985); and Nielsen, "Rights and Consequences."

8 H. Kleist, *Michael Kohlhaas* (New York: The New American Library, 1960).

9 Kai Nielsen, "On the Ethics of Revolution," *Radical Philosophy* 6 (1973): 17-19; and Kai Nielsen, "Violence and Terrorism: Its Uses and Abuses," *Values in Conflict*, ed. B.M. Leiser (New York: Macmillan Publishing Company, 1981) 435-49.

10 G.E.M Anscombe, *Ethics, Religion and Politics* (Minneapolis: University of Minnesota Press, 1981); and A. Donagan, *The Theory of Morality* (Chicago: The University of Chicago Press, 1997). For a response, see Kai Nelson, *Ethics Without God*, revised edition (Buffalo, N.Y.: Prometheus Books, 1990) 128-162.

11 See Nielsen, "Philosophy Within the Limits" 3-41; and Nielsen, "Rights and Consequences."

12 Barry 76.

13 R. Miller, "Marx and Aristotle: A Kind of Consequentialism," *Marx and Morality*, ed. Kai Nielsen and S.C Patton (Guelph ON: Canadian Association for Publishing in Philosophy, 1981) 325-52; Barry 40-70.

14 M Hollis, "Dirty Hands," *British Journal of Political Science* 12 (1982): 385-98.

15 Walzer 161.

16 Walzer 162.

17 Walzer 165.

18 Walzer 166-167.

19 Walzer 167-168.

20 Walzer 174.

21 Walzer 171.

22 Walzer 174.

23 Kai Nielsen, "Universalizability and the Commitment to Impartiality," *Morality and Universality*, ed. Kai Nielsen, Potter, and Mark Timmons (Dordrecht: Reidel, 1985) 91-105; and Kai Nielsen, "Justice, Equality and Needs" *Dalhousie Review* 69 (1989): 211-27.

24 Nielsen, "Rights and Consequences."

25 Walzer 160.

26 Walzer 160.

27 Kai Nielsen, *Naturalism Without Foundations* (Buffalo, New York: Prometheus Press, 1996) ch. 1.

28 It might be thought that I am in a kind of pragmatic self-contradiction here. I deny that there are any unconditional categorical prescriptives, but is not "Choose the lesser evil" just such an unconditional categorical prescriptive? It is not, because it, like "Do good and avoid evil," is an empty formal "principle" that does not, by itself, guide conduct. Where we give "evil" content so that the above maxim, *so supplemented*, can guide conduct, we get something that is neither unconditional nor certain. That such and such is evil can perhaps always be coherently challenged. At least there never will be a contradiction in denying that so and so is evil. Unconditionally and certainty are bought at the price of emptiness. I do not say that we can prove this must be so, but I do say that when we look at how things go, including how our language-games are played, that is what we find. There is no pragmatic self-contradiction here. I am not taking a transcendental stance to prove that nothing can be transcendental. There is a useful collection of contemporary essays on absolutism and its consequentialist critics, in Joram Graf Haber, ed., *Absolutism and Its Consequentialist Critics* (Lanham, Maryland: Rowman & Littlefield Publishers, 1994).

NINE

Dirty Hands in Politics: On the One Hand, and On the Other

MICHAEL YEO

At the most generic level, the dirty-hands problem concerns conflicting obligations under circumstances in which to fulfil the one is to contravene the other. In the circumstances of dirty hands, no matter what choice the agent makes—including not choosing—someone will be seriously harmed or wronged, or some principle held dear will be otherwise negated. The agent's hands will be dirty whichever course is taken.

Reflection upon such forced choice situations challenges our moral intuitions and the various theories philosophers have developed to give coherence to our moral lives. Such reflection is especially unsettling when the dirty-hands problem is set in a political context involving a conflict between obligations of state and ones of public morality. Here troubling questions arise about the commensurability of politics and morality, and about whether it is possible for politicians or state officials to be politically effective and to keep their hands clean at the same time. If, or to the extent that, politics goes hand in hand with the possibility of dirty hands, what implications follow concerning the integrity of public morality and the complicity of ordinary citizens in dirty deeds done by those acting on their behalf?

At the outset of any attempt to grapple with these questions, it must be acknowledged that the conceptualization of the dirty-hands problem is itself an issue. I shall take Michael Walzer's conceptualization as my point of departure for the analysis to follow.[1] His account has become a standard reference (albeit, contested) on the problem of dirty hands in politics and captures well its historical antecedents in moral and political philosophy. Moreover, because his analysis sets up the problem in such extreme and stark terms, it brings into clear view certain of its dimensions that I wish to explore.

I shall argue that, among dirty-hands deeds, acts of deception are most revealing of the torturous logic of the dirty-hands problem in politics.[2] Walzer's dirty-hands doer, I shall argue, will have good reason to lie, or at least will be willing to lie if he[3] must, to those on whose behalf he acts dirty-handedly. The corollary of this is that these ordinary citizens are subject to being deceived and susceptible to illusion. This obtains not just with respect to this or that particular event or action but also with respect to their fundamental beliefs about the kind of society in which they live and the relationship between politics and morality in their society.

If what is said above is true, the ordinary citizen's becoming aware of the dirty-handed truth will be an experience of disillusionment. At least, that is how things must appear from the standpoint of Walzer's dirty-hands doer, who presumably will have passed through some such experience. However, whether this is how things will, should, or must appear to an ordinary citizen presented with the dirty-hands problem is open to debate.

Walzer's View

Walzer situates the conflicting obligations that bind the dirty-hands doer as belonging to different orders. On the one hand, there is the political realm, where powers are concentrated such that decisions may have consequences of great gravity and magnitude. He claims that this realm is, and should be, governed by a utilitarian imperative.

On the other hand, there is the moral realm, in which ordinary citizens conduct their private affairs (and which also commands the allegiance of the politician or official). Walzer believes that its ethic is deontological or absolutist.[4] Some acts are simply wrong—categorically—and "known to be bad quite apart from the immediate circumstances in which they are performed or not performed."[5] In any society these acts can be discerned from "the moral teachings good men accept—and whose acceptance serves in turn to mark them as good." This is the official morality of the society, what the society would wish to publicize about itself in a press release, so to speak, or what its members would wear proudly as a badge of honour: "Our fine and noble society is one in which…"

Although the imperatives of these two realms need not mandate conflicting directives for action, in principle they can, and in the circumstances of dirty hands they do. Such circumstances will be ones in which serious harms are at stake and cannot be averted without seriously contravening an important moral principle. Walzer believes that, given the reality of politics in a dirty world, such circumstances will and must sometimes arise for at least some politicians, although it is to some extent a matter of luck whether a particular politician will ever find himself caught in such unfortunate circumstances. He also believes that, when they do, the politician should resolve the issue on the side of the political imperative, which means that, from a moral standpoint, his hands will be dirty.[6]

As Walzer represents it, the dirty-hands deed is a deed that, under the circumstances, is both politically required (as opposed to plain corruption, or unadulterated badness, which answers no such requirement[7]), and morally forbidden. It is only against the background of what are thought to be clean hands that dirty hands are dirty. For something to be a dirty-hands deed it is not enough that it be wrong according to external principles; it must be wrong according to the morality of the society in which it occurs. For example, in a society in which bribery is publicly accepted as a way of doing politics and business, acts of bribery would not qualify as dirty deeds; nor would acts of torture in a society that officially sanctioned the torture of political prisoners under certain circumstances.

The dirty-hands deed, as conceived by Walzer, is thus double-handed. On the one hand (clean), there is some clean principle, rule, or obligatory action (let us call it [A]). On the other hand (dirty), there is an opposing dirty-handed imperative ([-A]). Under dirty-hands circumstances, what the one hand forbids, the other requires, and both hands are joined in the same person.

The possibility of being thus double-bound raises doubts about the commensurability of politics and morality and ultimately about the integrity of morals. "The argument," Walzer tells us, "relates not only to the coherence and harmony of the moral universe, but also to the relative ease or difficulty—or impossibility—of living a moral life."[8]

Dirty-handed Contradiction

Walzer's account of the dirty-hands problem presents us with a stark contradiction. To illustrate this, it will be helpful to consider one of his examples, which, as is common in the dirty-hands literature, deals with torture:

> He [the dirty-hands politician] orders the man tortured, convinced that he must do so for the sake of the people who might otherwise die in the explosions—even though he believes that torture is wrong, indeed abominable, not just sometimes, but always. He had expressed this belief often and angrily during his own campaign: the rest of us took it as a sign of his goodness.[9]

This politician appears to subscribe to two contradictory beliefs:

[A] Torture is always wrong (absolutism, deontology)
[-A] Torture may sometimes be right (utilitarianism)

How can this apparent contradiction be reconciled? One option for reconciliation would be to qualify the beliefs so as to remove the contradiction. For example:

[A] is true (right) for some people (the public)
[-A] is true (right) for other people (politicians)

However, Walzer sets up the problem such that [A] and [-A] obtain for one and the same person, as is clear from his example. When this politician "angrily" denounced torture during his campaign, he was not saying that it was wrong for the public, but right for state officials. No one would bother to denounce torture by ordinary citizens. Presumably, even after this experience, he will continue to denounce torture categorically—in public.

An alternative option for reconciliation would be to suppose that the politician does not hold these beliefs at the same time. There are two main scenarios for this. On the one hand, it could be that the politician converts from belief in [A] to belief in [-A], from absolutism or deontology to one variety or another of utilitarianism. "I used to believe [A], but now I believe [-A]. I now believe that [A], and other statements containing categorical terms like 'always' or 'never,' are false. Rightness, I now believe, depends on the balance of good over bad consequences."

Along similar lines, his revised view might be that [A], and other like statements, are guidelines only—handy rules of thumb that archive utilitarian wisdom, but no substitute for calculations based on data from particular circumstances. It is useful that [A] be widely believed and taken absolutely, and that people as a rule feel guilty when they break the rules, because usually (but not always and for everyone) it will be better to follow the rules than to do on-the-spot calculations.

On the other hand, we might suppose that Walzer's dirty-hands doer changes his mind in the direction of some version or other of deontology. Perhaps he revisits [A] in light of [-A], which he now thinks of as a special exception that does not really contradict [A], or that overrides it.[10] He believes he has only to modify [A] to accommodate this special case (e.g., by relaxing the "always"). He resolves to restructure official morality and revise his old campaign speech to sanction torture under certain circumstances. In effect, this will mean that, under the specified circumstances, torture would no longer be a dirty deed.

Or perhaps he finds instead that, having tried, he cannot reconcile [-A] with morality. Therefore he changes his mind again to revert back to his initial belief in [A]. "[A], like [-A], will have dirty consequences," or so he might say in his next campaign speech, running as a repentant dirty-hands doer, "but these will not be intended, and where intentions are pure, the hands are clean." Perhaps he will really believe this, or at least half-believe it.

Walzer permits none of these sensible, even if contentious, reconciliations. His politician does not change his mind. He believes both [A] and [-A] at the same time. That is what defines him as a dirty-hands doer of the Walzer variety.

Dirty-handed Deception

Walzer sets up the dirty-hands problem such that the dirty-hands doer, to all appearances, is in a contradiction. He is committed both to [A] and [-A] (whatever the content—principles, rules, acts—with which we fill in these letters). To dignify this by calling it a paradox, as Walzer does, does not make the contradiction go away. Moreover, he does not allow for this contradiction to go away, or otherwise to be reconciled.

How must this appear to those on whose behalf the dirty-hands doer acts? A commitment to both [A] and [-A] in moral terms—that is, from the standpoint of "the rest of us," the ordinary citizens—must surely appear either as a serious confusion, or as a lie. Faced with someone who espoused both [A] and [-A], or who espoused the one and acted on the basis of the other, it would be reasonable to conclude that he was either hopelessly confused, or a liar; in any event, that he did not truly believe both at the same time.[11]

However, it is quite improbable that this contradiction, at least so starkly put, would appear at all to the public, because in all likelihood no politician would publicly proclaim allegiance to both [A] and [-A]. And this not just because such a claim would appear absurd ("surely you cannot believe both at the same time"), but because he would probably have good reason to conceal [-A].[12]

One reason would be self-protection. If, as Walzer specifies it, the dirty-hands deeds is, by definition, forbidden by official morality, it will not play well if disclosed. This reason, however, would not be good enough to compel the dirty-hands doer to lie to his fellow citizens about his deeds. Walzer's doer, after all, is someone who, given his commitment to [A], is prepared to accept responsibility (and punishment) for his dirty deeds.

However, the self-interested desire to avoid adverse personal consequences is not the only reason that might figure in the deliberations of Walzer's dirty-hands doer. This doer, in virtue of the same principle that mandated his dirty-hands deed, might also, and I believe would likely, be compelled to lie to those on whose behalf he acts (and indeed to do so against an [A] prohibition forbidding this lie, to which he is himself bound, in earnest). For example, lying may be necessary (at least for some period of time) in order to ensure that the deed is effective, or to avert such harm as might come from disclosure of the deed.

Lying might also be necessary (according to the political, utility imperative, and in whatever way the dirty-hands deed is necessary) to preserve the moral order, or to ensure the credibility of the society's press release. Since the dirty-hands deed cannot be publicly reconciled with official morality, it may be necessary that it be covered up, suppressed, or otherwise concealed (perhaps to be uncovered by those who would probe beneath surfaces and question official statements, reports, press releases, etc.).

Depending on the circumstances, lying might also be necessary to protect the innocence of those on whose behalf the deed was done. If it were indeed done on their behalf—by someone acting as their agent, who did what needed to be done—disclosure of the deed could pull them into complicity and dirty their hands as well.

For any number of reasons that would be compelling for a dirty-hands doer, it may be necessary that the one hand (clean) not know what the other hand (dirty) is doing. Of course, whether it will in fact be necessary (in whatever way the dirty deed itself is) for the doer to lie about his deed will depend upon the circumstances. I believe that, at least in many cases, such circumstances as someone with Walzer's dirty-hands doer's commitments will think sufficient to warrant the deed will be deemed similarly sufficient to warrant its concealment.

Certainly lying figures prominently in what has become the standard literary reference for the dirty-hands problem, Sartre's *Dirty Hands*,[13] as the following excerpt shows:

HUGO: And do you think that the living will agree to your schemes?

HOERDERER: We'll get them to swallow them little by little.

HUGO: By lying to them?

HOERDERER: By lying to them sometimes.

HUGO: You—you seem so real, so solid! How can you stand to lie to your comrades!...I know better than you what lies are like. In my father's home everybody lied to himself, everybody lied to me. I couldn't breathe until I joined the party. Then for the first time I saw men who didn't lie to other men...

HOERDERER: I'll lie when I must, and I have contempt for no one. I wasn't the one who invented lying...We shall not abolish lying by refusing to tell lies, but by using every means at our disposal...

HUGO: All means are not good.

HOERDERER: All means are good when they're effective.

In Sartre's play, the dirty-hands deed is doubled. On one level, it is compromise with the dirty enemy. At a second level, it is lying about this compromise, concealing it from comrades, which is required in order for the compromise to be effective, if not for other reasons. Arguably, this lie is the featured and paradigmatic dirty-hands deed in the play.

In any event, if lying does not always accompany the dirty-hands deed, as it does in Sartre's play, it very well could, and would, if the circumstances required. If the dirty-hands doer does not lie, this will be because he need not, and not because he will not. Presumably, he would decide whether to lie by using the same deliberative principle that mandated his dirty-hands deed, which, like lying, would have been forbidden by his moral commitments. Moreover, even if utilitarian calculation did not mandate lying in a particular circumstance, in principle it could, and if it did, that is what the dirty-hands doer would do. Like Hoerderer, he will "lie when he must."

This means, of course, that he will lie about lying. The dirty-hands politician, we might suppose, will have allegiance to the following two maxims:

[A] One must not lie to one's comrades
[-A] One must lie to one's comrades if circumstances require lying

However, for obvious reasons, he would not proclaim both [A] and [-A] to his comrades: [-A], under the circumstances, will be virtually unspeakable.

Of course, it could be argued that the doer need not subscribe, or profess to subscribe, to [A] thus specified. He will have moral commitments, to be sure, but not necessarily *this* moral commitment. This comes down to the question of what substantive content will be contained in society's moral order, written up and proclaimed in its press release, as it were. Walzer's answer to this, unsatisfactory as it may be, is to mark out the moral realm from "the moral teachings good men accept—and whose acceptance serves in turn to mark them as good."[14] Whether [A] belonged in the moral realm of society, and was therefore something to which the dirty-hands doer would have allegiance, would depend on whether it was included among those teachings.

An alternative way of answering this question is offered by Kant (whom presumably Walzer would count among the wise), who circumscribes the moral realm with reference to the categorical imperative to preclude whatever fails the universalizability test. This test has an analogue in the "publicity test" of his "Perpetual Peace" article:

All actions affecting the rights of other human beings are wrong if their maxim is not compatible with their being made public.[15]

Given that Walzer's dirty-hands doer has one foot in the moral realm, and accepting that Kant's publicity principle circumscribes this realm, we can suppose that he will be committed to the following:

[A] I will publicize whatever maxims guide my actions

However, since he will also have a foot in the political realm, which Walzer believes is organized according to some species of utility principle, he will also be bound by something like the following:

[-A] I will conceal my maxims from the public if, according to my calculations, I must (in order to ensure effectiveness, avert some harm, etc.)

Indeed, following [-A], he would proclaim [A] even in the knowledge that he was prepared to act otherwise. Regardless of whether he did in fact feel compelled to lie to the public, given his commitment to [-A,] anything he might promise or express pertaining to [A] would be unreliable—if indeed his commitment to [-A] were known.[16] The need to appear reliable would be all the more reason for him to conceal his allegiance to [-A].

Dirty-handed Complicity

If we follow Walzer, the pursuit of the truth about the relationship between morality and politics, if we take each seriously in its fundamental imperative, leads to a contradiction. This truth ([A] and [-A])—whatever content we assign to [A], using whatever test or standard—has the logical features of a lie. Indeed, the good dirty-hands doer, a good man concerned with truth, must live a lie because he believes both [A] and [-A], but he must also (it follows from his commitment to [-A]) pretend in public not to believe [-A], and conceal the fact that he is a dirty-hands doer. At least he will be willing to do so if he must.

And what of the public? They believe—the dirty-hands doer would want them to believe—[A], and not to believe [-A], as true of their society: "Ours is a fine and noble society..." However, [A] is not true (or clean). More precisely, it is only a half-truth, or a half-lie, the other half about which they are in the dark. Indeed, in the society's press release, this other half of the truth, [-A], is denounced (the dirty-hands doer might even be leading this denunciation), attributed perhaps to less "civilized" societies, or to occasional renegades operating within the society without authorization.

Believing this, the "rest of us" are in illusion, or so it must appear from the standpoint of Walzer's dirty-hands doer, who would have good political reasons to support this illusion. Most people do not have the right stuff to maintain the belief both in [A] and [-A] at the same time—a condition which is so dizzying that, even for the very exceptional dirty-hands doer, it is the cause of great anguish and suffering. It may therefore be politically necessary that one hand not know what the other is doing—that the dirty hand do things on behalf of the clean one that the clean one could not live with while continuing to be good and clean, and that it therefore do them behind its back.

On the one hand, if the clean hand really does not know what the dirty hand is doing on its behalf, and moreover does not know that hands would also be dirty even if [A] were rigorously adhered to, it is in illusion. This illusion keeps it clean and innocent (or so it seems), and demarcates ordinary citizens from dirty-hands doers.

On the other hand, if the clean hand learns about the dirty hand—that [-A] is so, and indeed is unavoidable and no accident in relation to [A] in the circumstances of a dirty world—it is dirtied by this truth and becomes complicit. After all, it is joined to the dirty hand in the body politic. The dirty hand is the body politic's other hand.

Suppose that the two hands were not joined. If the dirty hand were not really our other hand, doing its dirty work on our behalf, there would be a fortuitous solution to the problem. If, for example, the dirty hand were the hand of Fate, a benign Fortuna acting on our side but not at our command, doing what we would forbid ourselves to do but which is nonetheless good for us, we might thank God for it.

Some loathsome villain—without whom we would all be better off and the world less evil—threatens us. We would like to strike him down but have forbidden ourselves the means to do so. Indeed, it is largely our resolve in this regard that makes us different from such villains. Fortunately, the hand of Fate intervenes: he has a heart attack. We get the good outcome, but our hands are clean. We have no complicity because the matter was out of our hands.

The situation would be virtually identical if the dirty-hands doer were able to conceal his deed, if one hand really did not know what the other hand was doing. The clean hand would be in illusion (not knowing the whole truth), but therefore would be innocent. As it turns out, the heart attack that killed the villain was caused by a poison slipped into his food, unknown to him and us, by one of our dirty-hands doers. This doer, a moral man as Walzer represents him, would be and feel guilty for doing something he earnestly believed to be morally wrong, notwithstanding that, as a public servant, he believed it had to be done to protect us from the evil ways of the world. And for political reasons, he would also suffer this guilt in silence if this were necessary to maintain us in our innocence.

Dirty-handed Illusion

By definition, [-A] is contrary to morality, and ordinary citizens, insofar as they are morally bound, will forswear [-A]. However, to the extent that dirty hands really are unavoidable, or that [A] needs [-A], or that by itself [A] will also be dirty, they will be in illusion. Several ways of being can be distinguished with respect to how someone stands with respect to this (alleged) illusion.

I. WHOLE-HEARTED ILLUSION: BLISSFUL IGNORANCE

This would be whole-hearted belief in [A], without any suspicion of dirty-handed [-A], or any thought that [A] is, or could be, dirty. Perhaps many people believe this when they are young and idealistic.

II. HALF-HEARTED ILLUSION: BAD FAITH

In a society that pays any lip service to truth and freedom in its official press release, in which the pursuit of truth is associated with the dignity of being human, it is unlikely that dirty hands [-A] can be kept entirely from public view. There will be a press officially dedicated to freedom and truth (albeit perhaps not as free and true as it would have us believe). There will be philosophers and artists who believe it is their responsibility to uncover illusion and to disclose what is true. There will be reports, from time to time (but usually long after the fact, when the dirty-hands deed is long since done, and the doer perhaps dead). Such reports will jeopardize the society's illusions about its morality.

Particular instances of dirty hands will be uncovered from time to time (usually long enough after the fact that people can dismiss this as something that happened *then*, but wouldn't or couldn't happen *now*).[17] That may be harmless enough. A certain amount of dirty-hands truth made public may even be useful. Its ritual denouncement could help prop up the illusion that the society takes truth very seriously (which by itself is true) and add credibility to its press release.

Moreover, the commitment to truth may not be quite as whole-hearted as it is officially said to be. Perhaps the dirty-hands doer (and the corrupt or plain bad dirty doer as well) can count on a certain tendency to illusion issuing from the wish to believe that [A] is true, even to the point of not squarely facing contrary evidence or argument in order to maintain the belief. Deception may be aided by proneness to self-deception.

There may an intermediary reality between clean hands and dirty hands, or innocence and guilt—a dirty illusion, a way of knowing, and yet not knowing. Perhaps everybody knows, yet does not know, that politicians (and not just bad ones) will lie and do things on our behalf that are incompatible with our proclaimed image and that they are expressly forbidden to do. Perhaps they know in the same way that circumstances may arise in which the hands of politicians would be dirty even if they scrupulously adhered to [A]. They know these things enough not to be surprised by disclosures of [-A], but not enough to displace the belief in [A]. That is, they know enough about [-A] to actively ignore it, or to conceal it from themselves in bad faith.

At least, things might appear thus from the standpoint of Walzer's dirty-hands doer, for whom the truth of the matter is that [-A] is no accident or aberration in relation to [A]. Perhaps, in a way, everybody knows this, but half-heartedly enough to continue to pay lip service to [A] by itself. This would be a retreat back into illusion, but the illusion would not be quite the same any more.

III. LOSS OF FAITH IN MORALITY AND POLITICS: CYNICISM

There will be some who, confronted with evidence of [-A] will scorn [-A], and give up on [A] as well, but only half-heartedly. "I am not under any illusions about morality and politics. I know about dirty hands. Yes, and I was foolish ever to have believed [A]. Politicians are liars. The bad ones lie for themselves, and the good ones lie for us, but they are all liars just the same, at least if they want to get elected. It has always been thus, and could not be otherwise."

Although those who speak this way will have gone so far as no longer to believe [A] whole-heartedly, they continue to half-believe it. For it is from the standpoint of half-hearted commitment to [A] that they pass judgement on politics. They are cynical because the world has not lived up to their [A] expectations, but nonetheless they cling to [A] as the standard against which they scorn politics.

IV. LOSS OF FAITH IN POLITICS: THE BEAUTIFUL SOUL

There will be some who, confronted with evidence of dirty hands [-A], will give up on politics, wash their hands of it (or so they might believe), but cling to morality nonetheless as having a local truth. Concluding that the city of God and the city of Man cannot be reconciled, they will elect for the city of God and withdraw into a sphere of innocence—an insular religious community, perhaps.

This, too, would be an illusion, insofar as this soul or this community must be located in some ungodly body or place and have some trade with the ungodly. At the very least, they will owe their safety and security to those who are dirtying themselves with politics on their behalf. The lambs would be eaten up by the wolves and would not enjoy such peace and comforts as they do were it not for certain of their kind who learn the ways of the wolf and become wolf-like themselves. Moreover, even a tent city deep in the desert will require politics of some sort, at least insofar as these souls need to sustain some kind of economy, mediate disputes, ensure their propagation, and so on, which needs could place their kind in the circumstances of dirty hands.

V. LOSS OF FAITH IN MORALITY: THE WILY UTILITARIAN

There will be some who, confronted with evidence of [-A], will conclude that [A] by itself would not be any cleaner, or would not be sustainable, and that all things considered [-A] commands the allegiance of rational beings living in a dirty world. They will give up on morality, or rather subsume morality under the utilitarian rule of politics. Morality, at least the absolutist type that passes for morality in the society's press release, will be dismissed as an illusion.

Some of these utilitarians might to all appearances be indistinguishable from deontologists. They might agree with Walzer that it would not be good (useful) if everyone converted to utilitarianism, and that society is best served if most ordinary citizens are deontologists and subscribe wholeheartedly to [A]. These citizens will be in illusion, but that is as it should be. And to support this illusion, wily utilitarians might even feign to be deontologists themselves, or otherwise prop up as the official morality of society something they believe in their hearts to be false, or at best half-true.

And just as wily utilitarians may not be distinguishable to all appearances from deontologists, so too they may be indistinguishable from Walzer's dirty-hands doer, who will differ from the wily only in that he really does believe [A], rather than merely pretending to believe for strategic reasons.[18]

From Walzer's point of view, this wily position would be illusory. [A] is not merely useful (or harmful, as the case may be) but categorically compelling for good men. If [A] were not (also) true, there would be no morality in the proper sense of the term—no genuine moral dilemmas, no guilt, no freedom. Morality in [-A], if it can be called that, would be reduced to technique: calculating, predicting, and so forth.

VI. FAITH IN THE FACE OF [-A]:
THE RESPONSE OF THE RIGHTEOUS MORALIST

There will be some who, confronted with evidence of [-A], will become indignant about it. However, rather than wash their hands of politics, like cynics or beautiful souls, they will insist that it be conducted under the imperative of [A], which they will reassert against [-A]. They will believe themselves complicit in [-A] to they extent that they do not explicitly forbid it. They will insist that politicians forswear the dirty-hands deed option and commit themselves to the principle of publicizability. Political roles will be carefully limited and monitored to minimize the occasion for dirty-hands deeds. No room will be left for equivocation. A clear message will be sent that [-A] is unacceptable, and that those caught red-handed doing [-A] will be punished.

From the standpoint of Walzer's dirty-hands doer, the moralist's crusade to bring politics under the rule of morality will be based on illusion. Dirty-hands deeds are not just incidental to politics, something we could do without and still do politics in a dirty world. In any event, in the circumstances of dirty hands, the hands of someone who chose [A] would be dirty all the same, whatever the moralist might say to convince himself that he can wash his hands of the dirty consequences of [A].

A Back-Handed Solution to the Dirty-hands Problem

Walzer claims that, given politics and morality in a dirty world, circumstances may very well arise in which it is necessary for politicians or state officials to get their hands dirty. Moreover, he believes that under such circumstances the political imperative should prevail against the countervailing moral one.

Walzer's claim to necessity could be construed in a number of different ways. It could be taken to mean that politicians may find themselves in circumstances from which it will be impossible to emerge with clean hands, whether they follow the imperative of [A] or of [-A]. It could mean that good men, under certain circumstances, will feel compelled to do things that they know are morally bad if they are to fulfil their political obligations. It could mean that any society needs men who will do things, under certain circumstances, that it needs done but regards as morally impermissible in any circumstance. It could mean that [A] needs [-A], even while disavowing it (of course, [-A], by definition, needs [A]). Or, to use a metaphor, it could mean that society forbids the breaking of eggs, but needs omelettes, and leaves the logic for the dirty-hands doer to sort out (he will produce omelettes as needed, quietly, and without requiring society to draw disturbing conclusions about what must have been necessary for these omelettes to be produced).

The claim to necessity, in any of these (or yet other) senses, is open to debate, whether the grounds be empirical, logical, or conceptual. Certainly there are many dubious assumptions and rebuttable arguments in Walzer's analysis. However, as fruitful as it might be to engage him on these points, I believe that, practically speaking, the issues can be distilled into a relatively simple question: should good men and women with a serious commitment to truth lend any support to political dirty-hands deeds? I believe that the answer to this question should be an unequivocal "no."

Imagine a society in which the dirty-hands issue has become a public issue. I submit that the right thing to do would be to lend our hands on the side of the righteous. We will champion the principle of publicity and launch a clean-hands campaign. Our motto: "whatever is not publicized in [A] is not permissible, is dirty by definition. Zero tolerance for dirty hands." Institutions will be reviewed and shaped in accordance with [A] to tie the hands of our officials. We will carefully communicate what officials acting in various capacities are and are not authorized to do on our behalf, and send a clear directive that none of our public servants are to do anything we have not authorized them to do. If they are thus tempted, we will want them to throw their hands up in the air: "But my hands are tied, I cannot do [-A]."

We will encourage men and women who are good, and who forswear [-A], to go into politics. We will make it clear we want good people only, and not good men who have learned to be bad. We will say: "Some claim that one cannot practice politics effectively without getting one's hands dirty. Let's prove them wrong!"

Ours is a society, we will say in our press release, in which [A] prevails, but not simply as a matter of fact. Indeed, as a matter of fact, [A] does not prevail, but we believe it can and ought, as an obligatory end towards which we will strive, and in the pursuit of which we forbid ourselves to use immoral means because this would be inconsistent with the kind of end that [A] is.

Would all of this make us fools? On the one hand, suppose Walzer is wrong, and dirty hands in politics are not necessary. The class of dirty-hands deeds, in Walzer's sense, is empty. There are no bona fide dirty-hands deeds, just dirty deeds. Then we would have done the right thing.

On the other hand, suppose he is right. Dirty-hands deeds are necessary (whatever this means). Our press release will be an illusion. Even so, we will have done the right thing! Indeed, we will have done precisely what a good dirty-hands doer would have had us do. Indeed, such a doer (or a wily utilitarian) might well lead the clean-hands campaign!

So even though, standing with the righteous champions of clean-hands politics, we will be in illusion, our reforms will not be inconsistent with those that Walzer's dirty-hands doer would endorse. We will champion [A], and campaign against [-A]. But that is precisely the platform that the dirty-hands doer (and the wilely utilitarian) would run on (but with the resolve to do [-A] when necessary, and in concealment)! After all, if it is debatable whether [A] needs [-A], [-A], by definition and as a matter of logical necessity, needs [A].

And what will we have lost? Good men and women will have gone into politics. If Walzer is right, if dirty hands are necessary, they will learn this for themselves. Faced with this knowledge, these good people will either abandon politics, or learn to be bad from the school of hard knocks. In any event, they will be precisely the sort of people who, if dirty-hands deeds are to be done, Walzer (and the righteous) would want to play the dirty-hands part. People who go into politics already having learned to be bad are suspect, their commitment to [A] dubious: perhaps they are just plain bad.

So, despite what we have publicized and forbidden, dirty-hands deeds will be done regardless, if dirty hands really are unavoidable. And if the good people who become dirty-hands doers (or wily utilitarians who only pretended to believe the moralist platform during the campaign) are really good at their job, we will not know what they have done for us. Indeed, the good dirty-hands doer will do everything possible to secure us in the illusion that we were right.

And if from time to time, despite the efforts of the good dirty-hands doer to conceal the dirty-handed truth, there should emerge rumours or reports of [-A], we will be indignant. "That is not permitted," we will say. "It was not authorized by us, indeed it was expressly forbidden. Whoever would do this is an outlaw, a criminal!" And this is precisely what the good dirty-hands doer would have us say!

And if someone is caught red-handed, doing dirty deeds, he will bow his head and accept whatever punishment is coming. (Perhaps this punishment will even be meted out by a judge caught in the dirty-handed circumstance of having to punish someone for doing what, in some sense, had to be done.) And with the doer's earnest acceptance and demonstration of guilt, faith in the moral order will be preserved, and perhaps even strengthened. "Yes, a dirty deed was done," we will say, "but it was an outlaw deed, not authorized by us. It was not our deed. And that this outlaw has been found out and punished for his deed, from the standpoint of our [A], demonstrates the rule of [A] in our society, that ours is a fine and noble society in which..."

And all of this will have come to pass just as the good dirty-hands doer would have willed it!

Notes

An earlier version of this essay was first presented to the Dirty Hands Workshop held at York University, December 1993.

1 Michael Walzer, "Political Action: The Problem of Dirty Hands," *Philosophy and Public Affairs* 2:2 (Winter 1973): 161-80.

2 Lying is explicitly at issue in one of the examples Walzer uses, but he does not accord lying any exemplary significance as a dirty-hands deed. I believe that my claims about the special importance of lying for the dirty-hands problem follow from his exposition, even though he does not draw out these implications.

3 The use of the masculine here and throughout this paper is in recognition of the gender dynamics of this problem. This dynamic is exemplified in Conrad's *Heart of Darkness*: "I laid the ghosts of his gifts with a lie....They—the women I mean—are out of it—should be out of it. We must help them stay in that beautiful world of their own, lest ours gets any worse," Joseph Conrad, *Heart of Darkness and the Secret Sharer* (Toronto: Bantam Books, 1981) 81. On the gender dynamics of the dirty-hands problem, see Sharon Sutherland, this volume.

4 It is because Walzer represents morality in absolutist terms that the conflict between morality and politics appears as stark and intractable as it does in his analysis. Otherwise, the conflict could be resolved with reference to concepts like 'exception to the rule' or 'overriding obligation.' For the purpose of my analysis I will accept Walzer's account, it being understood that the dirty-hands problem appears entirely differently if we begin from a more flexible, conciliatory view of morality. For a discussion of absolutism and morality, see Stuart Hampshire, "Morality and Pessimism," *Public and Private Morality*, ed. Stuart Hampshire (Cambridge: Cambridge University Press, 1978) 1-22; esp. 7-10.

5 Walzer 168.

6 Of course, the circumstances are such that, were the politician to resolve the issue on the side of the moral imperative, his hands would be also be dirty (from the standpoint of his political responsibilities).

7 Corrupt or plain bad deeds pit private against public interests, whereas dirty-hands deeds pit public interest against public morality. Probably the vast majority of seriously immoral acts that actually occur under political auspices (as opposed to fictitious ones philosophers often use as examples) are simply corrupt or plain bad. I believe that philosophers who write about the dirty-hands problem have some responsibility to take care not to (inadvertently) lend support to corruption and evil. For example, if acts of torture could conceivably be politically obligatory under certain very specific circumstances for some very compelling reason, it should also be noted that such acts typically occur for reasons far less noble.

8 Walzer 161.

9 Walzer 166.

10 Bernard Williams, whose views on dirty hands are in some respects quite similar to Walzer's, considers, and rules outs, several such ways of reconciling the problem of dirty hands. See Bernard Williams, "Politics and Moral Character," *Public and Private Morality* 55-73; esp. 60-4.

11 An alternative explanation would be to regard this as an instance of Orwellian 'double think.' David Shugarman also refers to Orwellian doublethink in the context of the dirty-hands problem. See David Shugarman, "The Use and Abuse of Politics," *Moral Expertise: Studies in Practical and Professional Ethics*, ed. Donald MacNiven (London: Routledge Press, 1990) 198-231; 215-6.

12 Walzer (168) says of his dirty-hands doer that "if he were a moral man and nothing else, his hands would not be dirty; if he were a politician and nothing else, he would pretend that they were clean." I accept that the dirty-hands doer—as Walzer describes him—would not pretend that his hands were clean *in order to escape being held accountable* (which is what I think Walzer has in mind), but that he could and very well would *for other reasons*.

13 Jean-Paul Sartre, "Dirty Hands," *No Exit and Three Other Plays* (New York: Vintage Books, 1955) 222-3.

14 Walzer 168.

15 Immanuel Kant, "Perptual Peace," *Kant's Political Writings*, trans. H.B. Nisbet, ed. Hans Reiss (Cambridge: Cambridge University Press, 1970) 93-130; 126.

16 What Kant (130) says, albeit with a slightly different subterfuge in mind, applies here as well: "This subterfuge of a secretive system of politics could, however, easily be defeated if philosophy were to make its maxims public, would it but dare to allow the philosopher to publicize his own maxims."

17 Goodin concedes that it may be "inevitable that any big lie will eventually be exposed" but adds that, by the time it is exposed, its sting may be neutralized in one way or another. Robert Goodin, *Manipulating Politics* (New Haven: Yale University Press, 1980) 42-3.

18 Deontologists will believe [A], and will not believe [-A]. Wily utilitarians will pretend to believe [A] (assuming that this is useful), but also (or really) believe [-A]. Walzer's dirty-hands doers believe both [A] and [-A]. To all external appearances, and given the possibility of deception, these three may be indistinguishable.

TEN

Bribery, Business, and the Problem of Dirty Hands

A.W. CRAGG

It is clear from the news that business ethics has become a widely discussed topic both within the business community and among the wider public. Some might take this as evidence of moral decline. Since media attention to business ethics is frequently attracted by evidence of moral corruption, this inference is not surprising. On the other hand, it might equally well be argued that the increasing attention to the ethical dimensions of business practice is a sign of rising standards and a public that increasingly is not prepared to tolerate unethical behaviour.

Corruption in international business transactions is a case in point. Leaders in the business community privately confirm that it is widespread. Transparency International, an international anti-corruption coalition, describes the problem as endemic around the world. In both government and business circles, this fact is frequently used to justify corrupt business practices as inevitable or unavoidable if companies are to avoid losing contracts. This view is not just informally expressed. Until very recently it has been embedded in legal systems (in Europe, for example) where bribery of foreign officials was accepted as a legitimate business expense for tax purposes. In these cases, bribery was not just legally condoned, it was actually supported, often unwittingly, by the tax-paying public.

Paradoxically, very few, even among those who have condoned bribery as unavoidable given the current international business environment, see the practice as benign or unproblematic. Most would prefer to operate in a business environment where it was not a factor. As a result, some countries are beginning to take unilateral action. The American "Foreign Corrupt Practices Act" is perhaps the best example of such an initiative. Other countries are moving more cautiously, hoping to find ways to discourage corruption without putting companies operating under their legal jurisdiction at a competitive disadvantage. It remains the case, however, that widespread corruption continues as a fact of life, particularly in international business. This raises a question. Where the costs of being ethical are high, is it ethical to be ethical? Like much about business ethics, the very question suggests a contradiction. Yet the idea to which it points is real enough. Indeed, it is one which is frequently voiced in private conversations with seasoned business leaders, who sometimes point to the lack of realism on the part of those advocating inflexible business standards and to the harm that an uncompromising ethical posture can cause individuals and the companies to whom their welfare is frequently tied.

In fact the possibility that one's responsibilities might require, and therefore justify, unethical conduct under certain conditions is one which has been extensively discussed by some of the most distinguished philosophers in the history of ideas. The focus for those discussions, however, has not traditionally been business; rather, it has been the realm of public affairs. At issue in these discussions is the view that people in positions of public trust fail in their responsibilities when they put moral standards ahead of the public interest. Machiavelli summarizes this view well when he advises that:

> A Prince cannot observe all those things which give men a reputation for virtue, because in order to maintain his state he is often forced to act in defiance of good faith, of charity, of kindness, of religion. And so he must have a flexible disposition, varying as fortune and circumstances dictate...he should not deviate from what is good, if that is possible, but he should know how to do evil, if that is necessary.[1]

A modern defence of that view is offered by Michael Walzer who argues that:

> It is by his dirty hands that we know [the moral politician]. If he were a moral man and nothing else, his hands would not be dirty; if he were a politician and nothing else, he would pretend that they were clean...politicians necessarily take moral as well as political risks committing crimes that they...think ought to be committed.[2]

Like many others, Walzer holds that, in serving the public interest, public servants, particularly politicians, may be required to override basic moral and legal imperatives in pursuit of their duty.

In what follows, I propose to ask whether this view is applicable only to officials in public life. Does it have wider application? The question is important, because the arguments frequently cited to justify decisions by political leaders to "dirty their hands" in the pursuit of an important public good normally imply that public life is a special case whose characteristics or objectives excuse unethical behaviour on the part of public officials in certain situations. What is true of public life, it is frequently implied, is not and could not be true of private enterprise or business. I shall argue that this view is mistaken. And for purposes of illustration I shall use the example of bribery.

Let me offer a preliminary note of caution. The view that public officials are not, and ought not to allow themselves to be, constrained by moral norms that apply in private or personal life might be argued in a number of different and incompatible ways. My discussion will be directed only to those accounts that recognize that the conduct of public officials ought, in the normal course of events, to be constrained by ethical considerations. When these constraints are justifiably overridden, the result is justified (or excusable) moral wrongdoing, but wrongdoing for all of that. The result is genuinely dirty hands, not hands which only appear sullied to the politically naive, with their limited understanding or experience.[3] Let us turn then to the argument.

Justifying Dirty Hands in Public Life and in Business Affairs

I will begin by drawing a series of parallels between the responsibilities of public and business leaders.

1. Where dirty hands are concerned, is public life a special case? The argument that it is might go like this:[4] the primary or overriding goal of public life is to advance the public good. On occasion, the pursuit of that goal can be expected to create the need for actions that run counter to the interests as well as the rights of private individuals, or to clash with the personal moral obligations of public office holders to others, whether groups or individuals.[5] When this occurs, and the public good in question is substantial, overriding ethical constraints in pursuit of that good is obligatory, even though immoral.

In contrast, it might be argued, the goal of business in a market economy is to advance private goods, usually the wealth of the owners or shareholders. Since the purpose of morality (we shall here suppose) is to bring the pursuit of self-interest under the discipline of moral rules or principles, an appeal to the goods which businesses typically pursue by its very nature cannot justify overriding substantial moral imperatives.

This argument and arguments of this form, I suggest, are flawed. They only seem persuasive in public argument because of the justified importance which is often given to protecting the interests of the state.[6] The welfare of the state is important for many good reasons. But, in the absence of arguments attributing to the state a special metaphysical status, it is important because of the necessity to function well and smoothly for the welfare of its citizens. Seen from a moral perspective, then, the good at which public life aims is just the good of individuals, or groups, or the public at large. To put it as utilitarian theorists sometimes do, the object of public life is, or ought to be, the pursuit of the greatest good of the greatest number.

Why, then, should we not let this form of argument convince us that public life is a special case for which there is no parallel in business? We might begin by noting that the distinction between public life and the world of business affairs may well have been true at an earlier stage in the history of economic development, when the activities of business generally impacted private interests only. I do not propose to argue the point here. However, if it ever was true, it no longer is. Perhaps the evidence that best links that fact to the kind of argument we are here considering is the considerable moral pressure put on politicians and governments from time to time to rescue particular business enterprises that have fallen on hard times. For example, in recent years, a large number of trust companies in Canada and banks in the United States have failed as a result of excessive exposure to collapsing real estate markets. In many of these cases, the public interest has been interpreted to require rescue of the companies themselves, or at least of their depositors, through the infusion of tax dollars.

What this example illustrates (and examples from other areas of business are readily available) is the fact that, in a modern economy, the actions of corporations can and do impact in morally significant ways on the lives of many people. That is to say, in modern economies, private economic activity can both contribute to and damage the public good. When this is the case, public intervention is thought to be justified. Neither is this only the case for large public corporations. Small business enterprises, too, can make significant contributions to the welfare of those directly touched by their activities.[7]

It follows that the public is as clearly a stakeholder in the world of business as it is in the world of public affairs.

2. Let me now point to a second parallel between public affairs and the world of private enterprise. Reflection quickly reveals that the kinds of considerations that make unethical conduct problematic for public officials make it equally problematic in the realm of business, and vice versa.

Bribery, for example, normally requires deliberate deception. It is frequently unfair and unjust. It corrupts moral character. It undermines the proper functioning of the democratic process and the marketplace. It can be used to rationalize and excuse failure. It can destroy reputations and undermine worthwhile initiatives. And so on. Recent experience shows that all of this is true whether the offerer and/or the recipient is a business person or a public official.[8]

3. Let us turn then to a third parallel. As with people in public office, business people do face situations in which acting morally would seem to be morally problematic. For some commentators, analysts, and participants, situations of the sort here described are a commonplace of business. International business is a realm from which examples are frequently drawn. Lane and Simpson point to this perception in commenting on the disposition of outsiders to assume that bribery is a way of life in developing countries and a necessity in business transactions.[9] Since the bribery in question frequently involves public office-holders, we can assume that many people view bribery as an endemic feature of third-world political systems and perhaps of foreign systems in general.[10]

Many situations, as described by those caught in them, appear at first blush to leave business people seeking, for example, contracts or permits with little choice but to offer bribes. However, as Lane and Simpson go on to point out, the outsider's perspective is not the only one. The assumption that bribery is widespread, or an unpleasant but unavoidable cost of doing business internationally, is normally thought to be a response to business realities. Those who challenge it are frequently described as naive or unrealistic, descriptions that echo commentaries made by seasoned politicians, their agents, and other observers of the political scene.

Values and assumptions about the values of others are not just responses to reality, however. They also shape perceptions and interpretations of reality in powerful ways. The assumption that bribery is a way of life colours the interpretation of requests, refusals, interventions, and negotiations. The assumption of widespread corruption becomes an interpretive device that enervates the search for imaginative solutions, provides convenient excuses for failure, and may well undermine the position of the honest among those charged with public or business responsibilities, whose various interventions and initiatives are thereby exposed to misinterpretation and misrepresentation.

That is to say, in business as in politics, the assumption that bribery is widespread or an essential ingredient of success, whether or not that success is in the pursuit of genuine goods, is not benign or morally neutral. To the contrary, it is morally suspect just because it is self-fulfilling. It shapes expectations and invites a parallel response on the part of those with whom one is attempting to do business, whether in the public or private sector.

4. All this having been said, however, it would be unreasonable to suggest that avoiding bribery is a matter simply of unilateral decision on the part of those seeking to fulfil their public duties on the one hand or their business responsibilities on the other. Once again, there is a clear parallel here between the requirements of public office and the conduct of business. The environment in which politics and business are conducted is malleable. But it is not infinitely malleable. Situations in which acting unethically seems the only way to fulfil legitimate and important responsibilities, for example offering a bribe or a pay-off, are sufficiently well documented that they cannot be dismissed or ignored.

What is morally troubling about many of these situations is the fact that all of the options apparently available to those caught up in them generate severe ethical tension. Any decision will be open to serious moral criticism. In these cases, the rigid refusal on the part of a public official to "dirty his or her hands" can have serious consequences for the public welfare. Equally, there are situations in which the rigid refusal of a business manager to offer a bribe or yield to extortion can have serious consequences for one's own company, its employees and one's own career, with all that may imply for one's dependents.[II]

5. Essential to the defence of dirty hands is the view that it is an inevitable feature of public life. Those having public responsibilities must be prepared to face morally unpalatable tasks. While they cannot expect public adulation for this, they can take consolation, at least, in the knowledge that their actions were compelled by their position of responsibility.

Once again, it should be clear that, if this view is true of those holding public office, it must also be true of business. If public officials are justified in ignoring moral restraints in the name of the public good, then surely business people are as well. Further (as in public life) because unethical behaviour, even where justified, is almost inevitably the kind of behaviour which cannot be publicly revealed without attracting severe public censure, public plaudits for acting unethically in the public interest cannot be expected. However, those whose unethical conduct is required by appeals to the public good can console themselves with the knowledge that their decisions were required by their position and were therefore morally justified.

6. We are now in a position to complete our characterization of those accounts which take the view that public officials, and by implication businesspeople, are sometimes required by their responsibilities—and therefore justified in their decision—to act unethically. As previous discussion illustrates, the view that the responsibilities of public office may require that one

get one's hands dirty implies that: (i) the act of overriding moral rules can be justified by an appeal to the consequences of not doing so; (ii) immoral means can be employed for beneficial as well as evil ends; (iii) when morally reprehensible means are used to advance or protect an important public good, their use is morally defensible; (iv) pursuit of public goods, whether by leaders in the public or private sectors, can require heroic leadership.

David Shugarman, in a perceptive analysis of "dirty-hands theory," adds to this list a characterization of public life to which those who believe that moral politicians must be prepared to "dirty their hands" also frequently subscribe. He argues that those who take this view typically see political life as carried on in an atmosphere akin to warfare, where social relations are marked by intense rivalry, duplicity and violence.[12]

What is intriguing about this account is how closely it, too, fits an apparently widely shared view of the nature of business. Discussion of corporate leadership seems often to imply that corporations require "heroic" leaders if they are to succeed in a world of untrammelled global competition. The task of "heroic" leaders is to take tough, morally unpalatable decisions in the interests of productivity and competitive advantage. The good which is appealed to for justificatory purposes in these circumstances is frequently the wealth-generating impact of the resulting economic activity for a particular society or community as a whole, as well as the particular benefits to employees and their dependents and to owners and shareholders.

Justifying Dirty Hands: An Evaluation

What this discussion identifies is the view of both business and politics which underlies the proposal that leaders in both sectors must be prepared to "dirty their hands" in pursuit of their responsibilities to their primary stakeholders. It is a view, I would suggest, that is unpalatable, problematic, and, in the end, inconsistent. Central to dirty-hands theory is the view that ethical behaviour, is and ought to be, the norm in political affairs. However, the effect of the theory is to make unethical behaviour not just an exception, but rather an obligation. That is to say, this approach to the justification of dirty hands implies, as Machiavelli saw so clearly, that unethical conduct is a fundamental ingredient of public life. As we have seen, the theory has the same implications for business in a market economy whose central characteristics are competition and survival. It follows on this view that recourse to unethical conduct is justified wherever success in a competitive marketplace, in which the welfare of those dependent on the activity in question may be at risk, requires it. What this view also implies is that unfairness, inefficiency, moral corruption, and self-deception are also inevitable characteristics of public life and private sector economic activity.

What options are available to those who would reject the view of democratic politics and free-market business enterprise just set out? There would seem to be three.

The first obvious option is to reject the view that unethical conduct in business or public life is ever justifiable. The difficulty with this view is that it misunderstands the nature of the kinds of dilemmas that people shouldering heavy responsibilities in the public or private sectors can and do encounter. An essential characteristic of these dilemmas is the fact that for any action to be taken, it seems an ethical principle must be overridden or sacrificed. For example, the possibility of succeeding in a business venture through bribery will generate a serious moral dilemma only where not bribing is likely to have costly implications for those to whom one feels a moral responsibility. When such a situation is encountered, therefore, all available solutions will carry high moral costs.

There is a second option. Some moral theories, utilitarianism for example, imply that for any moral dilemma there is always a "best in the circumstances" solution.[13] Theories of this sort accept the proposition that, at least in some circumstances, the end justifies the means.

I am going to simply assume, for the purposes of this discussion, that this option will not bear careful scrutiny.[14] Showing at the level of theory why this might be so is not possible in the space available here. Let me simply point out that this option does not fit easily with a good deal of human experience. Experience tells us that moral conflicts and dilemmas often appear to the people caught up in them to have no right answers. All available options require the sacrifice of important moral values. For example, refusal to offer a bribe, where it is required, might well put a company out of the running for an important contract. Company jobs might thereby be jeopardized, with serious implications for the individuals involved. In this situation, the immediate benefits of sacrificing a moral principle will be clear. On the other hand, the morally objectionable quality of bribery is not diluted by considerations of a consequentialist kind. The result is that, in situations of this kind, there is a compelling need to solve problems to which there would seem to be no right answer, morally speaking.

There is a final option which deserves serious scrutiny. I want to suggest that there is a perfectly acceptable sense, in which, faced with the kinds of dilemmas our discussion rests on, morality simply breaks down. That is to say, it may well be characteristic of serious moral dilemmas, of the sort that business people do sometimes encounter, that there *are* no morally acceptable solutions available. What one decides to do, faced with this sort of dilemma, is best seen as a matter of personal choice. To put it in another way, it is a mistake to think that there must be a morally acceptable solution to all moral dilemmas. Some apparently intractable moral dilemmas may be just that: intractable. To suggest that there is a superhuman perspective from which theoretical utilitarian calculations can be generated which will point to the right answer, or the best solution, or the lesser evil, seems simply mistaken.[15]

What does this imply for bribery, for example? The answer is that, in at least some severe cases, to bribe may very well not be morally prohibited. But neither, in these cases, would it be a breach of ethics to refuse to offer a bribe, even where the consequences of refusing might well prove severe for company stakeholders.

It is important to differentiate this option clearly from the second which has been rejected. What this option suggests is that it may well be the case that, in some situations faced by business people, there may well be no right answers, morally speaking. It follows that those caught in situations of this nature are not morally culpable for failing to do the "right" thing. None of the options from which a course of action will have to be chosen will be morally justifiable. It follows that, in these kinds of situations, the decision is bound to be controlled by non-moral considerations.[16]

Leaving the matter here, however, is clearly unsatisfactory. More needs to be said. For anyone who understands the central role of ethics in the building of sound social relationships, the suggestion that individuals might find themselves having to decide on a course of action where the chief options were neither justifiable nor unjustifiable, morally speaking, requires deeper analysis. At the very least, one must acknowledge what is easily forgotten, namely, that morality has to do not simply with guiding individual choices but also with shaping and evaluating social environments. What needs to be emphasized here is the deeply problematic character of any environment in which individuals are required to choose among options all of which require that important moral values be sacrificed or overridden. Addressing the social, political, or economic forces that drive individuals into having to cope with intractable moral conflict is, or should be, one of the central functions of moral criticism.

Business ethics, then, is not only, or even primarily, about ethical management or ethical decision-making. It is also, perhaps even primarily, about shaping the social, economic, and political environment of business. A central criterion for measuring the ethical quality of that environment is the extent to which those working in it find themselves driven toward "dirty-hands" decisions, decisions for which there are, morally speaking, no right answers. Intractable moral dilemmas do not point to unethical business people. Rather, they point to corrupt business environments. Ethical companies will recognize this fact and remove, themselves and their employees from them insofar as they are able. They will also support efforts on the part of governments, voluntary section coalitions,[17] and industry-wide alliances towards systemic reform.

This view of business and business ethics, based as it is on a particular view of morality and moral theory, has several virtues. It leaves those faced with what are appropriately described as impossible moral choices free of moral censure. Nevertheless, it does not condone their decisions. Rather, it isolates those decisions as exceptions, significant deviations from normal business practice, and symptomatic of moral pathology in the business environment. The result is to bring the focus of moral critique to bear on the social, political, and economic environment of business and its reform. In so doing it acknowledges the important role of moral values which, like efficiency, honesty, and fairness, lie at the foundations of market economies, while acknowledging openly the realities of doing business in a less-than-perfect world.

The discussion suggests a final query. Does what we have said about business apply equally to public life? Does the parallel we have been tracing go all the way down? This is not a question for which an answer is readily available. Central to it are arguments about the ultimate compatibility of public and private interests. If there are fundamental moral tensions built into public life, moral conflict may be an irreducible feature of democratic politics. David Shugarman explores this issue at length in the article to which I have already referred. His defence of the ultimate compatibility of public and private (or individual) interests is, in my view, the right one. His account takes the parallel I have been developing a final step. Irresolvable moral conflict can be removed from public life only where the shape of public life is informed by thoroughgoing moral reflection. The same, I have argued, is true of the world of business. If this is correct—and it should be acknowledged that it is only partially supported by preceding discussion — then bringing it home to politicians and business people alike should be one of the central tasks of business ethics.

Notes

An earlier version of this essay was first presented to the Dirty Hands Workshop held at York University, December 1993.

1 Niccolò Machiavelli, *The Prince and the Discourses* (New York: Modern Library, 1950) 101.

2 Michael Walzer, "Political Action: The Problem of Dirty Hands," *Philosophy and Public Affairs* 2:2 (Winter 1973): 161-80; 168 and 179.

3 Exactly which of the various "dirty hands" theories this caveat rules out is a matter of argument. A cursory reading of Machiavelli, for example, might seem to include him as one who thinks that politicians can indeed dirty their hands. On other interpretations, however, Machiavelli may be one of those who believes that moral prescriptions do not apply to public leaders in the normal course of events. Determining which of these interpretations is the sounder is not a discussion I shall pursue further here. My concern is with those who believe that public officials should normally be guided in the performance of their duties by moral strictures, but that, on occasion, they must ignore or override moral constraints if they are to fulfil their obligations. On these occasions, it is argued, public officials are justified in acting immorally.

4 Limits of space and time allow only a brief sketch of the kind of argument that typically underlies the position being examined. However, for our purposes in this discussion, only a brief sketch is required.

5 This statement of the argument assumes that in the life of a contemporary democracy, the interests and rights of individuals will come, from time to time, into conflict with the pursuit of public goods. Whether this assumption is justified is an ongoing debate in political theory. For the purposes of this discussion, however, all that is required is acceptance of the fact that such situations can and do occur in contemporary democratic societies. It is this fact which generates the dirty-hands problem.

6 David Shugarman points out that it is "reasons of state" that are typically thought to justify immoral conduct on the part of public officials: David Shugarman, "Ethics and Politics: The Use and Abuse of Politics," *Moral Expertise: Studies in Practical and Professional Ethics*, ed. Don MacNiven (London and New York: Routledge, 1990) 208.

7 Various Canadian commentators have suggested, for example, that over 80 per cent of new employment is likely to be generated by small-business activity. It is clear from this statistic that the activities of the small-business sector in Canada impacts directly on the public good.

8 For an interesting recent exploration of this theme, see Richard T. De George, *Competing with Integrity in International Business* (New York: Oxford University Press, 1993). Examples of the negative impact of bribery in particular and corrupt practices in general are so plentiful that citing examples seems almost redundant. However as a reminder, I offer the following short list: recent political upheavals in Italy centred around political corruption, Watergate, the British Airways/Virgin Airways scandal, and the Lockheed Tristar/Nippon Air scandal.

9 See H. Lane and D. Simpson, "Bribery in International Business: Whose Problem Is It?," *Journal of Business Ethics* 3:1 (Feb. 1984): 35-42.

10 Canadian business people are as prone to these assumptions as others in North America and perhaps Europe. It is interesting, therefore, to see similar assumptions operating in reverse. An interesting example is offered in V.S. Naipaul's novel *A Bend in the River* (New York: Modern Library, 1997). One of his characters, Nazruddin, a person of Indian extraction who grew up on the east coast of Africa, recounts his experiences with corruption in the business community in Canada, the effects of which are financially debilitating and lead him to migrate to England, where he eventually settles (242 ff).

11 One of the most widely cited cases in North American textbooks that has these characteristics is the Lockheed scandal. The reality of bribery in international business should not be exaggerated, however. De George points out in *Competing with Integrity* that an American study in the 1980s found that prohibiting bribery by law resulted in a loss of business for fewer than 1 per cent of 250 companies surveyed in the study.

12 Shugarman 208.

13 R.M. Hare, in *Moral Thinking: Its Levels Methods and Point* (New York: Clarendon Press, 1981), is a good example of such a theorist. Hard cases of the sort just described are not paradigms around which to build an account of moral deliberation and moral reasoning whether in business or elsewhere. They represent moral aberrations, moral conflicts for which there seem to be no right answers. In this we are in agreement. Hare argues, however, that right answers to difficult moral dilemmas can be found by moving to a higher level of moral reasoning. The reasoning required is the kind typically engaged in by moral theorists, or at least those of a utilitarian persuasion. Further, it is a level of reasoning which may be simply impossible to apply effectively in particular cases for very human reasons: lack of time, obscurity of facts, moral

complexity, lack of required moral intelligence, and so on. On this, I think, he is mistaken.

14 It has been extensively scrutinized, of course. One example is that offered by Shugarman 198. Other examples include standard critiques of utilitarianism, for example those contained in Bernard Williams and J.J.C. Smart, eds., *Utilitarianism: For and Against* (New York: Cambridge University Press, 1973).

15 As R.M. Hare, to whom I refer in note 13, suggests.

16 This proposed option is bound to be greeted with scepticism by some readers. It is worth pointing out, therefore, that what is being suggested is not unique to business settings. War, severe civil strife, and natural catastrophes like famines also create conditions in which morality ceases to guide because there are no right answers. The excruciating character of these situations is best illustrated in the accounts of partisans and others who, during the Second World War, were faced with choices imposed by Nazi decree, all the options of which could only be described as evil. Existentialist ethics could be said in many respects to constitute a response (though in my view an incorrect one) to such experiences. Triage situations sometimes faced by medical personnel offer other examples, as do situations occurring in times of severe famine or other natural disasters. Insisting that morality must provide solutions in such cases is what is here being challenged. This insistence inevitably drives one toward accepting that the end justifies the means or toward some form of irrationalism ethics.

17 Transparency International is an example. It is a non-governmental voluntary-sector organization that has come into existence in this decade to expose corruption in international business transactions. Further information about its work can be obtained by contacting the author of this paper.

ELEVEN

Hands: Clean and Tied or Dirty and Bloody?

MICHAEL MCDONALD

The dirty-hands dilemma is not unique to politics. It is a general feature of life in organized communities, that is, communities with authority relationships between leaders and followers. It applies as well to those with substantial power in the private sector or in other non-public sectors. Accordingly, I will speak about "leaders" rather than "politicians," and "organizations" rather than "states," in addressing the generic issues presented in the dirty-hands problem.

In Part 1, I begin with a discussion of the assumptions underlying the dirty-hands dilemma. In Part 2, I consider *tied hands* as a strategy for establishing a trust relationship: leaders deliberately tie their hands to assure followers that their hands will remain clean. I contrast this with *dirty hands* which I argue are usually *hidden hands*. In Part 3, I offer some reflections on dirty hands in their most extreme context, namely *bloody hands*. Finally, I provide some general conclusions.

Assumptions

The dirty-hands problem is constructed from two main elements: highly desired consequences (the first element) that can only be achieved through immoral actions (the second element). Leaders have to decide whether or not to perform actions that violate morally significant constraints in order to produce highly desirable results or, even more poignantly, to prevent highly undesirable results for their organizations. Morally significant constraints should be understood as involving both moral rules and moral character, for one of the significant risks of dirtying one's hands is becoming a morally undesirable sort of person.

Amoral leaders can be thought of as Machiavellian.[1] Amoral leaders will, without remorse, dirty their hands to advance or protect the organization's good. They don't care about moral rules or virtues. Their motto could be,

"Clean hands are for wimps." By contrast, moralistic leaders refuse to dirty their hands. Without regret, they pass up opportunities to promote or protect the organization's good. Because it would be wrong and contrary to moral character, the good consequences foregone or the evil consequences that ensue are as nothing to moralistic leaders. Their motto might well be, "Clean hands at any price!" Only so-called "moral" leaders will find these choices hard. For them, both the moral constraints and the opportunities to protect or promote the organization's good matter. They don't want dirty hands, but are willing to get their hands dirty for the good of the organization. Tongue in cheek, I would ascribe to them the Mackenzie King-like motto of, "Dirty hands if necessary, but not necessarily dirty hands."

In much of the theoretical discussion about dirty hands, it is assumed that leaders have the following beliefs:

a) The aim is the good of the organization and not the leader's good.

b) There is only one way of achieving the good in question.

c) The only way to achieve the organization's good is to act to violate a moral rule and/or degrade one's moral character.

In practical as opposed to theoretical contexts, I believe it is essential to question each of these assumptions:

a) It may not be true that the consequences to be achieved by dirty-handed actions are genuinely good for the organization. They may only be desirable from a narrower, partisan or even self-serving perspective. Consciously or unconsciously, then, the leaders and their followers may use the dirty-hands dilemma as an excuse or even justification for actions that are venal, abusive, or even morally horrifying, as in the case of bloody hands (see Part 3). Motivations for such behaviour may be concealed from others and even from oneself. Self-deception about the nobility of one's intentions is a major problem for leaders, especially in closed societies and in hierarchical organizations in which there is a lack of critical scrutiny (e.g., the police and the military). Indeed, one of my worries about the dirty-hands argument is that it provides too easy an out for leaders who engineer or accept situations in which there remain only dirty-handed options. They structure or manipulate the choice context to eliminate clean-handed alternatives, and then shed crocodile tears about the terrible moral costs they, as leaders, must pay.

b) It may well be that there are alternative courses of action that can bring about consequences that are as ethically desirable as those achieved by leaders dirtying their hands. Again, I see self-deception as a special problem in contexts where the organizational culture discourages internal criticism and disparages criticism from outsiders. In these contexts, it is easy for insulated leaders to deceive themselves into thinking there are no palatable alternatives to dirty-handed actions. As well, they may lack the will to find clean-handed strategies. Identifying and pursuing clean-handed alternatives to dirty-handed actions requires attention, imagination, and energy—commodities that leaders may well want to expend on projects other than that of keeping their hands clean.

c) It may be false that moral rules, properly understood and contextualized, forbid the supposedly dirty-handed action, or alternatively that the action in question involves a serious breach of the rules applying to those with a leadership role. Hollis, for example, has argued that the rules applying to political roles provide morally legitimate openings for contravention of *prima facie* moral rules that apply to us as private citizens.[2] In a well-known article on lawyer's ethics, Wasserstrom has argued for a similar exception for professionals in the form of "role-differentiated responsibilities."[3] In short, there may be a mistaken generalization from "Acts of type x are *generally* impermissible" to the claim that such acts are "*always* impermissible." Here, the problem may lie on the side of those who accept the simplistic views of leadership roles fostered by media-seeking pundits and politicians.

It is important for ethical and political theorists and researchers not to casually or quickly dismiss worries about whether (a), (b), and (c) actually obtain. They see themselves as hunting for the "big game" trophies of theory, e.g., consequentialism vs. deontology or a tragic as opposed to a well-ordered moral universe. But many of us working in applied ethics today are called upon to act as consultants and commentators on ethical issues. We should take care in offering remarks on moral theory in practical contexts, especially when our words may be misconstrued or misused to wrongly inculpate or exculpate leaders faced with difficult choices.

Clean Hands as Tied Hands

One of the sources of our discomfort with dirty hands is that leaders, and often their followers as well, want to have it both ways. They want the advantages of hand-tying moral rules and also of being able to break those rules whenever greater net advantages are likely to be secured. That leaders can often have it both ways is a result of the opacity or non-transparency of their actions and dispositions to many, if not most, of their followers.

But there are situations in which the dirty-handed option is sufficiently unattractive to recommend against its adoption by rational agents. My colleague Peter Danielson describes the general context of these situations:

> I happen to have a solution looking for a problem like this. I can show that some ethical strategies are evolutionary successes. Social evolution can be trusted to solve social dilemmas if some participants can identify others' cooperative dispositions and use them to discriminate whose behaviour they accept. These conditional strategies are effective because if you know I won't cooperate unless you do, you have a new reason to cooperate. Unfortunately, this theory of *Artificial Morality* doesn't apply to people, except in small face-to-face groups, since it is difficult for us to discern the dispositions of strangers.[4]

Danielson's general point is important. Given sufficient transparency and mutual vulnerability, conditional co-operation both resolves social dilemmas and emerges as a dominant strategy. I want to apply his general lesson of a "solution seeking a problem" to the dirty-hands situation. In the face-to-face context just described, there would be an evolutionary advantage in rational individuals *tying their own hands* in order to secure co-operation with other rational agents ("I will tie my hands if you will tie yours," or even "I will tie my hands to see if you will tie yours"). By "tying one's hands," I mean taking steps that, at least for the time being, ensure one's own co-operation and disable one from acting uncooperatively with another. While the first agent is at least temporarily at the mercy of the second, he has effectively communicated his wish to cooperate with that second. If the second accepts the cue and co-operates, then both are better off. If the second rejects the cue in order to take temporary advantage of the first, he invites a tit-for-tat response. Reciprocity invites reciprocity; non-reciprocity generates non-reciprocity.

A variety of useful social conventions for resolving potential conflicts could be created in this way, whether deliberately or spontaneously.[5] Two salient aspects of the leader-follower relation could emerge: first, followers accept the authority of their leaders; and second, leaders are expected to use their authority for purposes authorized tacitly or expressly by members of the group. I would suggest that it is plausible to picture the creation of a leadership role in a small group as a hands-tying activity on the part of potential leaders and their followers. Members of the group agree to have some of their members act as chiefs, captains, judges, or ambassadors; to lead the group into battle or out to sea; to judge their conduct; or to carry on negotiations with neighbouring groups. Acting in this organized way is seen as more effectively securing the followers' interests, rights, goals, or ideals than going leaderless.[6]

The key to making this work is that both followers and leaders tie their hands, and tie them in ways that are evident to others. The creation of leadership roles is filled with the risk of betrayal. Followers may try to hitch a free ride; leaders may seek to serve their own rather than the group's good. Hence, what is crucial in creating leadership roles is that followers not undermine their leaders and—directly to the point for the dirty-hands question—that leaders not betray their followers. Under these circumstances, betrayal is unilaterally untying one's hands to secure the advantages of individual defection from the social agreement without paying the price of simultaneous defection by others. To pursue the tied-hands metaphor further, leaders must have tied their hands with real knots, not slip knots; otherwise they will not attract enough followers to reap the benefits of cooperation.

Hence, under the circumstances Danielson pictures, there would be an evolutionary advantage for the clean-handed over the dirty handed. Over the long run, they will do better than leaderless groups or ones in which leadership relations are highly unstable due to a lack of reciprocity.

I now want to argue that in this context, a dirty-hands choice situation tests the limits of the leader/follower relationship. Recall that in a dirty-hands situation, a leader is faced with a choice between either respecting certain constraints on action and character or breaching them to achieve some good for the group. In the small group context just described, it seems to me that either the authority constituting constraints would be revised to allow the action, or they would not. They would be revised if new constraints were seen as both feasible and mutually beneficial. The leader's hands would only be seen as dirty when judged from the perspective of the old conventions. Hence, the leader's hands could be made clean by new, mutually beneficial conventions.

But the revision of leadership generating conventions may be neither feasible nor desirable. Changing the constraints or convention around leadership may not be feasible because the group lacks mechanisms for self-consciously revising the constraints in question, e.g., spontaneous constraints. Or it may be a traditional society with only customary law.[7] It may not be mutually beneficial, because the greater good for some members may be achieved at the expense of the justified expectations of other group members. In this situation, there are no emergent new conventions to clean the leader's hands. The leader really has dirtied her hands and, depending on how badly they are soiled, the very existence of her authority is at issue.

As social relations become more opaque, it becomes harder for follow-ers to be sure that leaders have tied their own hands; we cannot then rely upon evolutionary mechanisms to promote the emergence of the trust rela-tionship that underlies the leadership role. We turn to non- or semi-trans-parent warrants for trust—promises, pledges, oaths of office, and other indications of contract—and to relations of status in which trust is pivotal, such as parent/child, professional/client, employee/employer.[8] Thus, in large-scale anonymous relationships, it is fair to say that a good deal of the power enjoyed by leaders depends on trust being given in the absence of the conditions predicated by Danielson.

Besides opacity, there is the issue of power. In the face-to-face situation pictured by Danielson, no one has a monopoly (or oligopoly) on power; there is mutual vulnerability and the need for co-operation all round. Reciprocity is the name of the game. As the power imbalance between leaders and followers increases, followers are at greater risk. By virtue of the positions they occupy, leaders have control and knowledge which their fol-lowers lack. The power relationship may be highly asymmetrical. Two remedies suggest themselves: (a) to prevent the relationship from becoming too asymmetrical, and (b) to find trustworthy leaders. Since this paper is about dirty hands and the abuse of trust, my main concern is with (b). In any case, some imbalances of power are not easily eliminable: for example, those between adults and small children, the healthy and the very sick, or the able and the severely disabled. Nor is it always desirable to remove significant asymmetries. For example, in war or other "going for broke" situations, nations or other organizations may do better with highly centralized forms of leadership than with more egalitarian and democratic forms of authority.

It is often a matter of considerable debate as to exactly what a particular trust relationship between a leader and follower entails, but suffice it to say that as the power and knowledge imbalance increases, it becomes harder to picture the relationship as a contract between equals in which the leader's abuse of power may be effectively countered by the follower's disobedience. Moreover, because contractual specificity is not as morally persuasive in relationships characterized by power imbalances, trusts are generally broader and less explicit than contractual arrangements. Fiduciary respon-sibilities also typically involve the exercise of virtues, whereas contractual relationships are less demanding in this regard.[9]

Thus, it seems to me that at the core of our—the relevant public's—rela-tionships with leaders is the issue of trust. Trust is a response to both the opacity of social relationships and the imbalances of power. That is, we expect our leaders in the public, private, and not-for-profit sectors to act as guardians of entrusted interests. Those in high public office exercise a trust on behalf of citizens, as do CEOs on behalf of stockholders and other primary stakeholder groups, including employees. Our leaders bear a fiduciary relationship to us and thus have fiduciary responsibilities.

Of course, the extent and nature of fiduciary relationships varies from social role to social role and from society to society.[10] In business and professional ethics (broadly conceived as examining occupational roles in the public, private, and not-for-profit sectors), I believe that there is a growing tendency to give a fiduciary, as opposed to a contractual, reading to many key relationships of managers and professionals to less powerful stakeholders. Much depends, of course, on the nature and extent of the power imbalance in question and the largely implicit assumptions upon which, say, professionals and clients enter a relationship. The same, I think, is true of high public office or high private station. In both public and private spheres, there is controversy about the sometimes rapid changes in public expectations about the nature and extent of particular trust relationships. Suffice it to say that:

a) Morally, there is a great deal at stake in such discussions.

b) While there may be similar patterns, it is important not to over-generalize about such relationships. Thus, the moral responsibility of accountants to clients is generally much more circumscribed and focused than that of physicians. Moreover, there are significant differences between the public and private sectors and even within each of these sectors.

c) Insofar as the social relationship is socially desirable, it is important to avoid either under- or over-estimating the nature or extent of the trust relationship. Over-estimation makes it difficult to recruit morally decent people to positions of trust and also increases public cynicism about leaders in all sectors (public, private, and not-for-profit). Under-estimation tends, I believe, to ignore the significant power imbalances that often obtain in such relationships.

What would constitute ethically carrying out one's fiduciary responsibilities as a leader? I believe that Annette Baier has provided the basic criteria for an answer in her 1986 article "Trust and Anti-Trust."[11] The test is whether the trust relationship could survive the unmasking of the trusted persons' motives and methods to those who trust in them. If I knew what the trusted person has done on my behalf and why she has done it, would I still trust her, or would my trust turn to its opposite—anti-trust or suspicion? Would I go so far as to sever the relationship? Baier's test is to introduce transparency into opaque relationships. This hypothetical test mimics the face-to-face situation Danielson describes.

Baier's criterion for warranted trust suggests both inward- and outward-looking tests. For the leader, it suggests this self-reflective question: "If my actions were made known to my followers, would they still willingly follow?" Yet such self-administered, hypothetical informed consent is by itself seriously insufficient. There needs to be outward tests of trust in the form of effective and usable accountability relationships.[12] From time to time, information must be provided, the books must be opened, and the record revealed. There must be reasonable opportunity for reviewing and renewing, or withdrawing, the mandate of those in a position of trust. It is essential that such reviews actually take place and not be portrayed as either superfluous or disloyal.

Both the review of significant information about the performance of leaders and the renewal of their mandates may well require the establishment of other trust relationships. As investors in pension funds, mutual funds, stocks, and bonds, we need auditors to go over the books on an on-going basis and boards with independent and knowledgeable directors to ensure managerial competence and responsibility. As citizens, we need reports from auditors general, parliamentary enquiries, and even royal commissions. We also need a vigorous opposition and a free press to probe the actions and intentions of government and public officials. As to renewal processes, we need honesty in both public elections and stockholders' meetings. We also need various safeguards to protect the interests of minority groups, be they members of a linguistic or cultural minority or minority shareholders. Such safeguards require, again, individuals who will play an institutional role in protecting our interests, in particular judges, lawyers, and juries.

The need for such intermediaries raises the *Quis custodiet* question. So in turn we need effective accountability relationships to review the actions of our intermediaries and renew the trust relationship. How far one carries this is, in part, a question of efficiency and cost as well, ultimately, of trust.

Bloody Hands

I would now like to examine the dirty-hands issue in regard to the far nastier context of bloody hands. Matters are more serious with bloody hands than with dirty hands. We move from dishonesty, insincerity, fraud, and the like to the terrain of assault, murder, and even genocide. There is a qualitative difference tied up with major differences in the possibility of compensation in the case of dirty, as opposed to bloody, hands. In principle, it is possible to make whole the victim of dirty hands, but not so the victims of bloody-handed actions, the victims of ethnic cleansing or genocide.

Nevertheless, especially with bloody hands, it is important to distinguish between two cases.[13] The first is one in which the blood on the hands of politicians, business leaders, or others is the blood of those to whom they have a direct contractual or fiduciary relationship. That is, the blood is *our blood*, where *our* refers to us and our fellow citizens, employees, shareholders, partners, etc. The second is the case in which leaders get their hands bloody to benefit us; the blood on their hands is that of outsiders and not insiders.

In the case in which the hands of leaders are covered with the blood of their followers, I will assume that their power and authority as leaders depends significantly on the trust given them by their followers. Now, one possibility is that there is not a real, but only an apparent, betrayal of trust. On Baier's trust test, followers might not withdraw their trust even though they knew that the blood was literally their own or that of their fellow citizens, workers, comrades-in-arms, etc. Altruism, self-interest, or a combination of the two could motivate such a dirty-hands escape clause in the social contract between leaders and followers. Thus, in the event of a maritime disaster, passengers would want the ship's captain and crew to save at least some of them rather than letting all perish. That is, there may be built into some fiduciary relationships emergency or catastrophe clauses which allow a partial, albeit bloody, exit for some, but not all, of us.

But this exit may well not be open. A leader might not have won, and would not now retain, the allegiance of followers if these knew that their leader intended to sacrifice them or their comrades. Indeed, the evidence might be overwhelming that they gave no such license. What is to be said then? I don't think appeals to higher goods, or better overall consequences, suffice. After all, such a leader's power is in large part constituted by trust. In this situation, bloody hands really are a betrayal of the trust relationship, because the leader has no moral warrant for bloodying his hands.

But what about the other case—the one in which the proposal is to let leaders cover their hands with the blood of others, i.e., of non-followers or outsiders to the social unit in question? Let me assume that neither leaders nor followers collectively have a right to the outsiders' blood (e.g., it is not self-defence or a just war). So if our leader does this, he acts wrongfully. Yet it is not clear that this is an act of betrayal, for it is possible that the bloody deed may fulfil rather than betray the bonds between leader and followers. Alternatively, it may break these bonds. Followers as moral individuals might not have given their trust had they known that it was to be used in such a bloody way—even though this may well be to their individual and collective advantage. So in order to decide if the blood of innocent others is on the heads hands of all or some of the people as well as on their leaders, we need to look at the nature of the trust relationship as it historically unfolds between leaders and followers.

This case of bloody hands is genuinely unlike the other cases discussed in this paper. In them, the choice of a dirty-handed option by a leader at least raises the possibility of the abuse of trust or the destruction of reciprocity. However, when the blood on the hands of the leader is that of outsiders, for insiders it may well be the fulfilment of trust and reciprocity. The dark spectre of ethnic, class, ideological, or religious warfare falls into this category when, for example, group solidarity manifests itself in the removal and murder of minorities.

Conclusion

In this paper, I have expressed my disquiet with dirty- and bloody-handed leaders. Part of my disquiet is based on scepticism about the extent to which the dirty-handed option is the right thing to do, all things considered. I think it is all too easy to slip from the dirty-hands "dilemma" to the dirty-hands "rationalization." The main source of my disquiet is with the violation of the reciprocity and trust that followers place in their leaders. In the case of bloody hands, my worries are, if anything, even greater, for the fulfilment of trust in the cause of evil must never be regarded as morally justifiable.

Notes

An earlier version of this essay was first presented to the Dirty Hands Workshop held at York University, December 1993.

1 However, in this book the editors have used the term "moral Machiavellism" to refer to those who subscribe to the morality of dirty hands. See also, Ian Greene and David P. Shugarman, *Honest Politics: Seeking Integrity in Canadian Public Life* (Toronto: James Lorimer, 1997) 164-67.

2 Martin Hollis, "Dirty Hands," *British Journal of Political Science* 12 (1982): 385-98; 394.

3 As Richard Wasserstrom notes, the onus lies on those who defend such role-defined exceptions to general moral rules: "Lawyers as Professionals: Some Moral Issues," *Ethical Theory and Business*, ed. Tom L. Beauchamp and Norman E. Bowie (New Jersey: Prentice-Hall, 1979).

4 Peter Danielson, "Pseudonymity, Evolution, and Computer Mediated Ethics," draft paper for the American Association for the Advancement of Science-American Bar Association National Conference of Lawyers and Scientists Invitational Workshop on Legal, Ethical, and Technological Aspects of Computer and Network Use and Abuse, Irvine, CA, 17-19 December 1993. I think it is also unlikely that such behaviour would emerge in the presence of major inequalities untempered by moral sentiment.

5 I have in mind here the sort of unplanned conventions that arise spontaneously out of a background of shared social experiences, e.g., first come first served. See Robert Sugden, "Spontaneous Order," *Journal of Economic Perspectives* 3:4 (Fall 1989): 85-97.

6 It is worth noting that such co-operators need not be asocial, self-centred maximizers. They may well be quite sociable and other-centred in their focal concerns.

7 H.L.A. Hart, *The Concept of Law* (Oxford: Oxford University Press, 1961) 77ff.

8 I think modern moral philosophy has overly relied on a contractual model of human relationships and underestimated the importance of relationships of status both in theory and practice. In large part, this is due to the dominance of liberal thought in contemporary moral philosophy and jurisprudence.

9 Michael Bayles, *Professional Ethics* (Belmont, CA.: Wadsworth, 1987) 69-99.

10 Compare to Michael Walzer, *Spheres of Justice: A Defense of Pluralism and Equality* (New York: Basic Books, 1983). See also, Walzer, "Political Action: The Problem of Dirty Hands," *Philosophy and Public Affairs* 2:2 (1973): 160-80.

11 Annette Baier, "Trust and Antitrust," *Ethics* 96 (1986): 231-60.

12 I am assuming that the parties are not in the sort of situation Danielson envisions.

13 The same distinction can be made with regard to dirty hands as well. However, due to the generally lesser gravity of dirty hands, I have only explored the two contexts in the case of bloody hands.

TWELVE

Ethical Politics and the Clinton Affair

IAN GREENE AND DAVID P. SHUGARMAN

The vote by the US House of Representatives in December, 1998 on whether to impeach President Bill Clinton could be regarded as a debate about the acceptability of dirty-handed politics. At various stages in the charges and counter-charges concerning his affair with Monica Lewinsky it was suggested, usually by those sympathetic to the president, that what would normally be morally dubious behavior should be excused, given the importance of the man and the office and the great disruption to American politics that would be caused by his impeachment or forced resignation. What makes this particular case so difficult to analyze is the complex set of subplots surrounding it. To treat it as an instance of presidential dirty hands, however, would be to misconstrue both the meaning of that term and Clinton's bumbling attempts to cover up his sexual escapades in the White House.

In digging up evidence about Clinton's affair, the media, Republican partisans and special counsel Kenneth Starr invaded his privacy. Linda Tripp's tape-recording, for public consumption, of her conversation with her friend Monica Lewinsky is morally wrong and in several states is illegal. To backers of Republican efforts to track Clinton's life, such dirty-handed acts were justifiable if they led to the exposure of what they believed to be the sins of a bad man. But from the point of view of US citizens, politicians should be allowed privacy in their personal lives, and prying into their personal affairs is not acceptable.[1] And in a succession of opinion polls taken throughout 1998, the vast majority of Americans indicated that their disapproval of Clinton's dalliance with Ms Lewinsky, and his lying about it, were not to be confused with their opinion of his performance as President.[2] Moreover, if Clinton had lied only in front of the media and his family, there would be no grounds for impeachment. But he lied under oath while testifying before a grand jury and in a deposition he gave in the lawsuit against him by Paula Jones. So the question is whether the repeated lie was big enough or important enough to count in the constitutional category of "high crimes and misdemeanors" and thus to justify impeachment.

Another critical question is whether Clinton encouraged others to cover up both his affair and his lying about it, because orchestrating a cover-up might constitute the crime of obstructing justice. There is also the question of whether efforts made by the White House to help Lewinsky find a job could reasonably be seen either as providing a public office favour in return for the president's personal sexual gratification, or as an incentive to support his denial of the affair. Finally, the investigation of the Lewinsky-Clinton affair by independent counsel Kenneth Starr resulted from an initial investigation into allegations that Clinton had been involved in some shady dealing years earlier in the Whitewater investment debacle. The Starr Report indicated that no case could be made that any Clinton wrong-doing had occurred in the Whitewater scandal. Instead, it focused on his sexual improprieties and his attempts to deny them. Adding to the complications of dealing ethically with the matter of Clinton's public ethics was the fact that views on the seriousness of his lying were, with few exceptions, a matter of party affiliation, and Starr was closely associated with the right wing of the Republican Party.

So what are the appropriate principles that ought to be used in judging Bill Clinton's behaviour, and how do they bear on what could be alleged as his recourse to dirty hands?

We argue that the principle of mutual respect is the ethical foundation of democratic government.[3] As Ronald Dworkin states: "...individuals have a right to equal concern and respect in the design and administration of the political institutions that govern them... [T]hey possess [this right] not by virtue of birth or characteristic or merit or excellence but simply as human beings with the capacity to make plans and give justice."[4] It is around the core value of mutual respect that other pillars of our democratic tradition have taken shape: representative legislatures, freedom of expression, the rule of law, social equality, respect for human rights, and the expectation of integrity in governing. The Clinton case highlights the issues of integrity in public life and respect for the right to privacy.

Integrity is honesty modified by concern and respect for our fellow human beings. As Stephen Carter puts it, "one cannot have integrity without being honest ... but one can certainly be honest and yet have little integrity."[5] For example, an elected official could promise to find a good job for his mistress. By keeping the promise, he is honest. But he has violated the respect he owes to others who were cut out of that job. Telling a lie is dishonest. But telling the whole truth at every possible instant in time does not necessarily mean acting with integrity. We all face situations where we must be the bearers of distressing news, but we can often choose the time and the circumstances for presenting the news so that we can maximize the respect we show for the recipient.

So integrity is actually a complex ideal, closely related to the principle of mutual respect. People show their respect for one another by being straight with each other and by tolerating differences in lifestyles and beliefs—as well as by adhering to other crucial corollaries of treating fellow citizens as equals, such as dealing with others fairly, keeping promises, maintaining public trust when given it, and respecting others' autonomy, including their right to privacy. The Clinton affair raises the political problem of how these principles can be applied in the most effective and ethical way.

From the President's testimony before a grand jury on 17 August, 1998 and his five-minute speech to the American nation on television the same evening, it is clear that he lied to the American public. He did have sexual relations with Monica Lewinsky, although he had categorically denied this at a meeting with reporters at the White House on 26 January, 1998. Yet in his explanation and apology for lying, Clinton offered no excuse or justification related to his public office. Rather, he said he was mainly concerned with protecting himself from the embarrassment of his own conduct, and second, he wanted to protect his family and their privacy from outsiders. Clinton was dishonest, but can his dishonesty be justified? It is difficult to fathom how his admission of sexual activity with a young woman would have contributed to integrity in American public life, or for that matter, how his honesty would have enhanced the life of Ms Lewinsky or strengthened either his relationship with his family or their public image. It is equally difficult to defend his show of solemnity and feigned sincerity for millions of television viewers as he decided to move from keeping a private relationship confidential to deceiving the public.

Clinton claims that his adulterous behaviour is a matter between him and his wife and daughter. In his August 17 television address, he said, "It is private and I intend to reclaim my family life for my family. It's nobody's business but ours." Here, of course, we need to remember that it is difficult for a politician to make an objective judgment about the difference between the public good and one's personal interests in such cases. At first glance, Clinton's deny, deny, deny strategy may appear to be an instance of a politician forced to dirty his hands. And if he was lying because he sincerely believed that the public good is not served by confessing his private sexual habits and accepting the political consequences, there is some basis for treating this episode as a dirty-hands matter. A dirty-hands situation is one in which a public official knowingly does something wrong, conceals it, but justifies—to himself and a few confidantes—the wrong, as well as the concealment, as being for the public good. Clinton came close to making a dirty-hands claim—lying for the public good—when he asserted that the prying into his private life had distracted him and the citizenry from attending to all the challenges of preparing for the next century. But it is hard to see how either his indiscretions or his attempted cover-up of them could be construed as dirty-handed activities when what is meant by such a phrase is the adoption of unseemly or repugnant methods to serve a great public interest. Clinton's sex acts could hardly be regarded as serving a grand public purpose, and even the suggestion that he lied in order to refocus attention on national priorities is questionable. Being up-front about the affair when he was first questioned about it would have put an end to the speculation and the prying. More to the point, his own explanation and apology for lying had to do with saving himself and his family, not the nation, from embarrassment.

Therefore, Clinton's situation is not so much an example of dirty hands as it is a case of a politician attempting to protect his private life from public scrutiny. This raises the question of a politician's right to privacy, and his or her capacity to separate private activities from public responsibilities. Politicians can justly claim that their private lives are off limits to the public when the one does not intrude on the other, when public responsibilities and the leadership role are not affected by situations in one's private life. A politician can claim that it is not in the public interest to have his or her sexual activities made transparent—which is not the same as claiming that engaging in such activities and then trying to keep them secret are done to serve the public interest.

Sissela Bok has written that it is not uncommon for public officials to want to keep their private lives secret. She holds that maintaining secrecy as a means of protecting their private lives is justified to a point:

> A great deal of deception [practiced] by public figures concerns their private lives. Information about their marriages, their children, their opinions about others ... all are theirs to keep private if they wish to do so. Refusing to give information under these circumstances is justifiable—but the right to withhold information is not the right to lie about it. Lying under such circumstances bodes ill for conduct in other matters.[6]

Clinton chose to lie about the allegations of his affair with Lewinsky rather than to remain silent. An interesting contrast is the behaviour of former Canadian Prime Minister Pierre Trudeau. When questioned by reporters about his sex life prior to his marriage, and about his marriage later on, Trudeau made it a point never to answer, no matter how embarrassing the allegations. There is no evidence that he ever lied about his private life, because he refused to comment on it. Perhaps the most glaring contrast, because of paradoxical similarities, is the treatment enjoyed by and accorded to John F. Kennedy. Kennedy apparently had remarkably similar sexual proclivities to those of Clinton. Areas of the Kennedy White House were devoted to parties that the President had with a succession of women who were smuggled in and out. Yet Kennedy was never confronted about his sexual activities, nor did he ever face questioning about how his private life might intrude on his public duties.

From the perspective of ethical politics, there are several critical questions that bear on Clinton's conduct. First, did the President fail to keep his private life and public responsibilities separate, and did he abuse the powers of his office by using others to advance both his private and political interests? Specifically, did Clinton take advantage of a White House intern by encouraging her to think that she could expect public office favours in return for sexual favours? And since Clinton lied about his affair with Lewinsky when he appeared before a court dealing with the Paula Jones lawsuit, did he encourage others to lie under oath on his behalf? If the answers to any of these questions turn out to be yes, then the President has been involved in serious ethical misconduct. Based on scrutiny of the Starr Report, and evidence placed before the House, we are of the view that the answers to these questions are no and that the President did not violate his responsibilities of office. There was nothing comparable to Richard Nixon's lies to cover up the subversion of democratic political processes in the Watergate scandal. The verdict, reached by the US Senate on 12 February, 1999, accords with this conclusion.

Our view is that politics-and-sex issues must be judged from the perspective of mutual respect rather than from a position of prevailing social standards or taboos about sex. For example, Quebec's Premier Duplessis was known to have provided public office favours to the family members of one of his mistresses.[7] The use of public office prerogatives to obtain personal sexual satisfaction is a clear violation of mutual respect. If we focus on Duplessis's extra marital sex alone—as distinct from his use of public office favours to obtain it—this is a personal rather than a political matter, although on a personal ethical basis it would be enlightening to know whether he treated his wife with fairness and respect. In Clinton's case, there is no evidence that he either forced himself on Ms Lewinsky or used his power as President to entice her to do something she otherwise would have refused to do. Their liaison was between two consenting adults.

The Starr investigation exposed the fact that Clinton was sexually promiscuous, that he was dishonest with his wife and daughter, and that he compounded that dishonesty by lying to the public and under oath. But his lying was about his sexual infidelities, not his activities as President. The failing is primarily a personal, familial one, a failing of a husband and father. He engaged in an all-too-common lie, understood by many as often used (and often excused) in keeping intimate details about one's private life and intimate relations out of the public eye. An important aspect of mutual respect in a democracy is the privacy we accord to each other to engage in intimate relations free from surveillance by the government, corporations or others. If we don't respect people's right to privacy and the importance of boundaries separating the public from the private, if we encourage the monitoring of our every move, and public truth-telling on erotic activities, then we open the door to Orwell's Big Brother of 1984 and widespread reliance on dirty hands as a means both of persecution and protection.

Finally, the Clinton impeachment scandal exposes a worrying characteristic of political practice in purportedly mature western democracies. Public lying, even when it is only about private matters, undermines the credibility of the individual perpetrator and of politicians in general. Those of us who teach political science courses have often heard our students say, "All politicians lie, and they lie often, so why should Clinton be singled out for blame?" Support for Clinton was frequently based on the judgement that he's the least bad of a very bad bunch. If the public's trust in their leaders drops too low, then clearly the system of government becomes vulnerable. For politics to be rehabilitated, politicians need the courage to tell the truth consistently, which may include the courage to avoid telling lies that would protect against personal embarrassment. While largely avoiding recourse to the tactics of moral Machiavellism, Clinton's response to his enemies, combined with their muck-slinging tactics, nonetheless contributed to the cynicism and lack of trust that is a becoming a staple of our political experiences.

Notes

1 See Michael Johnston, "Right and Wrong in American Politics: Popular Conceptions of Corruption," *Polity* 18:3 (1986): 367; and Sissela Bok, *Secrets: On the Ethics of Concealment and Revelation* (New York: Pantheon, 1982).

2 Canadians also think that politicians deserve to have private lives, and that invading this privacy is not ethical. See Maureen Mancuso, Michael Atkinson, Andrè Blais and Neil Nevitte, *Political Ethics: Canadians Speak Out About Their Politicians* (Toronto: Oxford University Press Canada, 1998).

3 Ian Greene and David Shugarman, *Honest Politics: Seeking Integrity in Canadian Public Life* (Toronto: Lorimer, 1997) Ch. 1.

4 Ronald Dworkin, *Taking Rights Seriously* (Cambridge: Harvard University Press, 1978) 180-82.

5 Stephen Carter, "The Insufficiency of Honesty," *Atlantic Monthly* 227:2 (February 1996): 74.

6 Sissela Bok, *Lying: Moral Choice in Public and Private Life* (New York: Pantheon, 1978) 176.

7 Jacques Bourgault and Stéphane Dion, "Public Sector Ethics in Quebec," *Corruption, Character and Conduct: Essays in Canadian Government Ethics*, ed. John Langford and Allan Tupper (Toronto: Oxford University Press) 70.

THIRTEEN

Retrospection and Democracy: Bringing Political Conduct Under the Constitution

S.L. SUTHERLAND

The standard conception of the dirty-hands problem looks at the desperate choices made by a political leader in terms of their consequences for his[1] soul: the focus is his moral condition as an autonomous moral actor. Therefore, reflection on dirty-hands scenarios naturally encourages judgments about the inherently compromising nature of politics; the fatalistic message is that political actors inevitably compromise their moral being by taking part in political action. Perhaps the single passage most cited to exemplify the supra-ethical stance of the political leader is a short speech from Jean-Paul Sartre's *Les mains sales*. In the passage, the leader of a revolutionary movement (Hoederer) seems to tease his apparently principled young secretary and eventual assassin (Hugo):

> How you cling to your purity, young man! How afraid you are to dirty your hands!…Purity is an idea for a yogi or a monk. You intellectuals and bourgeois anarchists use it as a pretext for doing nothing…Well I have dirty hands. Right up to the elbows. I've plunged them into shit and blood. But what do you hope? Do you think you can govern innocently?[2]

The speech is often lifted from the context of the play to make the point that it is somehow right for politicians to violate important moral standards prevailing outside "politics."[3] Yet a reading of the play shows that Hoederer's words ironically foreshadow the readiness of the bourgeois intellectuals of his party (who he does not understand are fully prepared to use him) to express in the blood of others the twists and turns of their thought. The play is about the period that inevitably follows upon a daring dirty-hands "political" act, when the protagonist loses "authorship" of his action because his proximate motives lose visibility and salience in all eyes except his own. The result is that all political action assumes its unique trajectory of effects and is retrospectively evaluated and assigned meaning in a phase of public, political, and social judgment.

This article, in which I challenge the internal validity of the dirty-hands problem as standardly presented and then try to salvage some insights that arise from the problem, is constructed in two parts. The first explores, through the defining features of the dirty-hands stand, whether it is possible to sustain the claim that it reveals a routine moral compromise at the heart of political action. The features of the classical dirty-hands problem that are isolated and challenged are the following: 1) that the political actor *must* be pressured into acting on consequentialist reasoning in the context of a psychologically-compelling narrative frame; 2) that he *must* then be judged as an individual in the context of a deontological ethics; and 3) that the exploration of the modeled or schematic dirty-hands situation captures the important aspects, or the heart, of politics.

The second part argues that it is important to study dirty-hands episodes for what we can learn about the capacity of our political structures to conduct thorough retrospective discussions about conduct in politics and public life, and to hold political actors to account for the impact of their actions upon the quality of political life—public life—and the processes that guide its unfolding. This argument is made on three main ideas: Dennis Thompson's concept of mediated corruption, which holds that strategic political actions undertaken to evade the deliberative phases of decision and the judgement of retrospective deliberation are to be seen as *moral* offences against the political system itself;[4] David Braybrooke and Charles E. Lindblom's persistent and evolving image of policy-making as an ongoing exploratory, remedial, and serial activity, more or less systematic;[5] and some of my own notions about how particular representative institutions are more or less good at the task of configuring and conducting a *retrospective* cycle of concentrated deliberation to weigh the earlier acts of the executive. I argue that the signal importance to democracy of the retrospective phase is that it enables politics to be thoughtfully remedial (and even directly corrective) in respect to these three: the quality of *process,* the quality of political *conduct* expected of public actors, and the taste for identifying desirable *substantial* or policy changes. By "process" I mean of course that public business should be conducted under the rule of law, but also, more generally, that it should be conducted with respect for deliberation and disclosure. The usefulness of this perspective, which emphasizes deliberation, systematic retrospection, and remediation, is investigated in three examples: Hollis's discussion of the sacrifice of Coventry; the use of the presidential pardon in American politics; and an evasion of ministerial responsibility by the Conservative government in Canada in 1991. I propose that it is best if retrospection and calls for restitution and penalties take place on a timely basis within the institutions of representative democracy, which in turn implies that responsible government has some advantages if this remedial phase can be pursued honestly.

Anachronisms and Flaws in the Dirty-hands World

The dirty-hands dilemma is a circumstance in which a political actor must strive to achieve the least-evil outcome for some group, where he must do wrong to do so, in secret, and where, in a successful effort, he is accountable only to himself. In his beautifully-crafted exposition of the Glencoe massacre, for example, Martin Hollis endorses what he says is Machiavelli's starting point: that " there [exist] evil persons who do not wish the good of the people and who do not keep faith; and that they can only be thwarted by marshaling the apparatus of legitimacy against them [the "faithless"]; and that this apparatus has to be used dishonestly."[6] The apparatus of legitimacy is the arm and power of the state. In 1692, the military hierarchy, "to pacify the tribes," inspired a night massacre of a clan that was negotiating in good faith, as shown by the fact that it allowed its assassins to be billeted on it, but would be strong enough to demand continued attention—were it not subjected to the more permanent solution by the apparatus of legitimacy. "Politics," Hollis concludes, "is an arena where the best is the enemy of the good, where we license our agents to pursue the good, and where they can succeed only if they operate partly beyond our ken and our control."[7]

Other much-cited dirty-hands situations include the following: the justification of political assassination as an action that can dramatically correct the course of history; whether it can be right to yield a targeted judge to terrorists in exchange for the safety of many innocent hostages; what to do if one should be so unfortunate as to stumble across a guerrilla leader who stipulates that if one will personally kill just one small peasant he will spare the rest of the doomed group; and whether, as a leader of a country in civil war, one ought to order that a captured opponent be tortured to extract information that one expects will save innocent lives.[8] In brief, the role of anyone but the leader (or, sometimes, collective leadership) in a dirty-hands problem is as the body count: the public is an unorganized collection of individuals on behalf of which the decision-maker must undertake "morally criminal acts," doing wrong to do right, deciding who shall live and who shall die, supposedly to save the largest number.

Consequentialism and its Limits

The representative dirty-hands scenario, as Benn notes, *anticipates* the costs and benefits of the eventual outcome of a decision.[9] It is therefore consequentialist in its form. The problem-solving by the individual caught in the dirty-hands situation thus suffers from the same fatal problems as does any system of reasoning that assumes that it is possible, at need, to elaborate a rational, comprehensive, robust predictive system that can give the rational actor direct and certain knowledge of the future behaviour of all active variables. Braybrooke and Lindblom identify three logical problems in relation to utilitarianism: no interpersonal calculus; no rule for bringing accounts of consequences to an end; and no rule for specifying reference groups for whom consequences count.[10]

Therefore, if the choice of features to notice and their weighting is personal and arbitrary, if one cannot know when to stop tracing effects, nor in regard to whom, and one has in addition to address the problem of getting and processing information about the few features one can identify, it seems correct to say that the dirty-hands hero is really only guessing. And if he is guessing, he cannot ground his belief that he has the "right" to take decisions for those his actions will affect in certainty that his strategy will factually turn out to be the best. Certainly he may make *probable* judgments, but given the essentially intuitive and arbitrary basis of his probability calculations, the legitimacy and rationality of secret unilateral decision-making—outside a compelling emergency situation—begins to seem dubious. Further, if one accepts that the dirty-hands hero can be allowed to simply relax the logical and information requirements before he can allow himself to "do wrong to do right" or engage in "lesser evils" decision-making, one seems to endorse a quietistic stance toward the kind of factors that may trigger a round of secret decision-making, and, indeed, one's own safety; one is issuing a blank cheque. And certainly a sole decision-maker might seek to reduce his uncertainty by consulting widely, but then the moral responsibility for his projected action would seem to be shared. The would-be dirty-hands decision-maker must therefore find his legitimacy as a political actor elsewhere than in certainty that his personal decisions will be economical in terms of the sacrifice imposed on those without the protection afforded by the positional power he enjoys. The one option available to the "prince of lesser evils" would seem to be that he must believe in his own inherent right to be the decider; that is, he must situate himself in the elitism of birth or of power. The only other route to legitimacy would be for the decision-maker to submit himself to an agreed, public process within which his role is circumscribed and reviewed; that is, to constitutionalism (below). This is the route to which the lone strategist and his bard are oblivious.

The Incoherence of the Moral Perspective of the Hero

A second common assumption is that the decider's consequentialist phase of strategic political decisions and actions, in which he tries to succeed using evil or perhaps only "lesser evil" sacrificial means, is naturally and suitably followed by a phase of scourging self-judgment. The dirty-hands leader in a wicked situation must *act* impersonally and efficiently for his followers. But then, once the well-intentioned expedient bad action has been accomplished in total secrecy, he must judge himself on deontological views. These hold that "...some principles of right and wrong, notably principles of justice and honesty, prescribe actions even though more evil than good would result from doing them."[11] Thus he must accept that he, as an autonomous moral actor, has chosen to use evil means, and heartily and sincerely condemn himself. Meanwhile, the practitioner-consequentialist alter ego stays alert and active: he must conceal all evidence of the wrong action by any means, keep the burden of his guilt to himself, and stiffen his resolve to carry on in this vein, because only by so doing can he fulfill his duty to his followers. Further, he must convince himself that at some level beyond ordinary morality he was "right" to have done wrong. Our actor is tempered—improved—by experiences from which ordinary persons would shrink. In short, the problematic has the heroic decider acting "politically," that is, as a consequentialist, but it also insists that he punish himself in private for being what he is on deontological moral principles: a failure. It further insists that the dirty-hands hero fuse these two metals into a source of tortured personal strength. But is this pose coherent (note that one does not say "possible")? I would submit that it is not; it is only a pose. The dirty-hands leader is always in consequentialist mode, no matter the conceits of nightfall.

The Generalization to all Politics of a Flawed Model

The third assumption, that the usual dirty-hands scenarios reveal the essential or true nature of political action in general, is also flawed. It involves a generalization from the particular scenario (as a modelled political problem) to a so-called universal character of "political action." But, as with any model of a problem, a dirty-hands scenario can shed light only upon the variables it explicitly takes into account in its specification of the causal conditions. And, even though it may be that internal validity is supported—that such a set of identified circumstances would plausibly interact to produce the predicted result (that an individual can be put under such pressure that she or he will choose for others without warrant)—this does not guarantee external validity.

External validity, that is, the appropriateness of generalizing to the world from an outcome resulting from the playing out of a dynamic in the model, is to be judged by the adequacy with which the model "experiment" in fact appropriately captured each of the telling or contingently important conditions of the domain *to which* it is hoped to generalize. Unless each of the causal features of the setting have been seized in the schematic problem, one must not generalize from the model or experiment to the setting from which the model was schematized. One must take into account again that the dirty-hands leader is, in effect, a primitive executive, unchecked by either assembly or judiciary. As Anthony King tells us, executives are the primitive core of government activity, being "already there" at the start of organized political life.[12]

Dirty-hands scenarios therefore exclude the prospect of the reciprocity between citizens and leaders which arises through the citizens' role—won through the victories of constitutionalism—in choosing and judging the governors, an arrangement that is regulated in its detail by the structure of justice that predates them both. There is no prior structure of justice in the raw "politics" of a dirty-hands problem because the problematic does not allow looking beyond the moment. The protagonist is caught in a game with the following rules: he is the only actor in his round; if he refrains from bold action, the innocent will pay; the only way he can save at least some innocents is with the blood of other innocents; and time presses. Because the dirty-hands executive acts outside a constitution, the dirty-hands problem would appear merely to be a model of the emergency situation in a preconstitutional world; as in feudalism, in a dirty-hands problem the noble has rights of life and death over the inhabitants of his territories and feels obliged to deal honourably only with other nobles.[13]

Political Action as Constituted by Rules Deliberated and Retrospectively Evaluated

Constitutionalism can be defined as, first, the belief in the rule of law; further, that the ideals and rules about how deliberation shall be realized and how the mechanisms of democratic procedure will operate should be formally expressed in normative documents that should guide the processes of government; and, finally, that these rules should try to ensure that the power of government will be linked to and subjugated in some way to the people.[14] Political activity in representative institutions must channel and control, and afterwards carefully study, assign meaning to, and sometimes condemn the use of power. This is so whether the political action is to be, or was, exercised within the state or externally; whether the action is routine; or, on the other hand, whether it involves the exercise of discretion in contexts that are poorly understood at the moment of crisis. No one could be so naïve as to believe that moral and political safety are *guaranteed* by constitutionalism through rule by law and the respect and adherence to democratic participation in decision-making that it underwrites, because, as noted, emergencies and unforeseeable situations will always arise to which leaders will respond. What constitutionalism adds is the strong probability, if not certainty, of the headache of the morning after: the *public* process of retrospection in which leaders' actions are reviewed.

The decisional phase of the executive is thus inevitably followed by phases of judgment. These subsequent rounds of discussion, whose form and impact is dictated by the contingent configurations of the representative institutions of each democratic state, operate to moralize and, indeed, politicize the events of previous rounds: there will be reassessment, redefinition, approbation or disapprobation, and formulation of new issues for the agendas of all parts of the institutional framework. *Public judgment* takes the place of the hero's self-judgment in the dirty-hands scenario. In addition, it must be remembered that retrospective deliberation also takes place outside the representative fora in the "big loose" systems of social judgment that represent the interplay between different views in what is now fashionably called "civil society." (These social and media contexts which once imposed normative control are now their own kind of *merdier*, because they are largely media-driven or media-appropriated for profit.) Sometimes retrospective deliberation will lead to new policy and occasionally to destitution or censuring of particular actors. Its cycles will be more or less open, timely, exploratory, inexorable, just, or remedial depending on the issues in question and the effectiveness of the actual structures of the representative institutions (as well as the vigilance of civil society in supporting the prior structure of justice) in a given society.

The above perspective on democracy as *both* a policy delivery system and as a conversational system has its origin in David Braybrooke's book about public debate over traffic congestion and his earlier book with Charles Lindblom, *Strategy of Decision*. Braybrooke and Lindblom say that public policy is "remedial, serial and exploratory."[15] What is argued next is that *particular* political institutions provide particular structures and routes for ongoing public conversations about public life that are inexorably serial but *differently* exploratory and remedial (and perhaps different in deterrent effect). My goal is to emphasize that political conversation does take place, not only in regard to the content and form of policy, but also, importantly, in regard to political action overall. In particular, I want to stress that these public conversations (within a particularly-structured set of rules in the community of conversation) retrospectively explore and pass judgement on the morality and general aptness or quality of previous rounds of political action and on the quality of conduct. Thus society struggles toward substantial public policy and public or political morality through its exercise of the deliberative opportunities provided under the procedural rules of its public life. Both phases of political life count mightily: for new policy, the first-round decision phase, and for maturing policies, the results of decisions, the style and quality of conduct of the leadership, and the phases of retrospective deliberation come into prominence. The importance of the retrospective phase, in a nutshell, is that it makes sense of what has passed and builds and strengthens the networks of reciprocity between leaders and society that draw citizens into civic life and responsibility.

David Carr's discussion of the narrative character of everyday experience is helpful. True foresight—comprehensive knowledge of future facts and an interpersonal calculus—being beyond reach, in our daily lives we ruminate on the probable consequences of possible courses of action on an "as if" basis. This "guessed" foresight/hindsight is essential to the storyteller's position: it is *necessary* to select and impose the frame for the story, actively constituting a point of view. Similarly, as Gadamer insists, the fissure that time creates entails that meaning must be reconstructed, and that, being reconstructed, it is different from what went before ("alienated"). The past is remade socially in a mediation with the present.[16] Building on these insights, one is led to conceive of a democratic community of inquiry as engaged in the construction of its own narrative on the meaning of events and actions as they flow past. The collectivity decides on the important variables and makes the decisions about "beginning-middle-end, suspension-resolution, departure-return, repetition, and the like."[17] The collectivity can then try to protect[18] itself—that is, to negotiate with the future (for what it wants it to be) on the basis of what can be reclaimed evidentially and made of policies and political conduct of the past. It can try to protect all of its members, even those of whom it disapproves.

The configuration of the representative machinery of different kinds of governments create different kinds of fora and schedules for political conversation and the crafting of the narrative on public life. (The British House of Commons has long been called "the great inquest of the nation.") One can hypothesize that a constitutional design that ensures that retrospective deliberation will take place *within* the representative institutions (accompanied by the "big loose" conversation outside) might have the following impact on the public policy process: allow it to be more effectively educational and exploratory because it can be made more systematic; make it more remedial because judgment can be more timely and more concentrated, bringing closer the possibility of corrective action; and make it calmer and more civil because the agenda for discussion and grievance will be to a large extent in the hands of the assembly, so that the utility of strategic overstatement is less.

More precisely in relation to a given democracy's capacity to handle dirty-hands episodes, it is useful to think about such episodes to discern by what means actors may have subverted the controls of particular configurations of political institutions, understood as rules for guiding behaviour. The choices political actors may have made under pressure should be seen as raw events to be studied and (politically) moralized in the course of the orderly, constitutionally-appropriate processes of retrospective deliberation and evaluation. The political mechanisms of each constitution can then be examined for their capacity to structure retrospective rounds of public discussion in a timely and transparent way, and so remedy, lay to rest, or systematically and continuously reformulate the issues embedded in the choices.

In regard to actions that undermine political life but which are not usually regarded as criminal, Dennis Thompson's rich conception of mediated corruption provides a framework. For the purposes of this article, the most important aspect of his definition states that acts that subvert the democratic process by undermining deliberation and thus competition are morally corrupt actions. Thompson stresses that mediated corruption "precludes deliberation about whether to deliberate." Actors become corrupting agents when they undertake to manipulate system rules for covert political gain, to consolidate their hold on power. Thompson uses the adjective "mediated" because the actions at issue, performed by politicians looking for "loopholes" in the system rules, are in his conception laundered through political practices that may in other contexts be legitimate:

> ...mediated corruption differs from conventional corruption with respect to each of these three elements [that normally define corruption]: (1) the gain that the politician receives is political, not personal, and is not illegitimate in itself, as in conventional corruption; (2) *how* the public official provides the benefit is improper, not necessarily the benefit itself or the fact that the particular citizen receives the benefit; (3) *the connection between the gain and the benefit is improper because it damages the democratic process, not because the public official provides the benefit with a corrupt motive.* In each of these elements, the concept of mediated corruption links the acts of individual officials to qualities of the democratic process. In this way, the concept provides a partial synthesis of conventional corruption (familiar in contemporary political science) and systematic corruption (found in traditional political theory).[19] [Italics added.]

Thus, although his conception of mediated corruption is broadly consistent with other theories of democracy, Thompson recommends that we might try founding respect for our democratic system more squarely upon the deliberative conception, "which prescribes that officials act on considerations of moral principle, rather than only on calculations of political power." This moral principle is that it is wrong to bypass or otherwise corrupt the democratic processes of deliberation and competition. In this conception, neither ends nor means are legitimate unless they have been addressed in legitimate *deliberative* procedures. This is not the same thing as saying that all things that are chosen through legitimate procedures are just or necessary. The "warrant of the democratic process" must be obtained for at least two basic reasons that have nothing to do with the eventual substantial decision's correctness: 1) to legitimate a substantial course of action—a policy—and, 2) to support the health of the democratic process itself. (In this regard, one must again insist upon the importance of the retrospective phase of a political process. "Loophole man" can be seen for what he is: a criminal of process.) The very idea of constitutionalism can thus be seen to incorporate the idea of deliberative democracy, and further, of deliberative democracy as "exploratory, serial, and remedial" (that is, as explicitly *retrospective* as well as active or positive).[20]

Thompson's idea suggests a standard by which to assess the effectiveness of the machinery of government of actual democratic systems. The morality of a political action can be judged, alongside other standards[21] by whether or not its agents anticipated that retrospective exploration of the meaning and effects of the act would occur, took this appropriately into account, and did not try to evade responsibility. The integrating instrument of the individualistic and structuralist views of responsible action is our prior conception, indeed our political-moral judgment, of what kind of democratic process we want.

The deliberation standard as a test of political morality suggests that contemporary political systems—configurations of institutions and rules—may differ in their capacity for engaging focused public discussion. They would therefore also differ in their characteristic vulnerability to dirty-hands decision-makers, to the extent that some architectural features may provide distinctive incentives to leaders to slip into secretive, consequentialist modes of thinking and acting. Certainly the requirements for deliberation are different, or at least differently configured, in different political systems.

Westminster Norms and Hollis's Treatment of the Coventry Sacrifice

The article by Hollis cited earlier makes an almost-offhand observation about the British Cabinet or Westminster system that, I submit, errs in an interesting and useful way in that it clearly illustrates the importance of how political rules and the opportunities for retrospection are configured. The "story goes," he tells us,

> ...that Churchill was told during the afternoon of 14 November 1940 that there was to be a massive air raid on Coventry that night. A word of warning would have saved hundreds of lives. Yet no warning was sent. For, if the Luftwaffe found themselves expected, they would know that their Enigma cypher had been broken and that was a consequence worth more in the war effort than hundreds of lives in Coventry. It might seem that Churchill had sacrificed his integrity to the war effort. But, on reflection, would it not have been self-indulgence to give the word? Did integrity not demand the keeping of a wider faith?[22]

But, in a note at page bottom, Hollis tersely informs us of the factual detail that "Churchill was given no such information." The note then dismisses the importance of Churchill's personal ignorance of the episode. Hollis finds that Churchill's personal integrity was engaged. Why? Because, Hollis says, "certainly those who deciphered the German signals did know; so the case can stand, even if Churchill is not the focus of it."[23] In other words, the anonymous officers who contingently did possess the information about the raid could have warned their fellow citizens in Coventry, but chose not to do so for wartime emergency reasons (with which we have no quarrel here), and thus sacrificed their moral integrity. And so did Churchill, vicariously.

But Hollis's involvement of the prime minister is not an accident, for he picks up the Coventry decision a second time. To me, it seems most likely that he assigns responsibility to Churchill as an autonomous moral actor because his own thinking is immured in the British framework of responsible government: the minister, as the head of administration, is politically responsible (must answer in public and must provide for redress or a rationale for not acting) for the actions of subordinates in his or her portfolio. Political responsibility so defined cannot, at least in theory, be denied. (If Hollis were American, the excuse of "deniability" would surely have crossed his mind in regard to his example, because deniability, or the contingent ignorance defence, is an explicit repudiation of the possibility of vicarious moral responsibility, and *thus* of political responsibility, at least in an expedient version of the American system of government.)

Certainly, under the British constitution, Churchill was *politically* responsible for the decision not to warn the people of Coventry, whether or not he knew of it in time. Political responsibility means that Churchill had to submit himself to answer for all aspects of the decision to the House of Commons. Any legal consequences, likely for the Crown, would follow, as would any electoral consequences for the government. But legal responsibility and political answerability are not the same thing as vicarious moral responsibility, nor is there any route by which they entail it. Churchill's political duty to the House of Commons and the nation would be to explain the reasons why the actual decision-makers thought that national security had to trump the rights to life of the citizens of Coventry. (If Coventry were answered for by a new war minister, that person would interpret and defend the government's past action in the public discussion.) One can imagine circumstances that would have seen the government politically blamed: if security on the Enigma project had been slack, the Luftwaffe had learned that the code had been broken, *and* Coventry was not warned.

But Churchill could only be *morally* responsible for the blood spilled in Coventry were it to be shown in evidence, retrospectively, that he had personally been involved in a series of events that led directly or indirectly to the tragedy. One can imagine that, in another set of contingencies, he might have let slip to a spy that the Enigma code had been broken, Coventry might have been struck, and he might next have tried to cover his fault by denying that he had had knowledge that the code had been broken, allowing officials to be blamed. In short, unless the retrospective political phase saw evidence emerge as to Churchill's personal fault, Churchill's personal moral integrity should be seen to have been utterly untouched by the Coventry event. One can note that the concept of mediated corruption adds the standard that Churchill would have been gravely at fault had he in any way evaded his duty to be briefed and make himself available to his officers—had he acted in such a way as to keep himself "out of the loop" of information.

Mediated Corruption and the American Presidency

The idea of mediated corruption as action that defeats the established lines of the system as they are understood by the main players and by citizens— action that precludes public deliberation—provides help to those wishing to grasp some of the dilemmas of the modern institution of the American presidency. One can offer as examples the Watergate and Iran-Contra scandals and their sequels. President Nixon apparently thought he had the right to order any action that he believed might be instrumental in maintaining the safety and stability of American life. This included breaking into the offices of the Democratic National Committee in the Watergate building. One reconstruction of a motive is that Nixon and his officials honestly thought that information could come into their hands that could help preserve the stability of the country. Another is that they wanted to collect partisan information to hurt their opponents in the forthcoming election. Or both motives could have figured. Nixon told David Frost on television that no law is violated if a president's staff members are simply doing whatever it takes to implement a presidential decision.[24] The opinion of the American courts was different, for Nixon's officials were tried and sentenced for criminal actions. Yet Nixon was not impeached because he resigned, and, further, he was never tried for any crime, because President Gerald Ford pardoned him prospectively, as phrophylaxis.

Likewise, both the Reagan and the Bush presidencies were haunted by the fear of the revelation of the scope of secret weapon sales to Iran in exchange for the release of American hostages and of the money used to make undeclared war on the Nicaraguan government. President Reagan ducked the question of his own political responsibility for the acts of several officials who reported directly to him, claiming that he had never been personally involved in these particular matters. President Bush subsequently, and likewise, long claimed that he had been "out of the loop" of information during the same events. In December 1992, at the end of his term of office, with proof of his personal involvement appearing ever more likely, Bush permanently short-circuited the possibility of a systematic deliberation about the question of both Reagan's and his own involvement by using the power of presidential pardon to prevent the impending criminal trial of his associates. In his announcement of the Christmas Eve pardons, President Bush claimed that the officials he pardoned had been motivated by patriotism, which made their deeds pure. Those who were prosecuting the cases, he said, were opportunistically trying to seize the law in order to criminalize what Bush called mere policy differences. "Thus did he define law-breaking as a public duty, and law enforcement as an extension of party politics."[25]

The very existence of the power to extend a full pardon before a case is tried may well have incited Reagan and Bush to use it in this way, and thus the power begs to be rethought, even if the actions which its use covered up might have been judged eventually to have been acceptable in the circumstances. So used, the presidential pardon deprives the deliberative evaluation phase of knowledge of the quality and correctness of the original round of decision-making and executive action. One sees that the power to pardon prospectively, combined with the solitary nature of presidential decision-making in foreign policy in general, and in the emergency situation in particular, trumps constitutionalism. But—and this is important to remember—the prospective pardon does not stop or slow continued media and public speculation. In fact, it feeds it. Thus the use of the pardon to evade disciplined conversation conduces to media fantasy, florid conspiracy theory (one need only think of Oliver Stone's film *JFK*) and the erosion of the public's belief in the legitimacy of their system. One can close by noting that the tactic of providing political chiefs with "deniability" can be given a small amount of dignity by redefining it as conspiracy to commit *deliberate* negligence.

Mediated Corruption in Canadian Parliamentary Life

One can find a rich example of mediated corruption in Canada in the 1991 episode in which an Iraqi diplomat who had served as his country's ambassador to the United States in the lead-up to the Gulf War was, with uncommon speed, admitted to this country as a landed immigrant within weeks of his first inquiries. The media coverage and opposition interest that greeted the discovery of his residency at the end of the war created a normal requirement for the government to answer opposition questions in the House of Commons—to submit itself to a retrospective and deliberative moment. But the ministers of the Conservative government whose departments had been involved flatly refused to give reasons for the admission, on the grounds that they had not been engaged in person, as natural persons, in the decision, and thus they could not provide answerability in the House of Commons—they had been "out of the loop." Next these ministers, consulting with the Clerk of the Privy Council and other senior officials in the executive's main support agency, the Privy Council Office, devised and implemented an inquiry into the conduct of officials by a government-dominated House of Commons committee.[26] (The assignment of seats to parties in committees in the same proportions as seats are held in the House of Commons is a condition of responsible government.)

By re-framing its problem in a such a manner, the government formally constituted itself as a dirty-hands actor, debasing the political processes for partisan gain. The manipulation of the deliberative option was corrupt in the following ways:

a) it evaded its duty as a responsible government to provide political answerability to the House of Commons for the admission decision;

b) it sacrificed the rights to natural justice of the individuals who were designated to take the blame (and to thereby protect ministers) by pretending that the ministers were only co-operating with "Parliament" in making their officials available for questioning, whereas *de facto* the committee could not have become seized of the issue without direct government management of the House of Commons' committee agendas;

c) it knowingly allowed its MPs to aggressively cross-examine the accused officials, thus play-acting for the public in show trial fashion in order to legitimate the "verdict," one shamelessly arrived at by a partisan vote directed by the government, an action that amounts to gross manipulation of the system of legitimation;

d) it knowingly used "national security" rationales as a shield for itself, and to protect from scrutiny the government's reasons for which the individual in question had been admitted, and the issues of whether, and how, blame should be fixed for having mishandled the case (*assuming that it had been mishandled*), actually silencing all attempts to provide a fuller explanation of the event and its administration, one that might have supported both the working-level bureaucrats and the merits of the applicant, which had been put into grave doubt by the government's initial panic and later steadfast denial of answerability.

In effect, the government strategy pretended that the admission of the diplomat to Canada was at best a dirty-hands dilemma that had been suffered by bureaucrats (between, perhaps, giving shelter to the enemy national or sending him home to die at the hands of his enemies). But bureaucrats cannot be the end of the line of responsibility in our system of government. As has been discussed in relation to the Hollis example, the working framework of the constitution provides that ministers are politically answerable in retrospect for everything that goes on in their ministries, present and past, whether they knew of it at the time or not. *Their duty is to know of it now, and to take responsibility from the moment forward for amelioration or correction.* In the absence of individual criminal action, the Crown is legally responsible. The government's behaviour here imitated American-style deniability (unacceptable even in that system), and did so without ceding an iota of the power of a Westminster-style government to control information and procedure. It illegitimately put into motion the powers and liberties of two very different systems of government.

Next, the government moved to prosecution of its enemies. It used the apparatus of parliamentary and civil service coercion to create what it pretended was a discovery. Documents were heavily censored or wholly suppressed. Two individuals, one civil servant and one political officer, were selected for blame by partisan vote. That one of the civil servants—a career bureaucrat of 25 years—was the nephew of the then-leader of the Opposition party was presented alternatively as the merest of coincidences, or as what one might expect, given the Government's pure presumption that his sense of duty would be partisan.[27] In summary, the crime against the democratic process consisted in disarming and subverting the structure of justice of the formal retrospective phase of responsible government and turning it illegitimately upon two chosen victims who did not have standing in the representative institutions and could be handled like pawns.

Comparing Systems of Government

In systems of responsible government, the apportioning of blame for previous activity (or inactivity) is the defining political ritual of the adversarial assembly. Thus, retrospective deliberation can be at the centre of political life because "the system"—the living constitution—does have the capacity to see to it that the executive will be forced to respond to the political opposition and to signals from the electorate within short time periods, provided, of course, that secrecy is either not imposed or fails. The American system of separated institutions, in contrast, seems to concentrate on substantial debate about new political decision-making, and, further, on politically and legally regulating the amount of influence that the separated institutions, sharing power, can have on the substance of new policy in each instance. The institutional plan of American government appears to an observer to force intense *prospective* discussion of currently interesting or pressing political options by the device of distributing vetoes widely. What should be done? Who can do what? In some areas, such as health care, mobilizing the separate institutions of the political system to act in concert to undertake a substantially new direction virtually requires that the whole politically-active layer of society be in accord—that all interests with vetoes come together in positive engagement. The first substantial phase of decision being so deliberately undertaken, with so many procedural requirements, and drawing on all institutions, it is perhaps the case that formal, systematic retrospective deliberation inside the representative institutions is less important than in cabinet government systems where the executive controls the legislative program. What does get done has wide support. But in areas such as foreign policy and national security, the US president can act almost unilaterally and exempt himself and his officials from investigation. The sting is, as noted, in the fact that retrospective social and political judgment pursues its course in the "big loose" accountability system outside the framework of representative and government institutions. The "big loose" networks around government, increasingly laden with the covert political agendas of intense minorities, dominate the raw materials of the society's political retrospection.

In parliamentary systems, on the other hand, the executive *gets* power to act unilaterally by taking responsibility for anything that may occur in an area that is within the scope of a minister's powers. At any given time the "disaster-bring-forward" mechanism, from which the House of Commons takes its energy, can lay responsibility for any state of affairs at the feet of the government, which in turn can learn and respond on the spot. All the government has to do in order to get the jurisdiction and legitimacy to act remedially or in expiation of guilt is to accept retrospective, current, and prospective responsibility for a problem. Who can do what is not an issue. Here responsible government can come into its finest moments. But, it should be admitted, this phase seems increasingly to be shirked by parliamentary politicians and to be disregarded by the public and by scholars.

Conclusion

I have argued that the problem of dirty hands, as focused on the intentions of the lone political actor trapped in a vicious scenario, distorts our understanding of the nature of politics. Most obviously, it does not model the most difficult and interesting aspects of politics: those that aspire to democratic action under constitutionalism.

The dirty-hands problematic is deceptive in its assumptions that a sole political actor can routinely and somehow properly engage in efficient "lesser-evils" choices on behalf of the whole of society: to sacrifice people without the possibility of retrospection or retribution. As Evan Simpson points out, dirty-hands problems flatly pit expediency (or sympathy) against rights, often the right to one's life. In utilitarian thinking, as it is standardly represented, the welfare of the whole (again assuming it can be calculated) can trump the rights of individuals.[28] That conflicts sometimes exist between the rights of individuals and the needs or expediencies of the group, or between the needs and expediencies of individuals and the rights of a group, is a fact of public life. But here is where political institutions matter. Political responsibility, located in the public structures and processes of the political framework, must be engaged. The citizens must accept their duty, not to realize substantial justice in the aftermath of events (for which it will often be too late), but to ensure that the answerability phase of political life does operate in public, deliberatively and calmly. This is so not only for reasons of political education and justice, which I have emphasized, but also because it is important that the direction and rate of change in the regime rules under which the executive operates should be known and controlled by those who are the subjects of that regime.

The illusion that heroic wisdom can deliver lowest-cost sacrifices in dirty-hands situations is largely preserved by the suppression of deliberative politics, as was illustrated in the examples of side-tracked answerability in American and Canadian politics. Practical wisdom would suggest that it is a false economy to suppress the retrospective-deliberative process, because this process is the only hope that society has to be educated by the past in order to face the challenges of the future. Political institutions can and should help society to learn about its options and also to protect the integrity of the system itself by conducting formal retrospective deliberation in a framework of orderliness and civility that cannot be simply stolen for partisan purposes.[29] It seems fair to say that, because of Thompson's work, it becomes possible to understand "mere" process as having great substantial importance. Respect for process keeps the substantial choices of the future somewhat more open. Process alone is by no means enough, but it is good ground for a last stand. More realistically, it is often the only ground that remains after the commission of an injustice by those in the positions of power.

Deliberation in public institutions tends the networks of reciprocity and mutual restraints that bind individuals into society, conducing also, I think, to concern for distributional justice. This is because any serious discussion of how processes of answerability are to be arranged will also help to identify and clarify at least some of the social goals that such processes are designed to protect and fulfill. Again it would appear that process and procedure are not empty of substantial importance; process shades into substance at the same time as it underwrites the citizen's right to see what guides substantial choices.

As Bertolt Brecht tells us in his didactic theatre, secretive politics and disregard for process is a significant element of fascist politics. Brecht blames the collectivity for allowing political leaders to be tempted by too much freedom. He tells us that the apparatus of legitimacy is always vulnerable to being appropriated by adventurers – in fact, banal thugs – who would/will turn it into an apparatus of exploitation and suppression. For this reason Brecht reminds the citizen to stand on guard, because fascism, of which Hitler was only one example, waits always and everywhere to be reborn:

> Therefore learn how to see and not to gape.
> To act instead of talking all day long.
> The world was almost won by such an ape!
> The nations put him where his kind belong.
> But don't rejoice too soon at your escape—
> The womb he crawled from still is going strong.[30]

Notes

This is a new version of "The Problem of Dirty Hands in Politics: Peace in the Vegetable Trade," *Canadian Journal of Political Science* 28:3 (September 1995): 479-508.

The author wishes to thank in particular David Braybrooke of Dalhousie and the University of Texas at Austin for his unfailing generousity. Of my Carleton colleagues, Peter Emberley and Radha Jhappan made helpful comments on the text, while others provided pertinent ideas. David Shugarman and Ian Green must be thanked for providing the incentive to think about the subject. The anonymous referees for the first version published in the *Canadian Journal of Political Science* importantly assisted the development of the paper.

An earlier version of this essay was first presented to the Dirty Hands Workshop held at York University, December 1993.

1   The masculine pronouns are used because the dirty-hands problem is historically gendered, making the use of "she" anachronistic. Dirty-handed women before the contemporary era were typically those who incited or depended upon males to "do wrong to do right."

2   Jean Paul Sartre, "Dirty Hands," in *No Exit and Three Other Plays*, trans. Lionel Abel (New York: Vintage Books, 1955) 223-4. Abel's translation has been slightly modified here by using a literal translation of *la merde*. Sartre's original is as follows: "Comme tu tiens à ta pureté, mon petit gars! Comme tu as peur de te salir les mains... La pureté, c'est une idée de fakir et de moine. Vous autres, les intellectuels, les anarchistes bourgeois, vous en tirez prétexte pour ne rien faire. Ne rien faire, rester immobile, serrer les coudes contre le corps, porter des gants. Moi j'ai les mains sales. Jusqu'aux coudes. Je les ai plongées dans la merde et dans le sang. Et puis après? Est-ce que tu t'imagines qu'on peut gouverner innocemment?" *Les mains sales* (Paris: Gallimard, 1948) 104. In another place (193) he says "Tous les moyens sont bons quand ils sont efficaces [all means are good when they are effective]."

3   The point is paraphrased from C.A.J. Coady, "Politics and the Problem of Dirty Hands," *A Companion to Ethics*, ed. Peter Singer(Oxford: Blackwell's, 1991) 373.

4   Dennis F. Thompson, "Mediated Corruption: The Case of the Keating Five," *American Political Science Review* 87 (1993): 369-81.

5   David Braybrooke, *Traffic Congestion Goes Through the Issue Machine* (London: Routledge and Kegan Paul, 1974); David Braybrooke and Charles E. Lindblom, *A Strategy of Decision: Policy Evaluation as a Social Process* (New York: The Free Press of Glencoe, 1963); Charles E. Lindblom and David K. Cohen, *Usable Knowledge: Social Science and Social Problem Solving* (New Haven: Yale University Press, 1979); and David Braybrooke, Bryson Brown, and Peter K. Schotch, *Logic on the Track of Social Change* (Oxford: Clarendon Library of Logic and Philosophy, 1996).

6   Martin Hollis, "Dirty Hands," *British Journal of Political Science* 12 (1982): 396.

7   Hollis 398.

8 Assassination is a subject for Albert Camus, notably *The Just Assassins*, in *Caligula and Three Other Plays* (New York: Knopf, 1958); the judges problem is from Robert Nozick, *Anarchy, State and Utopia* (Oxford: Blackwell, 1974); the torture example is taken up in Alan Donagan, *The Theory of Morality* (Chicago: University of Chicago Press, 1977), 184-89; and the jungle parable is developed in Bernard Williams, "A Critique of Utilitarianism," *Utilitarianism, For and Against*, ed. J.J.C. Smart and Bernard Williams (Cambridge: Cambridge University Press, 1973) 98. But see also Williams's "Politics and Moral Character," *Public and Private Morality*, ed. S. Hampshire (Cambridge: Cambridge University Press, 1978) 55-74. The authors' various scenarios have taken on a life of their own. Michael Walzer, "Political Action: The Problem of Dirty Hands," *Philosophy and Public Affairs* 2 (1972-3): 160-180, perhaps contains the most direct discussion of the possibility of living a moral life as a public figure.

9 Stanley I. Benn, "Private and Public Morality: Clean Living and Dirty Hands," *Public and Private in Social Life*, ed. S.I. Benn and G.F. Gauss(London: Croom Helm, 1983).

10 Braybrooke and Lindblom, *A Strategy of Decision*, vii. It is because consequentialism seems to share the knowledge problems of utilitarianism that I disagree with those who say that a "lesser evils" approach to the problem is an improvement over the standard dirty-hands formulation. See Kai Nielsen, this volume. On dirty-hands dilemmas in private life see Anthony P. Cunningham, "The moral importance of dirty hands," *The Journal of Value Inquiry* 26:2 (April 1992): 239-50.

11 John Deigh, "Ethics," *The Cambridge Dictionary of Philosophy*, ed. Robert Audi (Cambridge: Cambridge University Press) 247.

12 "The [contemporary] executive...is neither more nor less than what is left of government...when legislatures and the courts are removed." Anthony King, "Executives," in, eds., *Handbook of Political Science*, ed. F.I. Greenstein and N.W. Polsby. Vol. 5. (Reading, MA: Addison-Wesley, 1975) 181.

13 For "nobles," one can read, in much modern dirty-handed politics, ideological group, university clique, gang, among other kinds of neo-tribal conspirators.

14 For an interesting exploration of democracies as communities of inquiry capable of intelligent collective adaptation, see Charles W. Anderson, "Pragmatic Liberalism, the Rule of Law, and the Pluralist Regime," *A New Constitutionalism: Designing Political Institutions for a Good Society*, ed. Stephen L. Elkin and Karol Edward Soltan (Chicago: The University of Chicago Press, 1993) 106.

15 Braybrooke and Lindblom vii.

16 See Joel C. Weinsheimer, *Gadamer's Hermeneutics: A Reading of Truth and Method* (New Haven: Yale University Press, 1985), 131-34.

17 David Carr, *Time, Narrative and History* (Bloomington: Indiana University Press, 1986) 60-65. On self-authorship and authenticity see 80-99. Carr says that to suppose that one can take full charge of the stories in which one figures (in private or public life) "is to succumb to the illusion of being or desiring to be God."

18 Note that I do not say "perfect." I believe that the most that can be done is to try to protect one another.

19 Thompson 377.

20 Thompson.

21 We are familiar with the standard of majority rule. In his 1987 book, Thompson develops an argument to the effect that morally justifiable decisions can be assessed against three additional sets of standards: generality, autonomy and publicity. Very briefly, "Standards of generality require that legislative actions be justifiable in terms that apply to all citizens equally....Standards of autonomy prescribe that representatives act on relevant reasons....Standards of publicity require that an intervention take place in ways that could be justified publicly." See Dennis F. Thompson, *Political Ethics and Public Office* (Cambridge: Harvard University Press, 1987) Chap. 4. The concept of mediated corruption is distinguishable from the publicity standard in that it specifically considers the form and requirements of the *system*, rather than simple exposure of a deed.

22 Hollis 391.

23 Hollis, note 5.

24 Michael Foley, *The Silence of Constitutions* (London: Routledge, 1989) 68.

25 Hugo Young, "If This Is The New Ethical Order, It Stinks," *Manchester Guardian Weekly*, 17 Jan. 1993: 5.

26 See, for a description of the inquiry, S.L. Sutherland, "The Al-Mashat Affair: administrative accountability in parliamentary institutions," *Canadian Public Administration* 34 (1991): 573-603.

27 Actually, *two* memoranda had gone to the undersecretary of External Affairs through the career advice stream of Chrétien's shop, both from Mr. Tony Vincent, a senior official, dated March 8 and April 2, the latter a reminder along with press lines. These memoranda were released to Ken Rubin.

28 Evan Simpson, "Justice, Expediency, and Forms of Thinking," paper delivered at the "Dirty Hands" workshop, York University, 12 December 1993. "Willingness to get one's hands dirty in politics expresses an orientation toward thinking in terms of welfare at the expense of principles of right. It is permanently subject to question from the alternative orientation but not to refutation."

29 Stephen L. Elkin, "Constitutionalism's Successor," *A New Constitutionalism* 124.

30 Bertolt Brecht, "Epilogue, " *The Resistible Rise of Arturo Ui* (London: Eyre Methuen, 1976).

FOURTEEN

Democratic Dirty Hands?

DAVID P. SHUGARMAN

Introduction

Dirty-hands activists believe that their illegal and immoral actions are necessary, obligatory, and therefore defensible. They are also convinced that they are doing what people in their constituency would want done and would support if they only knew and fully appreciated the reasons for them, which the nature of dirty hands makes very difficult. For example, Lt.-Colonel Oliver North testified before a congressional hearing into the Iran-Contra scandal that he and his co-conspirators had good reasons for running covert operations which contravened American law and his President's publicly declared policies and good reasons for lying about doing so at earlier congressional committee sessions. Public statements are one thing and serving the nation's interest by doing what your President really wants done is quite another, North suggested. People need to realize, he continued, that America "is at risk in a dangerous world," and that is why he and his scheming partners "had to weigh in the balance the difference between lies and lives." Here is the claim that lies are necessary to save lives, in this case the lives of Americans and those who support the American way of life. That, North was saying, was what he and his co-conspirators were all about. There was no reason for Congress or anyone else to be surprised or upset about the lying, North testified, because, "By their very nature covert operations are a lie. There is great deceit, deception practised." What that meant for the Iran-Contra operatives was making sure that no one outside a tight circle knew what they were doing. And that, unfortunately, included elected members of Congress, because, said North, there were "incredible leaks, from discussions with closed committees of the Congress."[1] Very similar responses came from a former head of a branch of Canada's security services when he was asked by a Royal Commission of Inquiry to explain why in the early 1970s his squad broke into offices of a news agency and a political party in Quebec, opened up hundreds of pieces of regular mail without court authorization, and recruited informers by using threats and force. He responded by stating that incidents of law-breaking in his section of the Royal Canadian Mounted Police were "so commonplace they were no longer thought of as illegalities," and that in his position one can either "betray one's duty to protect the public or break the law."[2] Similar testimony was presented to South Africa's Truth and Reconciliation Commission, chaired by Archbishop Tutu. Former members of the apartheid regime's security forces stated that arrested anti-apartheid activists were tortured because that was the best way of getting information from them about subversive activities.

These statements seem to be in keeping with recent philosophical defences of dirty hands. Early in the 1970s, just prior to the Watergate scandal, Michael Walzer wrote that "in politics it is easy to get one's hands dirty and often right to do so"[3] and went on to defend dirty election practices. And he also stated that when a moral politician is wrestling with whether to do something unscrupulous which will lead to something importantly good, "we want him to."[4] A few years later, Martin Hollis discussed the slaughter of one Scottish clan by another in the late 1600s to exemplify the dirty-hands issue and claimed that, "We order or at least license our agents to pursue policies which cannot be translated into action, if honesty and openness are required."[5] There are important "we's" in these comments and claims by practitioners and theorists of dirty hands.[6] What they imply can be summed up in two propositions: 1), dirty hands are a staple of politics; 2), they are also acceptable as democratic practices. The first proposition is the claim that dirty hands and politics are inextricably linked such that, (like love and marriage in the old song) you can't have one without the other. The second maintains that uses of cruelty and deception are, if not consistent with democratic principles, so important as exceptions that they have (or ought to have) the support of citizens and are therefore compatible with democratic politics. In what follows, I intend to question both these claims. And I will do so by considering both the theoretical and practical appropriateness of dirty-hands advocacy.

Politics as a Warrior's Realm

Those who share the dirty-hands mentality take much from Machiavelli. As with all major influential thinkers there are several Machiavellis, or several interpretations of his work. The Machiavelli emphasized in regard to dirty-hands arguments is the one who tells us that violence can be used for ill or good, who says, "A wise man will never criticize someone for an extralegal action undertaken to organize a kingdom or to establish a republic. He will agree if his deed accuses him, its consequences excuse him ... for it is those who are violent in order to destroy who should be found guilty, not those who are violent in order to build anew."[7] And if your country's safety is at stake, "you should pay no attention to what is just or what is unjust, or to what is kind or cruel, or to what is praiseworthy or shameful ... [Y]ou should adopt wholeheartedly the policy most likely to save your homeland's life and preserve her liberty."[8] This is the Machiavelli who recommends doing anything and everything for good purposes, and it is the reason we call defenders of dirty hands moral Machiavellians.

But what the moral Machiavellians conveniently ignore is that even when their mentor is calling for a republic, a popular government, he maintains that given the widespread corruption and lawlessness of his Italy, the leadership necessary to set up such a government must be invested in a single man. Speaking of this man, Machiavelli states it is essential "that all power lies in his hands" and that, remarkably, he "should have no other concern, no other thought, should pay attention to nothing aside from war, military institutions, and the training of his soldiers. For this is the only field in which a ruler has to excel."[9] And he adds that since rulers can't always win by fighting fairly, they need to adopt the beastly attributes of the lion and fox. You not only have to be ready to devour an enemy, you have to be cunning too. What should be noted here is that Machiavelli's acceptance and recommendation of cruelty as a legitimate method of seeking and exercising power, which seems bold, realistic, sophisticated or sick depending on the reader, has to be understood as coming out of a context in which torture of prisoners was legal, and is expressed by someone who was himself tortured.[10] Machiavelli had no experience of democracy, of living in a system with a bill of rights and constitutional constraints on office holders; his world had no Universal Declaration of Rights and no Covenant on Civil and Political Rights, both of which contain Articles that stipulate, "No one shall be subjected to torture or to cruel and inhuman treatment or punishment." Remarkably, the moral Machiavellians treat politics as if it has changed little from the lawless, embattled atmosphere of Machiavelli's Italy. Stanley Benn says the reason leaders today have to rely on the tactics Machiavelli recommends "is that they are champions and trustees of the public in a jungle world,"[11] while Martin Hollis maintains that democracies have to make way for the "Princely view" of dealing with difficulties rather than the citizen-centred one. This means that our leaders must be foxes, because "there are evil men about who do not wish the good of the people and who do not keep faith," and the only way of checking them may be for the "apparatus" of the state "to be used dishonestly."[12]

The dirty-hands mentality, then, sees politics as very much a realm for the crafty, well-intentioned, ruthless warrior. In this view, where the difficult role obligations of leaders are concerned, there is little difference among forms of politics. It does not matter whether we are talking about autocratic rule or democracy. The issues that pertain to Machiavellian "Princely" rule apply in all cases. The sole qualification is that although anything a Prince does will be praiseworthy and rewarding if it is successful, a democratic Prince is ultimately responsible to the people and is aware of the paradoxical nature of his official calling. So a hostile, war-like environment is assumed to characterize any polity. This permits moral Machiavellians to slide easily and disturbingly back and forth between conditions and principles of authoritarian rule on the one hand and democracy on the other. Furthermore, the version of democracy they have in mind— the only one that can be squared with the latitude granted leaders—is a highly elitist one requiring a very restrictive understanding of both the nature of citizenship and the relationship between citizens and leaders.

Interestingly, this approach, which commends itself as the most realistic appreciation of the nature of politics, cannot explain the fact that major crises in democracies are usually dealt with through recourse to democratic procedures and the rule of law rather than violence, and that two of the most significant and successful political movements of the twentieth century were Gandhi's non-violent challenge to British Imperial rule in India and Martin Luther King's non-violent civil rights struggle of the 1960s.[13] In contrast to Machiavelli's advice and that of his latter-day proponents, King held that "nonviolence demands that the means we use must be as pure as the ends we seek ... that it is wrong to use immoral means to attain moral ends. But ... it is just as wrong or even more so to use moral means to provide immoral ends."[14] One could respond that King is showing his naiveté here, or that he was insincere and deceptive. But both charges would be difficult to sustain.

Democracies and Dirty Hands

At issue in the controversy over the ethics of dirty hands are two very different understandings of democracy. On the one hand we have an election-focused, elitist version, and on the other a fuller, more participatory one. It is only the first that can accommodate dirty hands. A brief summary of their features is useful to highlight their differences.

The election-focused, elitist version emphasizes citizens' passivity and deference to leaders between elections. It grants elected representatives relatively unfettered discretion to be entrepreneurial: to do both the good and the dirty things that need be done while in office. In the elitist version, citizens' participation is reserved for elections, and the citizens' physical involvement, critical sensibilities, and judgement are held in abeyance until the next election and transferred to their elected representatives between elections. This was Max Weber's preferred model: "In a democracy the people choose a leader in whom they trust. Then the chosen leader says, 'Now shut up and obey me.' People and party are then no longer free to interfere in his business ... Later the people can sit in judgement."[15] The elitist model assumes that the majority of people have neither the wits nor the interest to deal with large, complicated, or technical issues, all of which are better left to the few who do have such talent. As Joseph Schumpeter put it, democracy along elitist lines means "making the deciding of issues by the electorate secondary to the election of the men who are to do the deciding."[16] This version of democracy assumes a categorical divide between governors and governed—such that, between elections, leaders are to citizens as authoritarian commanders are to their troops, or authoritarian as parents are to their children, or as allegedly innovative and active entrepreneurs are to relatively passive consumers, or as the boss is to the worker.

The thoroughgoing or participatory democratic model is very different.[17] It calls for elected leaders to exhibit transparency in decision-making, openness in their dealings with citizens, and accountability (which means, to answer) to the public for actions and decisions taken, or in some cases, not taken, *not every four or five years, but on an ongoing basis*. Contrary to the elitist version, this means that what representatives do as trustees of the public weal is not "their" business, it is the public's. Rather than expecting citizens to shut up between elections, an orientation to thoroughgoing democracy means willingness to dialogue with citizens and respond to their objections and appeals *during* the term in office, and a commitment to keep promises made or provide clear reasons why they have not been. Implied here are practices consistent with the democratic principle of mutual respect: the principle that, insofar as there is a collective interest in recognizing an equal right to self-development on the basis of cooperative association, "each has to refer his own action to that of others, and to consider the action of others to give point and direction to his own."[18] With regard to procedural priorities the principle requires institutions and institutional practices which scrupulously conform to the rule of law and politically balance a) general reliance on majority (and often plurality) decision-making—expressed through elections, referenda, legislative assemblies, and organizational meetings—with b) protection of individual and minority rights.

For citizens, a more participatory democracy implies attentiveness to the public agenda, equal opportunities to influence it and equal consideration in collective decision-making. There is furthermore, in this admittedly idealized and normative account of democracy, a fundamental role given over to constitutional definitions and interpretations of governmental powers and citizen rights which act as important constraints on executive and legislative initiatives and discretionary latitude generally. The democratic temper is oriented to both procedural and substantive measures that support and promote mutual respect, integrity, fiduciary accountability, and collective decision-making. Finally, the notion of a thoroughgoing democracy calls for democratic principles, institutional procedures, and social practices to inform relations not just between citizens and elected government officials but in the daily life and operations of a society.

Dirty Hands or Basic Humanity?

The theoretical defence of dirty hands has to be understood as an ethical argument which, from the perspective of those making the connection, sets out the best way of combining morality with power. Walzer presents two examples to demonstrate what dirty-hands acts are and why they ought to be approved. They are meant to illustrate the nature of the moral problems faced by decent politicians and to persuade us that choosing to be devious and cruel, despite our normal repugnance to so act, is at times the best way to operate. In my view they are, to the contrary, useful examples for showing serious weaknesses not only in Walzer's updated version of moral Machiavellism but in the dirty-hands position generally, especially when we consider its repercussions and implications for democratic politics.

The first of Walzer's examples I want to review is the one he regards as the more dramatic of the two. In point of fact it is, in Walzer's discussion, his second example. I want to begin with it because it is a cruelty case, clearly much "bloodier" than the other example, but I will argue that, ironically, in important respects it is not a persuasive example of dirty hands. Walzer presents us with a politician who comes to national power while his country is at war with a colony. He wins election on a platform promising decolonization and peace, and his commitments are genuine. However, as soon as the new leader arrives in the colony to negotiate a peace settlement, he finds that terrorists have placed bombs in various apartment buildings in the capital, and they are set for detonation within hours. Luckily, a terrorist leader has been captured who is thought, on good grounds, to know where the bombs are. But the terrorist won't talk. So the national leader, who had made it clear in his campaigning that he regards torture as an absolute evil, orders the man tortured to try to get him to divulge the whereabouts of the bombs before hundreds or thousands of innocent people are blown up. That is the end of the scenario. We don't know whether the torture tactics paid off or not.

Now, there is something terribly contrived, almost to the point of being incredible, about this example: if this is meant as a *realpolitik* illustration, it is difficult to believe that anti-colonialist forces would engage in terrorism the day that a new leader, elected on a platform of effectively giving up the fight against independence, arrives to negotiate a transfer of power. Also, the new leader might well have considered other options: prevailing upon the rebel terrorist to reconsider, given the new government and new policy; ordering the evacuation of everybody in the apartments within twenty-four hours (which might have the effect of weakening the terrorists' standing with their public and, furthermore, might have moved the terrorist leader to co-operate); but no, Walzer treats this as an *in extremis* situation. There is no other option; this is the politician's last chance to save lives. But we can set aside questions about the credibility of the scenario to focus on whether or not this is really an account of dirty hands and to examine what, for Walzer, is the moral of the story.

What is especially important to Walzer's account, and what makes his contribution to the dirty-hands problem so interesting and innovative, is that we are asked to understand that this is a leader who knowingly autho- rizes commission of a moral crime and is willing to accept a moral burden, which is his guilt. It is the acknowledgement and acceptance of guilt, says Walzer, that "is the only evidence he can offer us, both that he is not too good for politics and that he is good enough." The national leader is then Walzer's archetypal "moral politician" who is so because we see his dirty hands: "If he were a moral man and nothing else, his hands would not be dirty; if he were a politician and nothing else, he would pretend that they were clean."[19] This is a seductive account of an ideal leader landing in a crisis situation and dealing with it. He does so both by accepting a moral paradox that meets the social psychology of decent citizens and by express- ing that paradox as a result of his strength of character, his own individual psychology. I think there are important problems with such an account.

Consider some other difficult critical situations we could find ourselves in. Normally, we don't physically push people: but pushing someone out of the way of an oncoming vehicle is hardly a dirty-hands illustration—though he or she may be bruised and shaken by the push; and pushing or pulling a child away from another child whom the first child is about to strike with a dangerous object may be paternalistic, but it's not dirty hands. There is no reason in either of these cases for someone to feel guilty about intervening. Injury or deceit is not involved, but it is easy to imagine cases where either could be necessary. Imagine pretending to be wealthy and promising a mil- lion dollars to a gullible kidnapper who is about to beat up your spouse and child unless you pay a ransom; after he releases them, you renege on the promise. Imagine having to kill or torture someone to get a key he or she is carrying that will open the freezer in which this person has locked your spouse or child, when the police and locksmiths are hours away. You are a good person, you don't normally deceive people, you believe keeping your word is a mark of your integrity and humanity, you've never killed anyone, are against capital punishment, and feel strongly about the importance of Article 5 of the United Nations Declaration of Human Rights that forbids torture and inhuman treatment. In the extreme situations I've instanced, you wouldn't be wrong to do what you wouldn't normally do, and while you might regret having to do what you did, there would be no reason for you to feel guilty or to be punished.

I suggest here that in such cases, one has to see the need to move away from an absolutist deontology—the one that says, "I have a duty to myself and others never to depart from the moral principles I believe that I and everyone else must follow"—and to recognize when an exceptional circumstance, an extreme situation, requires making an exception to generally sound ethical principles. In this view, recourse to dirty hands is an extreme exception to democratic politics rather than a staple of it and resort to such tactics is the result of a failure of politics and a turn to war. We would be mistaken to think of this as a move or "surrender" to consequentialism. Of course, unless we thought about the consequences of our act and those of not doing it, we wouldn't know whether to call this an exceptional circumstance or not. But such a move is also consistent with the notion of duty to humanity, and can be an expression of our humanity—considerations fundamental to Kantian moral philosophy, though departing from Kant's own commitment to an exceptionless categorical imperative and his rejection of considering the consequences of actions. It is a mistake to see such a move as one away from principles, as unprincipled and compromising (using compromise in a derogatory fashion). It is misleading to depict the world as a place where most people can be expected to be, and expect others to be, pure deontologists *except* for "gifted" politicians who are expected to know that they cannot be.

Camus on Dirty Hands

In support of his analysis of the dirty-hands dilemma, and almost as a response to the objections of the kind that have been raised so far, Walzer turns to the insights of Albert Camus. In several of his works, but principally in *The Rebel*,[20] Camus addressed the ethical issues confronting those who resist suppression and injustice. In my view, his reflections speak to the importance of avoiding a stark either/or choice between deontology and utilitarianism in a way that is radically different from moral Machiavellism. But that is not the way Walzer sees him.

Walzer sees Camus as a delineator of the limits, as well as a defender of the importance of dirty hands. Camus's ruminations on the plight of heroic rebels are, for Walzer, an instructive lesson in the prescriptive logic that needs to be applied by practitioners of dirty hands. It is possible to interpret Camus in this way. There is his observation that rebellion and recourse to violence exist "because falsehood, injustice, and violence are part of the rebel's condition." And there is his note of seeming despair over the idea that the rebel committed to actively challenging injustice and oppression "knows what is good and, despite himself, does evil."[21] These statements sound like an affirmation of a root contradiction manifested in a tension between means and ends, and the inevitability of moral incoherence whenever we try to end injustices: in other words, a dilemma much like the one Walzer is describing. Furthermore, when Camus argues that a mark of the just assassin's (or rebel's) acknowledgement of limits to the use of violence is his willingness to be executed for his act so as not to have further acts repeated or himself rewarded,[22] it seems like he is making a case similar to Walzer's about the importance of acknowledging and facing up to guilt.

Nevertheless, interpreting Camus's advocacy of rebellion as a defence of cruelty and deception is a stretch. It takes his argument out of context and twists it and the examples he provides in a direction that is quite at odds with the central theme in his theoretical reflections. Camus is concerned to analyze abuses of power. His rebel resists and challenges power, he is not a manipulator of it. Camus deals with and criticizes cruelty used by those wanting power and wielding it in Europe, from the leaders of the French revolution and their intellectual supporters, through those central to the Nazi and Bolshevik regimes. He notes that these regimes have been war governments, for which he has no use. Much of his writing displays a distaste for politics and politicians, and there can be little question that a principal reason for such feelings is that the politics he grew up with were enveloped and dominated by considerations of war. His own life was significantly affected by a world war, the Cold War, and France's battles with Algeria and Vietnam. Camus's heroes are not and cannot be pacifists, he maintains, because that would leave the world open to the domination of tyrants and the slaughter of innocents. But his recommendations differ from the moral Machiavellians.

His approach to using violence in extreme cases instructs us to reject the mind set and rationale for dirty hands. When Camus says that our choices are not just those of the yogi or the commissar because both "reject the conciliatory value that rebellion ... reveals and [both] offer us only two kinds of impotence ... equally removed from reality, that of good and evil," he is rejecting not only the ascetic and the resolute militant, but both of the principal protagonists in Sartre's *Dirty Hands*: the brilliant defender of dirty hands (Hoederer), and the allegedly pure moralist (Hugo) who, despite himself, gets his hands dirty (because while he rails against lying, he practices deception to assassinate Hoederer).

The authorizers of dirty hands, according to its advocates, are men of power, usually in power. They are in office or fighting to get there. But Camus's rebel is not a figure holding office, he is a resistance fighter. He may lead or join an insurrection when great injustice calls for it, but will never use violence "in the service of a doctrine or reason of state."[23] Here Camus clearly parts company with ideologues of the right and left and with moral Machiavellians. It is important in this regard to understand his appreciation of the relationship of means and ends. For Walzer, the unsavoury means necessarily involved in securing a great end, while never morally justifiable, are excusable when weighed against the value of the goal. Thus, immoral means remain less significant, subordinate to moral ends. In this connection Camus cannot be invoked as a defender of dirty hands. The means-ends logic of the moral Machiavellians is simply incompatible with Camus's claim that although it is sometimes the case that the end justifies the means, the answer to the equally important question "What will justify the end?" is "The means."[24] This tells us that if the means necessary to a particular end are shameful, then we ought to choose a different end. In his portrayal of just assassins, the means are consistent with their goal: in assassinating the tyrant, they are careful to kill no others. Camus is telling us that every use of violence or deception needs to be attached to a limited goal which clearly circumscribes how far people may go to achieve their aims, and that we need to make sure that what Walzer calls, and what Camus would not call, dirty-handed activity is not regarded as the normal calling of moral politicians. Camus's acceptance of a politics of resistance and reform can only be (mis)understood as a defense of dirty hands if his rebel's active resistance to oppression and violence is regarded as a reversal of his stated beliefs. However, his rebel is not a pacifist in principle who then has to break with his principles, in the way that Walzer's hypothetical and archetypal moral politician does when he uses torture after swearing that he will never do so. Camus makes it clear that "Absolute non-violence is the negative basis of slavery and its acts of violence."[25]

Fair Elections?

The other example of a defensible dirty-handed move that Walzer provides focuses on trickery and illegalities rather than on cruelty, but in some respects it is more disturbing. It has to do with the rigging of an election. An honest leader deliberates on whether to make a deal with a corrupt ward boss. In return for delivering votes, the ward boss demands that the politician, once elected, pay him back with a number of school construction contracts. The politician would be buying votes and committing himself to deliver favours with public funds—patronage. Walzer suggests that when the stakes are high enough, his hypothetical candidate (is he hypothetical? Jack Kennedy apparently did make deals with the Mafia, as well as with shady ward bosses in Illinois to win Chicago, and the state in 1960) will set aside his scruples and make the deal. And, says Walzer, "we want him to make it, precisely because he has scruples about it."[26]

There are several serious problems with this example.[27] First, there is a potentially dangerous contagion effect of supporting and applauding people who contravene rules governing fair elections: if it gets around that this is what it takes to win, it will be difficult to expect others not to do so in the future.[28] A similar point was made by Justice Brandeis of the US Supreme Court seventy years ago: "Decency, security and liberty alike demand that government officials shall be subject to the same rules of conduct that are commands to the citizen. In a government of laws, existence of the government will be imperiled if it fails to observe the law scrupulously. Crime is contagious. If the government becomes a lawbreaker, it breeds contempt for law."[29] There is also something obviously contradictory about a supposedly democratic politician flouting fundamental values of democracy: " The cultivation of the capacity for judicious vice in the ruler sits oddly with the values of public accountability and relative openness characteristic of genuine democracy."[30]

Then (as was also problematic in the first example) the claim that citizens can know a politician and his psyche so intimately that they understand how badly he's going to feel is dubious. In the US people running for the kinds of positions where dirty hands might make a difference—governor, senator, president—spend hundreds of thousands, usually millions of dollars on public relations, advertising campaigns, and public opinion polls to project both an image and an attractive platform. During an election campaign, people have enough trouble getting important issues clarified without being expected to know a candidate's inner motives and deeply held moral convictions.

Additionally, Walzer's "we" in this case is outrageously presumptuous. While it no doubt includes members of Nixon's Committee to Reelect the President—who helped organize and finance support for the Watergate burglars and White House plumbers, and who were convinced they were supporting a great American to achieve great goals—it doesn't include me, nor should it include people who value democratic procedures and principles and are prepared to live by them, even when their agenda and candidates may be defeated.

The notion that winning elections justifies rigging them calls for a remarkably schizoid moral sensibility on the part of both leaders and led. It requires a belief in the tragic heroism of a moral expert who can be trusted to be dishonest because he has carefully weighed the ethical costs of dishonesty against the ethical benefits of what that dishonesty will bring and who will experience psychological trauma as a result. In fact, Walzer's example collides with the theory it is supposed to strengthen when we ask how his successful politician is to do penance. Why would a successful politician feel or admit guilt at having done something that paid off in victory and that was done with the assumed consent of his supporters? How would a successful politician be punished? By not electing him again? Why?

What this example recommends is excusing fraud at election time, nullifying the value of elections. People then consent to an empty mandate. But we cannot claim that the dirty hands are democratic, any more than we could use the term *democratic* to refer to bogus elections. The proposition that it is democratic for a democracy to disenfranchise itself is logically and practically incoherent. It is like saying that, as an example of their freedom, free persons will voluntarily submit themselves to slavery. In this regard, "free slaves" and "democratic dirty hands" are not paradoxes, they are oxymorons.[31]

Defensible and Indefensible Dirty Hands

There are a number of different facets or aspects of dirty-hands deeds; clearly, some are acceptable in extreme circumstances. In this regard there is the humorous example of the British military officer portrayed by Peter Sellers in the anti-war movie *Dr. Strangelove*. The Sellers character is stationed at a US nuclear-bomber air-command base commanded by a renegade madman who, using a secret code, signals American warplanes to drop nuclear weapons on Russian sites. When the British officer finds out what has happened, he first tries to reason with the base commander, then, realising he is dealing with insanity, tries to play along in order to extract the code and halt the bombing mission. When the base comes under attack by loyal American troops, the commander kills himself. The Sellers character attempts to phone the White House to inform the President of what has happened. But the base's military phone lines have been cut, and the only phone that is still working is a pay phone. The long-distance operator refuses to put a call through until Sellers pays for a connection, so he breaks into the coin depository of a nearby soda pop machine—and is berated by another soldier for this violation of private property, despite the fact that the change for the phone call might prevent a nuclear war.

So a good man tries deception, then breaks the law to try to avert disaster. This is a dirty-hands case, but in a conventional rather than Walzerian sense. The notion that the Sellers character should feel guilty for shooting up a pop machine or trying to deceive a crazed warmonger, and that he or we should think he has done something seriously wrong in order to do right, is as bizarre, ludicrous, and dangerously confusing as the situation he finds himself in. Of course, he has not had to torture or kill anyone to try to get the secret code, but, if he had, "we" would have thought it justifiable and we would not expect him to be punished for it.

Now let us consider two examples that come without any satirical intent and that are unacceptable. They concern recent unfortunate historical cases. MKULTURA was a program of mind-control experimentation funded and organized by the American Central Intelligence Agency and implemented at the Allen Memorial Institute of McGill University in Montreal by its director, Dr. Ewan Cameron. At least 77 persons who thought they were being given the best treatment possible to cure their psychological problems were instead used as part of a program to investigate mind-control techniques. They were given a hallucinogen (the drug LSD) and assorted other experimental drugs without their permission or knowledge. Stansfield Turner, a director of the CIA during Jimmy Carter's presidency, wrote that the unit conducting these experiments had an enormous grant of autonomy from oversight or review "and a few well-intentioned, but terribly misguided individuals badly abused the CIA's privilege of keeping secret so much of what it does." In a democracy, according to Turner, "we should never turn over the custody of [high ethical] ideals to any group of individuals who divorce themselves from concern for the public attitude. The crimes against humanity perpetrated by zealots ... are too many, [and] without accountability the temptations of acting in secret [are] too great."[32]

One response to MKULTURA offers an example, one of the few,[33] of a dirty-hands public servant who seems to have been troubled at the time and later aware that deceptive treatment and duplicitous use of mental patients was morally problematic and perhaps even wrong: appearing before the US Senate Select Intelligence and Human Resources Committee, one of the principal figures in charge of the MKULTURA program, Dr. Sidney Gottlieb, testified that all the work he did and authorized was "extremely unpleasant, extremely difficult, extremely sensitive." But, sounding like someone who saw himself as a noble warrior fighting the good fight of the Cold War, Gottlieb also testified it was "above all ... extremely urgent and important."[34] The fact that over seventy people had their psyches disturbed for years and, in some cases, had their lives ruined was a price they were unfortunate enough to be required pay for "desirable ends," such as counteracting the efforts of communist countries to brainwash Western operatives and soldiers. They paid by being subjected to the kind of brainwashing "we" wanted to be able to counter or inflict on the other side.

Our final example refers to the infamous presidency of Richard Nixon. In 1969-70, the Nixon administration secretly approved over 3600 B-52 air attacks against suspected Viet Cong and North Vietnamese installations in Cambodia. These attacks were kept secret from Congressional committees and authorities. Large parts of Cambodia were devastated, thousands of Cambodians were killed; it made no appreciable difference to how the Americans fared in Vietnam, but it contributed to the strengthening of the Khmer Rouge, who then ended up slaughtering their own people in one of the most brutal campaigns of this century. The secret bombing of a nation with which the Americans were not at war owed much to the devious minds and machinations of Henry Kissinger, Nixon, and Alexander Haig.

As Nixon's right-hand man in foreign affairs (first as national security advisor, then as secretary of state), Kissinger enjoyed a reckless, imperialistic, and hubris-filled tenure, apparently failing to appreciate that he was living in a democratic society in the twentieth century. Tony Judt points out that Kissinger was fascinated by, and identified with, the diplomacy and politics of Count Metternich and believed they were applicable to contemporary international relations.[35] However, Metternich operated in an early nineteenth-century hereditary Austrian empire. As Judt notes, this was a context where "all power was vested in the emperor and his ministers. There were no constitutional constraints, no electoral constituencies to placate or inform, no committees to consult. The imperial foreign minister and chancellor answered only to his emperor and to their shared view of the imperial interest."[36] Kissinger—a Noble Peace Prize winner, respected scholar, and towering figure in public policy—had hands which were continually filthy. He saw himself representing America's best interests and was unwilling and unprepared to let democratic demands get in the way of his Machiavellian maneuvers. Like his president, he was obsessed with, and talented at, concealment and the spreading of disinformation. The historical record shows, says Judt, that Kissinger was "resistant to the constraints of policy-making in a constitutional republic with multiple governing branches." As practical examples of an outstanding dirty-hands leader and dirty-hands programs, Kissinger, the bombing of Cambodia, and the MKULTURA program offer us powerful evidence for rejecting the arguments of moral Machiavellism.

What I think the examples show (and we could have added Lyndon Johnson's lies in 1964 about being the "peace candidate," Watergate, Iran-Contra, RCMP dirty tricks, and many others)[37] is that the dirty-hands position is terribly misleading, insofar as it seeks to convey a great truth about the close relationship between leadership, morality, and democracy. The picture painted of the dirty-hands leader is a composite of wily negotiator, clever manipulator, no-nonsense general, and "father-knows-best" moral actor. It is a highly romanticized view of leadership and a dangerous one. The only place we find such leaders is in hero-producing histories, fiction, and Hollywood movies. It is dangerous for precisely those reasons which Acton and Mill appreciated, and which ethical realists at times so acutely emphasize, but at other times unfortunately neglect: the use of power without checks and balances leads to its abuse.[38]

Dirty-hands defenders accuse their allegedly deontological opponents of being too moral (or of being moral purists), but the moral Machiavellian position is, in fact, buoyed by a moral righteousness of its own, the sense that, because of the high stakes and the nature of one's opponents, a leader needs to act in support of a cause in ways that are beyond normal judgements of good and evil. There may be something to this as an *in extremis* rationale, so long as we are addressing reactions in life and death situations and during war, but this is, I suggest, light years away from justifying electioneering trickery. Yet Walzer's treatment of the logic of dirty hands remains the same for both his dramatic and pedestrian examples.

With respect to *in extremis* issues, it is instructive to refer to the meaning of "hard cases" in law. Moral Machiavellians see politics as an arena of hard cases where leaders must repeatedly overcome adversity and prevent great suffering. When judicial decisions depart from normal principles of law to meet cases of hardship—suffering, privation, adversity—the term used to describe such an outcome is "hard case." It is generally recognized that "hard cases make bad law." In a like manner, we ought not to let hard, exceptional cases determine how we are to operate and understand the workings of ethical politics in a democracy. To deal with special circumstances, we may very well require the admission of exceptions to generally recognized, practical principles of ethical conduct. It is a mistake, however, to make the exception the rule.

Operating on democratic principles means that when an important plan of action is contemplated, a context of relevant information and the reasons for the plan should be widely disseminated, easily accessible, and addressed to the largest possible audience of citizens. As Sissela Bok argues, *where there is a case to be made for departing from accepted norms, reasons should, nonetheless, appeal to generally recognized considerations of justice in social relations.* We need to ask questions like: Does the recommended deviation prevent or reduce harm? Does it contribute to achieving benefit? Is it the thing to do because of considerations of fairness? Does it contribute to trustworthiness and so serve the cause of veracity?[39] If these considerations figured in political deliberations, and if citizens and not their representatives were to decide on the acceptability of probable risks, it would not be easy to get one's hands dirty in politics, and it would seldom be right to do so.

Moral Machiavellians, in contrast, contend that the only ways of dealing with dirty-handed politicians are for citizens to be willing to get their own hands dirty or to be spectacularly discriminating and psychologically prescient when choosing leaders. In other words, we should be electing leaders who we expect will do the nasty things they think need to be done on our behalf and then feel terrible about it, so terrible that they would welcome punishment. Indeed, Walzer tells us that the main failing in Machiavelli's own articulation of dirty hands is that "he does not specify the state of mind appropriate to a man with dirty hands."[40] So here the main checks on a leader's wide discretion and possible abuse of power are not constitutional rules, political institutions, nor democratic values, but rather the psychology of the individual mover and shaker. This is a position which has little practical purchase because, as Walzer himself points out, "In most cases of dirty hands moral rules are broken for reasons of state ... [and]moral rules are not usually enforced against [this] sort of actor largely because he acts in an official capacity."[41] In defending dirty hands and trying to find a place for them within democracy, Walzer is reduced to emphasizing the need for a political culture which values moral rules highly and takes their violation seriously, while simultaneously acknowledging that it is the remarkable individual who belongs to such a culture who is the quintessential dirty-hands politician. This is like recommending a recipe that is bound to be botched before it gets to the table.[42]

Conclusion

In this essay I have tried to show that both the allegedly inextricable connection of dirty hands and politics and the added putative link between dirty hands and democratic practice are highly problematic. My aim has been to bring out certain crucial features in both the theory and practice of dirty hands which are jarringly at odds with those of democracy, broadly understood. The obligations required of public officials to maintain integrity, trust, accountability, and publicity and to reinforce the value of mutual respect, are flouted, and their importance is trivialized. The democracy/dirty hands connection is only sustainable given a highly truncated, narrow, elitist version of democracy.[43] There is a connection of sorts between moral Machiavellism (the use of cruelty and deception for good ends) and an elitist form of democracy; however, in this connection, dirty-hands arguments and methods should be understood as both reflecting and shoring up a system of decision-making marked by autocratic features and dispositions that have much more to do with a military mentality and authoritarian paternalism than with thoroughgoing democracy.

Dirty-hands actions and actors are, I have tried to show, neither supra-ideological nor morally neutral. The assumptions of moral Machiavellism cannot be squared with a thoroughgoing democracy. Rather, they go with the view that the major decisions and moves that are needed to further such ends are so complicated tactically, strategically, and morally, and so subject to obstruction from hostile forces, that expecting consultation with or participation by the citizen at large is naive and counter productive. This means that there needs to be deference to elitist (ideally autocratic) and paternalistic leadership and reliance on the talents of great individuals or special elites who believe that they have grave professional responsibilities that set them apart from the average citizen and permit important exceptions to democratic expectations.

Merleau-Ponty's "in a world of struggle, no one can flatter himself that he has clean hands"[44] is a position shared by all dirty-hands theorists. For them, as Trotsky most boldly proclaimed, struggle is another name for war. Trotsky held that "there is no impervious demarcation between 'peaceful' class struggle and revolution," that every strike is an episode in a civil war, and that socialist movements cannot manage "without violence and lying." Any attempt to maintain the contrary—i.e., the contention that there is a fundamental distinction between peaceful struggle and war—was, said Trotsky, "a pathetic evasion."[45] And in war it is a matter of "our" morals against "theirs," and of not being hypocritical or weak-kneed when it comes to having to use violence and lies to defeat an enemy. My argument that dirty-hands theory is neither adequate description nor acceptable prescription, and my arguments that dirty-hands practices are undemocratic, should not be misunderstood as a denial that politics is often very much about struggle. It is a struggle over what laws are necessary and sensible to regulate social activities; over what is the best, moral way of organizing our lives, of promoting and making the best use of people's talents; and over how natural and collectively contributed resources should best be distributed. It is a struggle that, as Plato and Aristotle recognized almost two and a half millennia ago, and Marx rearticulated and re-examined a hundred and fifty years ago, is largely between classes and, in capitalist societies, between winners and losers in the marketplace and property sweepstakes. It is a struggle that has much to do with redressing grievances, making things right.

In a healthy, functioning democracy, that struggle is about, and is a reflection of, the opportunities citizens have to persuade each other of the merits of change, and of the substance and pace of particular preferred changes. It is about the mobilization of opinion and support, not of armed troops. It concerns defending and improving the workings of democracy, including the acceptance of procedures and practices that eschew those of war and dirty hands. And when violence or lying is used, it is because democratic procedures and principles have been thwarted, so that citizens' opportunities to be heard and treated with respect are denied and openness to change suppressed. Dirty hands may be defensible when democracy is denied or democratic processes are subverted, or when it's a matter of self-defence or the defence of others under attack, or when all other avenues have been exhausted—but only then. The notion that secrecy, law-breaking, and covert violence are necessary resources in the arsenal of those entrusted with the responsibility of promoting the principles and project of democracy and acting as democratic representatives should be seen not as a paradox but, in the words of C.A.J. Coady, as "corrosive of the basic ideals of democracy."[46]

In practice, supporting such ideals requires exhibiting an affirmation of politics and its distinctiveness over war; it means fighting for and within a context of free and open elections and the absence of intimidation, coercion, and punishment for peaceful political activities, and for the door to change remaining open. What this means, *contra* Trotsky, is the acceptance of the democratic legitimacy of class struggle, but *not* class war. The Sartrean and Trotskyist defence of "lying and worse" as "an inseparable part of the class struggle"[47] brilliantly expresses the pull of dirty hands—whichever side of the struggle one is on—but it is in fact quite at odds with Marx and Engels's declaration in the Communist Manifesto that "Communists disdain to conceal their views and aims."[48] And it is counter to the requirements of ethical democratic politics.[49]

Notes

An earlier version of this essay was first presented to the Dirty Hands Workshop held at York University, December 1993.

1 From transcripts of congressional committees of inquiry into Iran-Contra as cited by David Nacht, "The Iran-Contra Affair," *Ethics and Politics: Cases and Comments*, ed. Amy Gutmann and Dennis Thompson. 2nd ed. (Chicago: Nielson-Hall Publishers, 1990) 56.

2 *The Toronto Star*, 12 Jan. 1978 and 24 July 1980.

3 Michael Walzer, "Political Action. The Problem of Dirty Hands," *Philosophy and Public Affairs* 2 (Winter, 1973): 174.

4 Walzer 166.

5 Hollis, "Dirty Hands," *British Journal of Political Science* 12 (1982): 396.

6 W. Kenneth Howard also draws attention to the presumptive use of "we" in the dirty hands literature; see his "Must Public Hands Be Dirty," *The Journal of Value Inquiry* 11 (Spring 1977): 34.

7 Machiavelli, "The Discourses," *Selected Political Writings*, ed. D. Wooton, Bk. 1, Ch. 9: 108.

8 Machiavelli, "Discourses," Bk. 3, Ch. 34: 215.

9 Machiavelli, "Discourses," Bk. 1, Ch. 9: 108; "The Prince," *Selected Political Writings* (Indianapolis: Hackett, 1994) Ch. 14: 45.

10 See David Wooton's "Introduction" to his edition of Machiavelli, *Selected Political Writings* xi.

11 Stanley I. Benn, "Private and Public Morality: Clean Living and Dirty Hands", *Public and Private in Social Life*, ed. S.I. Benn and G.F. Gauss (New York: St. Martins, 1983) 167.

12 Hollis 396.

13 I have addressed the issue of reliance on law and constitutional measures in contradistinction to violence with examples more fully in my "The Use and Abuse of Politics" *Moral Expertise: Studies in Practical and Professional*, ed. Donald MacNiven (London: Routledge, 1990).

14 "Letter From The Birmingham City Jail," *Applied Ethics: A Multicultural Approach*, ed. Larry May and Shari Collins Sharratt (New Jersey: Prentice Hall, 1994) 243.

15 Max Weber, "Politics as a Vocation," *From Max Weber: Essays in Sociology*, ed. and trans., H.H. Gerth and C.W. Mills (New York: Oxford University Press, 1973) 42.

16 *Capitalism, Socialism and Democracy*, 3rd ed. (New York: Harper and Row, 1950) 269-270.

17 The term "thoroughgoing" was used by Robert Lynd to refer to an ideal democracy "in which social structure and all its institutions would have coherence in expressing and implementing democratic values." Robert S. Lynd, "Power in American Society," *Problems of Power in American Democracy*, ed. A. Kornhauser (Detroit: Wayne State University Press, 1957). Persuasive arguments that democracy is much more than a formal method for choosing or authorizing governments, that it requires effective participation by the populace in agenda-setting and decision-making and cannot be squared with elite rule in either political or economic organizations can be found in the work of John Dewey, e.g. *Democracy and Education* (New York: The Macmillan Company, 1916). The case against the narrow approach to democracy has been elaborated more recently, with differing

emphases, by e.g. C.B. Macpherson, e.g. *Democratic Theory: Essays in Retrieval* (Oxford: Oxford University Press, 1973) and his *The Life and Times of Liberal Democracy* (Oxford: Oxford University Press, 1976); Robert Dahl, *A Preface to Economic Democracy* (Berkeley: University of California Press, 1985) and his *Democracy and Its Critics* (New Haven: Yale University Press, 1989); and Alan Gewirth, *The Community of Rights* (Chicago: University of Chicago Press, 1996).

18 John Dewey, *The Political Writings*, eds. Debra Morris and Ian Shapiro (Indianapolis: Hackett, 1993) 111. Mutual respect both underlies and is expressed in the "one person, one vote" axiom of democracy, which in turn combines both a procedural and substantive standard. Mutual respect as a crucial aspect of social and political equality has been discussed by Bernard Williams, "Equality," *Philosophy, Politics and Society, Second Series*, ed. Peter Laslett and W.G. Runciman (Oxford: Basil Blackwell, 1969) 110-131; Ronald Dworkin, *Taking Rights Seriously* (Cambridge: Harvard University Press, 1978); more recently, Alan Gewirth emphasizes "the mutuality whereby human rights require that each person both respect the freedom and well-being of all other persons and have her freedom and well-being respected by all other persons." See Gewirth, *The Community of Rights* 19. In the revision of his theory of justice as fairness John Rawls notes that "fair terms of social cooperation" require cooperation "on the basis of mutual respect." See Rawls, *Political Liberalism* (New York: Columbia University Press, 1996) 303.

19 Walzer 167-68.

20 Albert Camus, *The Rebel: An Essay on Man in Revolt* (New York: Vintage Books, 1956).

21 Camus 285.

22 Camus's view that death somehow consecrates what the assassin has done is remarkable—and seems remarkably inconsistent—for someone who argued philosophically against suicide and opposed capital punishment on principle as adamantly as did Camus, but that is a puzzle that cannot be pursued here.

23 Camus 192.

24 Camus 292.

25 Camus 291.

26 Walzer 166.

27 When Kenneth Howard deals with the example, he finds it a trivial one or one that doesn't even bear the designation of a dirty-hands problem because it is too much like normal political activity! Howard, "Must Public Hands Be Dirty?" 32.

28 C.A.J. Coady, "Dirty Hands," *A Companion to Contemporary Political Philosophy*, ed. Robert E. Goodin and Philip Petit (Oxford: Blackwell, 1995) 426.

29 Mr. Justice Louis D. Brandeis, dissenting in *Olmstead v United States* 277 US 438, 475 (1928).

30 Coady 426.

31 See Ian Greene and David P. Shugarman, *Honest Politics* 173. Arguments that the term democratic ought not to be applied to cases where majoritarian decisions undermine basic democratic values and processes and reduce effective equal participation rights of citizens are presented by Dahl in *Democracy and Its Critics* 170-172 and Gewirth 324-325.

32 Quoted by Anne Collins, *In The Sleep Room* (Toronto: Key Porter Books, 1997) 32.

33 The case of Cyrus Vance's decision to resign from the Carter inner circle after lying to allies about the US's commitment not to use force to release American Embassy hostages in Iran would seem to be another. See Dennis Thompson, *Political Ethics and Public Office* 18, 19.

34 Collins 34.

35 Tony Judt, "Counsels on Foreign Relations" *New York Review of Books* XLV:13 (August 13, 1998): 54-60.

36 Judt 59.

37 These examples are discussed in *Honest Politics,* Ch. 7.

38 This and the preceding three sentences are, with slight revision, from Shugarman, "The Use and Abuse of Politics," *Moral Expertise: Studies in Practical and Professional Ethics,* ed. Don MacNiven (New York: Routledge, 1990) 215.

39 Sissela Bok, *Lying: Moral Choice in Political and Private Life* (New York: Pantheon Books, 1978) 75-77.

40 Walzer 176.

41 Walzer 149.

42 This and the preceding two sentences are from "The Use and Abuse of Politics" 215.

43 This connection was not adequately addressed in my earlier assessment of the contradictions existing between democratic expectations and dirty hands advocacy. See Ian Greene and David P. Shugarman, *Honest Politics* (Toronto: James Lorimer, 1997) Ch. 7.

44 Maurice Merleau-Ponty, *Humanism and Terror* (Boston: Beacon Press, 1969) 169.

45 Leon Trotsky, *Their Morals and Ours* (New York: Pathfinder Press, 1973) 28.

46 Coady 426.

47 Trotsky.

48 Karl Marx and Friedrick Engels, *The Communist Manifesto,* ed. Samuel Beer (New York: Appleton-Century-Crofts, 1955) 46.

49 This paper owes much to discussion with and comments by Ian Greene and Paul Rynard and to comments by Magnus Gunther, Gregory Baum, and David Bedford on earlier versions. It also benefitted from responses to related drafts presented to an international relations seminar at the University of Amsterdam organized by Henk Overbeek, and to a comparative politics seminar chaired by Frieder Schlupp at the University of Konstanz.

Selected Classic Statements on Dirty Hands

Niccolò Machiavelli

From *Selected Political Writings*, ed. and trans. David Wooten
(Indianapolis: Hackett, 1994) 45, 48, 53-55, 70, 128-29, 214.

FROM **THE PRINCE**

A ruler, then, should have no other concern, no other thought, should pay attention to nothing aside from war, military institutions, and the training of his soldiers. For this is the only field in which a ruler has to excel. ...

[M]any authors have constructed imaginary republics and principalities that have never existed in practice and never could; for the gap between how people actually behave and how they ought to behave is so great that anyone who ignores everyday reality in order to live up to an ideal will soon discover he has been taught how to destroy himself, not how to preserve himself. For anyone who wants to act the part of a good man in all circumstances will bring about his own ruin, for those he has to deal with will not all be good. So it is necessary for a ruler, if he wants to hold on to power, to learn how not to be good, and to know when it is and when it is not necessary to use this knowledge...

Everybody recognizes how praiseworthy it is for a ruler to keep his word and to live a life of integrity, without relying on craftiness. Nevertheless, we see that in practice, in these days, those rulers who have not thought it important to keep their word have achieved great things, and have known how to employ cunning to confuse and disorientate other men. In the end, they have been able to overcome those who have placed store in integrity.

You should therefore know there are two ways to fight: one while respecting the rules, the other with no holds barred. Men alone fight in the first fashion, and animals fight in the second. But because you cannot always win if you respect the rules, you must be prepared to break them. A ruler, in particular, needs to know how to be both an animal and a man....

Since a ruler, then, needs to know how to make good use of beastly qualities, he should take as his models among the animals both the fox and the lion, for the lion does not know how to avoid traps, and the fox is easily overpowered by wolves. So you must be a fox when it comes to suspecting a trap, and a lion when it comes to making the wolves turn tail. Those who simply act like a lion all the time do not understand their business. So you see a wise ruler cannot, and should not, keep his word when doing so is to his disadvantage, and when the reasons that led him to promise to do so no longer apply. Of course, if all men were good, this advice would be bad; but since men are wicked and will not keep faith with you, you need not keep faith with them....

A ruler, and particularly a ruler who is new to power, cannot conform to all those rules that men who are thought good are expected to respect, for he is often obliged, in order to hold on to power, to break his word, to be uncharitable, inhumane, and irreligious. So he must be mentally prepared to act as circumstances and changes in fortune require. As I have said, he should do what is right if he can; but he must be prepared to do wrong if necessary...

... In the behavior of all men, and particularly of rulers, against whom there is no recourse at law, people judge by the outcome. So if a ruler wins wars and holds on to power, the means he has employed will always be judged honorable, and everyone will praise them...

... Do not for a moment think any state can always take safe decisions, but rather think every decision you take involves risks, for it is in the nature of things that you cannot take precautions against one danger without opening yourself to another. Prudence consists in knowing how to assess risks and in accepting the lesser evil as a good.

FROM **THE DISCOURSES**

"If one had wanted to preserve liberty in Rome despite the progress of corruption, it would have been necessary to go beyond passing new laws from time to time and to construct new political institutions. For the institutions and ways of life one needs to establish if men are corrupt are different from those that are appropriate if they are good; if one has different materials with which to work, one must build a quite different structure. But these institutions would either have had to be reformed all at once, as soon as it was realized that as a whole they were no longer appropriate, or else they would have had to be revised little by little, as each particular institution was seen to be in need of reform. Both of these procedures are, in my view, almost impossible to carry out. For if you want to revise institutions little by little and one by one, you need to have some wise man proposing change, someone who sees problems almost before they have developed and catches them at the moment of their birth. In the whole history of a city there might easily prove to be not a single person as wise as this. And even if there were such a person, he would never be able to persuade others to recognize the truth of his arguments, for men who have been used to living in a particular way have no desire to change it, especially when they do not find themselves standing toe-to-toe with a problem, but rather are asked to accept its existence on the basis of someone else's conjectures and hypotheses. On the other hand, if one hopes to change the institutions at a stroke, when everyone has come to recognize that they are defective, then I maintain defects that are easy to recognize are hard to correct. For such reforms, ordinary measures are insufficient, for we are dealing with a situation where the ordinary measures have proved defective. So one has to adopt extraordinary measures, such as resorting to violence and civil war. One's primary goal must be to become sole ruler of the city, so that one can do with it as one pleases. In order to reconstruct the constitution of a city so that it fosters political liberty, one needs to be a man with good intentions; but people who resort to arms in order to seize power in a republic are people whose methods are bad. So you can see that there will hardly ever be an occasion when a good man, using wicked means, but using them in the service of good ends, will want to become sole ruler; or when a wicked man, having become sole ruler, wants to do good. It will not occur to him to use for good the power he has acquired by wicked means.

So I have now explained the difficulties that would have to be overcome if one were to try to preserve liberty in a corrupt city or to attempt to establish it from scratch. These difficulties are, in effect, insuperable. Even if one had the opportunity to carry out reform or revolution, one would have to introduce a constitution that was more monarchical than democratic. For men who were so ill-behaved that they could not be kept in order by the laws would need to be kept in check by a more or less arbitrary authority...

If you are discussing nothing less than the safety of the homeland, then you should pay no attention to what is just or what is unjust, or to what is kind or cruel, or to what is praiseworthy or shameful. You should put every other consideration aside, and you should adopt wholeheartedly the policy most likely to save your homeland's life and preserve her liberty.

Leon Trotsky

From "Their Morals and Ours" in Leon Trotsky, John Dewey, George Novack, *Their Morals and Ours: Marxist vs. Liberal Views on Morality.* (New York: Pathfinder Press, 1973) 36-39, 48-49; italics in original).

Civil war is the most severe of all forms of war. It is unthinkable not only without violence against tertiary figures but, under contemporary technique, without killing old men, old women, and children. Must one be reminded of Spain? The only possible answer of the "friends" of Republican Spain sounds like this: Civil war is better than fascist slavery. But this completely correct answer merely signifies that the *end* (democracy or socialism) justifies, under certain conditions, such *means* as violence and murder. Not to speak about lies! Without lies war would be as unimaginable as a machine without oil. In order to safeguard even the session of the Cortes (February 1, 1938) from fascist bombs, the Barcelona government several times deliberately deceived journalists and their own population. Could it have acted in any other way? Whoever accepts the end: victory over Franco, must accept the means: civil war with its wake of horrors and crimes.

Nevertheless, lying and violence "in themselves" warrant condemnation? Of course, even as does the class society which generates them. A society without social contradictions will naturally be a society without lies and violence. However there is no way of building a bridge to that society save by revolutionary, that is, violent means. The revolution itself is a product of class society and of necessity bears its traits. From the point of view of "eternal truths" revolution is of course "antimoral." But this merely means that idealist morality is counterrevolutionary, that is, in the service of the exploiters.

"Civil war," will perhaps respond the philosopher caught unawares, "is however a sad exception. But in peaceful times a healthy socialist movement should manage without violence and lying." Such an answer however represents nothing less than a pathetic evasion. There is no impervious demarcation between 'peaceful' class struggle and revolution. Every strike embodies in an unexpanded form all the elements of civil war. Each side strives to impress the opponent with an exaggerated picture of its resoluteness to struggle and its material resources. Through their press, agents, and spies the capitalists labor to frighten and demoralize the strikers. From their side, the workers' pickets, where persuasion does not avail, are compelled to resort to force. Thus 'lying and worse' are an inseparable part of the class struggle even in its most elementary form. It remains to be added that the very conception of *truth* and *lie* was born of social contradictions...

After the Paris Commune had been drowned in blood and the reactionary knaves of the whole world dragged its banner in the filth of vilification and slander, there were not a few democratic philistines who, adapting themselves to reaction, slandered the Communards for shooting sixty-four hostages headed by the Paris archbishop. Marx did not hesitate a moment in defending this bloody act of the Commune. In a circular issued by the General Council of the First International, which seethes with the fiery eruption of lava, Marx first reminds us of the bourgeoisie adopting the institution of hostages in the struggle against both colonial peoples and their own toiling masses and afterward refers to the systematic execution of the Commune captives by the frenzied reactionaries....

"Just the same," the moralist continues to insist, "does it mean that in the class struggle against capitalists all means are permissible: lying, frame-up, betrayal, murder, and so on?" Permissible and obligatory are those and only those means, we answer, which unite the revolutionary proletariat, fill their hearts with irreconcilable hostility to oppression, teach them contempt for official morality and its democratic echoers, imbue them with consciousness of their own historic mission, raise their courage and spirit of self-sacrifice in the struggle. Precisely from this it flows that *not* all means are permissible. When we say that the end justifies the means, then for us the conclusion follows that the great revolutionary end spurns those base means and ways which set one part of the working class against other parts, or attempt to make the masses happy without their participation; or lower the faith of the masses in themselves and their organization, replacing it by worship for the "leaders."

Max Weber

From "Politics as a Vocation," *From Max Weber*, ed. and trans. H. H. Gerth and C. Wright Mills (New York: Oxford University Press, 1973) 118-126; italics in original.

Now then, what relations do ethics and politics actually have? Have the two nothing whatever to do with one another, as has occasionally been said? Or, is the reverse true: that the ethic of political conduct is identical with that of any other conduct? Occasionally, an exclusive choice has been believed to exist between the two propositions—either the one or the other proposition must be correct. But is it true that any ethic of the world could establish commandments of identical content for erotic, business, familial, and official relations; for the relations to one's wife, to the greengrocer, the son, the competitor, the friend, the defendant? Should it really matter so little for the ethical demands on politics that politics operates with very special means, namely, power backed up by *violence*? Do we not see that the Bolshevik and the Spartacist ideologists bring about exactly the same results as any militaristic dictator just because they use this political means? In what but the persons of the power-holders and their dilettantism does the rule of the workers' and soldiers' councils differ from the rule of any power-holder of the old regime? In what way does the polemic of most representatives of the presumably new ethic differ from that of the opponents which they criticized, or the ethic of any other demagogues? In their noble intention, people will say. Good! But it is the means about which we speak here, and the adversaries, in complete subjective sincerity, claim, in the very same way, that their ultimate intentions are of lofty character. "All they that take the sword shall perish with the sword" and fighting is everywhere fighting. Hence, the ethic of the Sermon on the Mount.

By the Sermon on the Mount, we mean the absolute ethic of the gospel, which is a more serious matter than those who are fond of quoting these commandments today believe. This ethic is no joking matter. The same holds for this ethic as has been said of causality in science: it is not a cab, which one can have stopped at one's pleasure; it is all or nothing. This is precisely the meaning of the gospel, if trivialities are not to result. Hence, for instance, it was said of the wealthy young man, 'He went away sorrowful: for he had great possessions.' The evangelist commandment, however, is unconditional and unambiguous: give what thou hast—absolutely everything. The politician will say that this is a socially senseless imposition as long as it is not carried out everywhere. Thus the politician upholds taxation, confiscatory taxation, outright confiscation; in a word, compulsion and regulation for all. The ethical commandment, however, is not at all concerned about that, and this unconcern is its essence. Or, take the example, "turn the other cheek": This command is unconditional and does not question the source of the other's authority to strike. Except for the saint it is an ethic of indignity....

Finally, let us consider the duty of truthfulness. For the absolute ethic it holds unconditionally.... The politician will find that as a result truth will not be furthered but certainly obscured through abuse and unleashing of passion; only an all-round procedure may have consequences for a nation that cannot be remedied for decades. But the absolute ethic just does not *ask* for "consequences." That is the decisive point.

We must be clear about the fact that all ethically oriented conduct may be guided by one of the two fundamentally differing and irreconcilably opposed maxims: conduct can be oriented to an "ethic of ultimate ends" or to an "ethic of responsibility." This is not to say that an ethic of responsibility is identical with unprincipled opportunism. Naturally nobody says that. However, there is an abysmal contrast between conduct that follows the maxim of an ethic of ultimate ends—that is, in religious terms, "The Christian does rightly and leaves the results with the Lord"—and conduct that follows the maxim of an ethic of responsibility, in which case one has to give an account of the foreseeable results of one's action....

But even herewith the problem is not yet exhausted. No ethics in the world can dodge the fact that in numerous instances the attainment of "good" ends is bound to the fact that one must be willing to pay the price of using morally dubious means or at least dangerous ones—and facing the possibility or even the probability of evil ramifications. From no ethics in the world can it be concluded when and to what extent the ethically good purpose 'justifies' the ethically dangerous means and ramifications.

The decisive means for politics is violence. You may see the extent of the tension between means and ends, when viewed ethically, from the following: as is generally known, even during the war the revolutionary socialists (Zimmerwald faction) professed a principle that one might strikingly formulate: "If we face the choice either of some more years of war and then revolution, or peace now and no revolution, we choose—some more years of war!" Upon the further question: "What can this revolution bring about?" every scientifically trained socialist would have had the answer: One cannot speak of a transition to an economy that in our sense could be called socialist; a bourgeois economy will re-emerge, merely stripped of its feudal elements and the dynastic vestiges. For this very modest result, they are willing to face "some more years of war." One may well say that even with a very robust socialist conviction one might reject a purpose that demands such means. With Bolshevism and Spartacism, and, in general, with any kind of revolutionary socialism, it is precisely the same thing. It is of course utterly ridiculous if the power politicians of the old regime are morally denounced for their use of the same means, however justified the rejection of their *aims* may be.

The ethic of ultimate ends apparently must go to pieces on the problem of the justification of means by ends. As a matter of fact, logically it has only the possibility of rejecting all action that employs morally dangerous means—in theory! In the world of realities, as a rule, we encounter the ever-renewed experience that the adherent of an ethic of ultimate ends suddenly turns into a chiliastic prophet. Those, for example, who have just preached "love against violence" now call for the use of force for the *last* violent deed, which would then lead to a state of affairs in which *all* violence is annihilated. In the same manner, our officers told the soldiers before every offensive: "This will be the last one; this one will bring victory and therewith peace." The proponent of an ethic of absolute ends cannot stand up under the ethical irrationality of the world. He is a cosmic-ethical "rationalist." Those of you who know Dostoievski will remember the scene of the 'Grand Inquisitor,' where the problem is poignantly unfolded. If one makes any concessions at all to the principle that the end justifies the means, it is not possible to bring an ethic of ultimate ends and an ethic of responsibility under one roof or to decree ethically which end should justify which means....

The age-old problem of theodicy consists of the very question of how it is that a power which is said to be at once omnipotent and kind could have created such an irrational world of undeserved suffering, unpunished injustice, and hopeless stupidity. Either this power is not omnipotent or not kind, or, entirely different principles of compensation and reward govern our life—principles we may interpret metaphysically, or even principles that forever escape our comprehension.

This problem—the experience of the irrationality of the world—has been the driving force of all religious evolution. The Indian doctrine of karma, Persian dualism, the doctrine of original sin, predestination and the *deus absconditus*, all these have grown out of this experience. Also the early Christians knew full well the world is governed by demons and that he who lets himself in for politics, that is, for power and force as means, contracts with diabolical powers and for his action it is *not* true that good can follow only from good and evil only from evil, but that often the opposite is true. Anyone who fails to see this is, indeed, a political infant....

Whoever wants to engage in politics at all, and especially in politics as a vocation, has to realize these ethical paradoxes. He must know that he is responsible for what may become of himself under the impact of these paradoxes. I repeat, he lets himself in for the diabolic forces lurking in all violence....

Jean-Paul Sartre

From "Dirty Hands," *No Exit: And Three Other Plays*, trans. Lionel Abel (New York: Vintage Books, 1955) 221-4.

HUGO: The party has one program: the realization of a socialist economy, and one method of achieving it: the class struggle. You are going to use it to pursue a policy of class collaboration in the framework of a capitalist economy. For years you will have to cheat, trick, and maneuver; we'll go from compromise to compromise. Before your comrades, you will have to defend the reactionary measures taken by the government in which you participate. No one will understand: the hardened ones will leave us, the others will lose whatever political faith they have just acquired. We shall be contaminated, weakened, disoriented; we shall become reformists and nationalists; in the end the bourgeois parties won't even have to go to the trouble of liquidating us. Hoederer! This party is yours, you cannot have forgotten the hardships you endured to forge it, the sacrifices that were required, the discipline you had to impose. I beg you: don't sacrifice it with your own hands.

HOEDERER: What babbling! If you don't want to take chances you shouldn't be in politics...

HUGO: You think I'm the only one who has these ideas? Wasn't it for these ideas that our comrades were killed by the Regent's police? Don't you see that we'll betray them if we use the party to whitewash their assassins?

HOEDERER: I don't give a damn for the dead. They died for the party, and the party can decide as it sees fit about them. I pursue a policy of the living for the living.

HUGO: And do you think that the living will agree to your schemes?

HOEDERER: We'll get them to swallow them little by little.

HUGO: By lying to them?

HOEDERER: By lying to them sometimes.

HUGO: You—you seem so real, so solid! How can you stand it to lie to your comrades?

HOEDERER: Why not? We're at war, and it's not customary to keep each individual soldier posted hour by hour on operations.

HUGO: Hoederer, I—I know better than you what lies are like. In my father's home everybody lied to himself, everybody lied to me. I couldn't breathe until I joined the party. Then for the first time I saw men who didn't lie to other men. Everyone could have confidence in everyone else, the humblest militant had the feeling that the orders of the leaders revealed to him his own secret will, and if things got tough, each one knew why he was ready to die. You're not going to—

HOEDERER: What are you talking about?

HUGO: Our party.

HOEDERER: Our party? But we have always told lies, just like any other party. And you, Hugo, are you sure that you've never lied, never lied to yourself, that you are not even lying to me this very moment?

HUGO: I never lie to my comrades. I—Why should you fight for the liberation of men, if you think no more of them than to stuff their heads with falsehoods?

HOEDERER: I'll lie when I must, and I have contempt for no one. I wasn't the one who invented lying. It grew out of a society divided into classes, and each one of us has inherited it from birth. We shall not abolish lying by refusing to tell lies, but by using every means at hand to abolish classes.

HUGO: All means are not good.

HOEDERER: All means are good when they're effective...How you cling to your purity, young man! How afraid you are to soil your hands! All right, stay pure! What good will it do? Why did you join us? Purity is an idea for a yogi or a monk. You intellectuals and bourgeois anarchists use it as a pretext for doing nothing. To do nothing, to remain motionless, arms at your sides, wearing kid gloves. Well, I have dirty hands. Right up to the elbows. I've plunged them in filth and blood. But what do you hope? Do you think you can govern innocently?

Michael Walzer

From "Political Action: The Problem of Dirty Hands," *Philosophy and Public Affairs* 2:2 (1973): 160-80; 164-168, 174, 179.

"...[T]he sheer weight of official violence in human history does suggest the kind of power to which politicians aspire, the kind of power they want to wield, and it may point to the roots of our half-conscious dislike and unease. The men who act for us and in our name are often killers, or seem to become killers too quickly and too easily.

Knowing all this or most of it, good and decent people still enter political life, aiming at some specific reform or seeking a general reformation. They are then required to learn the lesson Machiavelli set out to teach: 'how not to be good'... No one succeeds in politics without getting his hands dirty... For sometimes it is right to try to succeed, and then it must also be right to get one's hands dirty. But one's hands get dirty from doing what it is wrong to do. And how can it be wrong to do what is right? Or, how can we get our hands dirty by doing what we ought to do?...

... We know he [the moral politician] is doing right when he makes the deal [with a dishonest ward boss] because he knows he is doing wrong. I don't mean merely that he will feel badly or even very badly after he makes the deal. If he is the good man I am imagining him to be, he will feel guilty, that is, he will believe himself to be guilty. That is what it means to have dirty hands...

... His willingness to acknowledge and bear (and perhaps to repent and do penance for) his guilt is evidence, and it is the only evidence he can offer us, both that he is not too good for politics and that he is good enough. Here is the moral politician: it is by his dirty hands that we know him. If he were a moral man and nothing else, his hands would not be dirty; if he were a politician and nothing else, he would pretend that they were clean....

That is the dilemma of dirty hands as it has been experienced by political actors and written about in the literature of political action. I don't want to argue that it is only a political dilemma. No doubt we can get our hands dirty in private life also, and sometimes, no doubt, we should. But the issue is posed most dramatically in politics for the three reasons that make political life the kind of life it is, because we claim to act for others but also serve ourselves, rule over others, and use violence against them. It is easy to get one's hands dirty in politics and it is often right to do so. But it is not easy to teach a good man how not to be good, nor is it easy to explain such a man to himself once he has committed whatever crimes are required of him....

In most cases of civil disobedience the laws of the state are broken for moral reasons, and the state provides the punishment. In most cases of dirty hands moral rules are broken for reasons of state, and no one provides the punishment. There is rarely a Czarist executioner waiting in the wings for politicians with dirty hands, even the most deserving among them. Moral rules are not usually enforced against the sort of actor I am considering, largely because he acts in an official capacity. If they were enforced, dirty hands would be no problem. We would simply honor the man who did bad in order to do good, and at the same time we would punish him. We would honor him for the good he has done, and we would punish him for the bad he has done. We would punish him, that is, for the same reasons we punish anyone else.... Short of the priest and the confessional, there are no authorities to whom we might entrust the task.

Select Bibliography

Adams, R.M. "Involuntary Sins," *Philosophical Review* 94 (1985): 3-31.

Anderson, Charles. "Pragmatic Liberalism, the Rule of Law, and the Pluralist Regime," in Stephen L. Elkin and Karol Edward Soltan, eds., *A New Constitutionalism: Designing Political Institutions for a Good Society*. Chicago: The University of Chicago Press, 1993.

Andrew, E. "Equality of Opportunity as the Noble Lie," *History of Political Thought* 10:4 (Winter 1989): 578-95.

Anscombe, G.E.M. *Ethics, Religion and Politics*. Minneapolis, Minnesota: University of Minnesota Press, 1981.

———. "Modern Moral Philosophy," *Collected Philosophical Papers*. Oxford: Blackwell, 1981.

Allett, John. "Bernard Shaw and Dirty Hands Politics: A Comparison of *Mrs Warren's Profession* and *Major Barbara*," *Journal of Social Philosophy* 26:2 (Fall 1995): 32-45.

Applbaum, Arthur Isak. "Democratic Legitimacy and Official Discretion," *Philosophy and Public Affairs* 21:3 (Summer 1992): 240-74.

———. *Ethics for Adversaries: The Morality of Roles in Public and Professional Life*. Princeton, NJ: Princeton University Press, 1999.

Arendt, Hannah. *Between Past and Future*. New York. Viking Press, 1954.

———. "On Humanity in Dark Times: Thoughts on Lessing," *Men in Dark Times*. New York: Harcourt Brace Jovanovich, 1955.

———. *Eichmann in Jerusalem: A Report on the Banality of Evil*. Middlesex, England: Penguin, 1963.

———. "Lying and Politics," *Crises of the Republic*. New York: Harcourt Brace Jovanovich, 1969.

———. *Lectures on Kant's Political Philosophy*. Ronald Beiner, ed., Chicago: University of Chicago Press, 1982.

Aristotle. *Nicomachean Ethics*. Terence Irwin, trans. Indianapolis: Hackett Publishing, 1985.

Baier, Annette. "Trust and Anti-Trust," *Ethics* 96 (1986): 231-60.

Barry, B. *Liberty and Justice*. Oxford: Clarendon Press, 1991.

Bayles, Michael D. *Professional Ethics*. Belmont, CA.: Wadsworth, 1989.

Benn, Stanely. "Private and Public Morality: Clean Living and Dirty Hands," in S. Benn and G.F. Gauss, eds., *Public and Private in Social Life*. New York: St. Martin's Press, 1983.

Berlin, I. *Concepts and Categories*. London: Hogarth Press, 1978.

Bok, Sissela. *Lying: Moral Choice In Public and Private Life*. New York: Pantheon, 1978.

———. *Secrets: On the Ethics of Concealment and Revelation*. New York: Pantheon, 1982.

———. *A Strategy for Peace*. New York: Vintage Books, 1989.

———. *Common Values*. Columbia, Mo.: University of Missouri Press, 1995.

Branch, Taylor. "The Odd Couple," *Washington Monthly* (October 1971).

Brandt, R. "Utilitarianism and the Rules of War," *Philosophy and Public Affairs* 1 (1972): 145-65.

Braybrooke, David. *Traffic Congestion Goes Through the Issue Machine*. London: Routledge and Kegan Paul, 1974.

Braybrooke David, and Charles E. Lindblom. *A Strategy of Decision: Policy Evaluation as a Social Process*. New York: The Free Press of Glencoe, 1963.

Braybrooke, David, Bryson Brown, and Peter K. Schotch. *Logic on the Track of Social Change*. Oxford: Clarendon Library of Logic and Philosophy, 1996.

Brecht, Bertolt. *The Resistible Rise of Arturo Ui*. London: Eyre Methuen, 1976.

———. "The Measures Taken," *The Measures Taken and Other Lehrstucke*. London: Erye Metheun, 1977.

Buckler, Steve. *Dirty Hands: The Problem of Political Morality*. Brookfield, Vermont: Ashgate Publishing, 1993.

Califano, Joseph. "Governing America," in A. Gutmann and D. Thompson, eds., *Ethics and Politics*, 1990.

Camus, Albert. "The Just Assassins," in *Caligula and Three Other Plays*, Stuart Gilbert, trans. New York: Knopf, 1958.

———. *The Rebel*. Anthony Bower, trans. New York: Vintage Books, 1956.

Carr, David. *Time, Narrative and History*. Bloomington: Indiana University Press, 1986.

Coady, C.A.J. "Politics and the Problem of Dirty Hands," in Peter Singer, ed., *A Companion to Ethics*. Oxford: Blackwell, 1991.

———. "Dirty Hands," in Robert E. Goodin and Philip Pettit, *A Companion to Contemporary Political Philosophy*. Oxford: Blackwell Publishers, 1995.

Cohen, M., T. Nagel, and T. Scanlon, eds., *War and Moral Responsibility: A Philosophy and Public Affairs Reader*. Princeton: Princeton University Press, 1974.

Collins, Anne. *In the Sleep Room: The Story of the C.I.A. Brainwashing Experiments in Canada*. Toronto: Key Porter Books, 1997.

Conrad, Joseph. *Heart of Darkness and The Secret Sharer*. Toronto: Bantam Books, 1981.

Cox, Archibald. "Ethics In Government: The Cornerstone of Public Trust," *West Virginia Law Review* 94:2 (Winter 1991-2): 281-300.

Cragg, Wes, ed. *Contemporary Moral Issues*. Toronto: McGraw-Hill Ryerson, 1992.

Cunningham, Anthony. "The Moral Importance of Dirty Hands," *The Journal of Value Inquiry* 26:2 (April, 1992): 239-50.

Dancy, Jonathan. "Caring About Justice," *Philosophy* 67 (1992): 447-66.

de George, Richard T. *Competing With Integrity in International Business*. New York: Oxford University Press, 1993.

de Wijze, Stephen. "Dirty Hands—Doing Wrong To Do Right," *South African Journal of Philosophy* 13:1 (1994): 27-33.

———. "The Real Issues Concerning Dirty Hands—A Response to Kai Nielson," *South African Journal of Philosophy* 15:4 (November 1996): 149-151.

Deigh, John. "Ethics," in Robert Audi, ed., *The Cambridge Dictionary of Philosophy.* Cambridge University Press, 1995.

Dewey, John. *Liberalism and Social Action.* New York: Putnam, 1963.

———. *The Political Writings.* Debra Morris and Ian Shapiro, eds. Indianapolis: Hackett, 1993.

Dobel, J. Patrick. "The Corruption of A State," *American Political Science Review* 72:3 (1978): 958-73.

Donagan, Alan. *The Theory of Morality.* Chicago: University of Chicago Press, 1977.

Draper, Theodore. *A Very Thin Line: The Iran-Contra Affairs.* New York: Farrar, Straus, and Giroux, 1991.

Elkin, Stephen. "Constitutionalism's Successor," in S.L. Elkin and K.E. Soltan, eds., *A New Constitutionalism: Designing Political Institutions for a Good Society.* Chicago: The University of Chicago Press, 1993.

Elshtain, Jean. *Democracy on Trial.* Toronto: Anansi Press, 1993.

Finer, Herman. "Administrative Responsibility in Democratic Government," *Public Administration Review* 1 (1940/1941): 335-50.

Fleishman, Joel, Lance Liebman and Mark H. Moore, eds., *Public Duties: The Moral Obligations of Government Officials.* Cambridge, MA.: Harvard University Press, 1981.

Foley, Michael. *The Silence of Constitutions.* London: Routledge, 1989.

French, Peter. "Dirty Hands," in Peter French, *Ethics in Government.* Englewood Cliffs, N.J.: Prentice Hall, 1983.

Gaita, R. *Good and Evil: An Absolute Conception.* London: Macmillan Press, 1991.

Garret, Stephen A. *Conscience and Power: An Examination of Dirty Hands and Political Leadership.* New York: St. Martin's Press, 1996.

Geras, Norman. *Discourses of Extremity: Radical Ethics and Post-Marxist Extravagances.* London: Verso, 1990.

Gewirth, Alan. "Are There Any Absolute Rights?," in J. Waldron, ed., *Theories of Rights.* Oxford: Oxford University Press, 1984.

———. *The Community of Rights.* Chicago: University of Chicago Press, 1996.

Gilligan, Carol. *In A Different Voice.* Cambridge, Mass.: Harvard University Press, 1982.

Goodin, Robert. *Manipulating Politics.* New Haven: Yale University Press, 1980.

———. *Utilitarianism As A Public Philosophy.* New York: Cambridge University Press, 1995.

Greene, Ian, and David P. Shugarman. *Honest Politics: Seeking Integrity in Canadian Public Life.* Toronto: James Lorimer, 1997.

Greenspan, P. "Moral Dilemmas and Guilt," *Philosophical Studies* 43 (1983): 117-25.

Gross, Michael. *Ethics and Activism: The Theory and Practice of Political Morality.* Cambridge: Cambridge University Press, 1997.

Gutmann, Amy and Dennis F. Thompson, eds. *Ethics and Politics.* Chicago: Nelson-Hall, 1990.

Gutmann, Amy and Dennis F. Thompson. "Moral Conflict and Political Consensus," *Ethics* 101 (1990): 64-68.

Haber, J, ed. *Absolutism and its Consequentialist Critics.* Lanham, Md.: Rownian & Littlefield Publishers, 1994.

Hampshire, Stuart, ed. *Public and Private Morality.* Cambridge: Cambridge University Press, 1978.

Hampshire, Stuart. *Morality and Conflict.* Oxford, Blackwell, 1983.

——. *Innocence and Experience.* Cambridge: Harvard University Press, 1989.

Hardin, G. "Living on a Lifeboat," *Bioscience* 24:10 (1974): 561-68.

Hare, R.M. "Rules of War and Moral Reasoning," *Philosophy and Public Affairs* 1 (1972): 166-81.

——. *Moral Thinking: Its Levels, Methods and Point.* Oxford: Clarendon Press, 1981.

Hart, H.L.A. *The Concept of Law.* Oxford: Oxford University Press, 1961.

Heidenheimer, Arnold J., ed. *Political Corruption: Readings in Comparative Analysis.* New York: Holt, Rinehart and Winston, 1970.

Hobbes, Thomas. *Leviathan.* London: Collins Clear-Type Press, 1962.

Hoffman, S. *Duties Beyond Borders.* Syracuse: Syracuse University Press, 1981.

Hollis, Martin. "Dirty Hands," *British Journal of Political Science* 12 (1982): 385-98.

Howard, W.K. "Must Public Hands Be Dirty?," *Journal of Value Inquiry* 11 (Spring 1977): 29-40.

Jackson, F. "Internal Conflicts in Desires and Morals," *American Philosophical Quarterly* 22 (1985): 105-14.

Jamieson, Kathleen Hall. *Dirty Politics: Deception, Distraction, and Democracy.* New York: Oxford University Press, 1992.

Johnson, Peter. *Politics, Innocence, and the Limits of Goodness.* New York and London: Routledge, 1988.

——. *Frames of Deceit: A Study of the Loss and Recovery of Public and Private Trust.* Cambridge: Cambridge University Press, 1993.

Jones, Donald G., ed. *Private and Public Ethics.* Toronto: The Edwin Mellen Press, 1978.

Kant, Immanuel. *Kant: Political Writings,* 2nd ed. Hans Reiss, ed., H.B. Nisbet, trans., Cambridge: Cambridge University Press, 1991.

Kernaghan, Kenneth, and John Langford. *The Responsible Public Servant.* Toronto: Institute of Public Administratrion of Canada, 1990.

King, Anthony. "Executives," in F.I. Greenstein and N. W. Polsby, eds., *Handbook of Political Science.* Vol. 5. Reading, MA.: Addison-Wesley, 1975.

Kleist, H. *Michael Kohlhaas: From an Old Chronicle.* James Kirkup, trans., New York: The New American Library, 1960.

Korsgaard, Christine M. "The Right to Lie: Kant on Dealing with Evil," *Philosophy and Public Affairs* 15 (Fall 1986): 325-49.

Kuflik, Arthur. "Morality and Compromise," in J. Roland Pennock and John W. Chapman eds. *Compromise in Ethics, Law and Politics.* New York: New York University Press, 1979.

Lane, Henry, and Donald Simpson. "Bribery in International Business: Whose Problem Is It?," *Journal of Business Ethics* 3:1 (Feb. 1984): 35-42.

Langford, John and Allan Tupper, eds. *Corruption, Character and Conduct: Essays on Canadian Government Ethics.* Toronto: Oxford University Press, 1993.

Lax, David and James Sebenius. *Manager as Negotiator.* New York: Free Press, 1986.

Levi, Isaac. *Hard Choices: Decision Making Under Unresolved Conflict.* New York: Cambridge University Press, 1986.

Lindblom, Charles, and David K. Cohen. *Usable Knowledge: Social Science and Social Problem Solving*. New Haven: Yale University Press, 1979.

Lukes, Steven. "Marxism and Dirty Hands," *Social Philosophy and Policy* 3 (1986): 204-23 (reprinted in Lukes, *Moral Conflict and Politics*, 1991).

——. *Marxism and Morality*. Oxford: Oxford University Press, 1987.

——. *Moral Conflict and Politics*. Oxford: Clarendon Press, 1991.

Lynd, Robert S. "Power in American Society," in A. Kornhauser, ed. *Problems of Power in American Democracy*. Detroit: Wayne State University Press, 1957.

Lyons, David. "Utility and Rights," in J. Waldron, ed., *Theories of Right*. Oxford: Oxford University Press, 1984.

Machiavelli, Niccollò. *Selected Political Writings*, David Wooton, ed., and trans. Indianapolis: Hackett, 1994.

——. *The Chief Works and Others*. Vol. 2. Allan Gilbert, trans. Durham: Duke University Press, 1965.

——. *The Art of War*. Neal Wood, ed. Indianapolis: Bobbs-Merrill, 1965.

Madsen, Peter, and Jay Shafritz, eds. *Essentials of Government Ethics*. New York: Meridian, 1992.

Mancuso, Maureen. *The Ethical World of British MPs*. Montreal: McGill-Queen's University Press, 1995.

Marcus, R. "Moral Dilemmas and Ethical Consistency," *Journal of Philosophy* 77 (1980): 121-36.

Marcuse, H. "Ethics and Revolution," in Richard T. De George ed., *Ethics and Society: Original Essays on Contemporary Moral Problems*. Garden City, N.Y.: Anchor Books, 1966.

McGinn, Colin. *Moral Literacy: How To Do the Right Thing*. Minneapolis: Hacket, 1992.

McLellan, David, and Sean Sayers. *Socialism and Morality*. London: The MacMillan Press Ltd., 1990.

Merleau-Ponty, Maurice. *Humanism and Terror*. John O'Neill, trans., Boston: Beacon Press, 1969.

Mill, John Stuart. *Utilitarianism, On Liberty and Considerations On Representative Government*. Toronto: J.M. Dent and Sons Ltd., 1972.

Miller, R. "Marx and Aristotle: A Kind of Consequentialism," in K. Nielsen & S.C. Patten, eds., *Marx and Morality*. Guelph, Ontario: Canadian Association for Publishing in Philosophy, 1981.

Moore, Mark and Malcolm K. Sparrow. "David Goldman and California Legal Services," in Moore and Sparrow, *Ethics in Government: The Moral Challenge of Public Leadership*. Englewood Cliffs, New Jersey: Prentice-Hall, 1990.

Morris, H. *On Guilt and Innocence*. Berkeley: University of California Press, 1976.

Nagel, Thomas. "War and Massacre," *Philosophy and Public Affairs* 1 (1972): 123-44.

——. "Ruthlessness in Public Life," in S. Hampshire, ed., *Public and Private Morality*, 1978.

——. *Mortal Questions*. New York: Cambridge University Press, 1979.

——. "Moral Conflict and Political Legitimacy," *Philosophy and Public Affairs* 16 (Summer 1987): 215-40.

——. *Equality and Partiality*. New York: Oxford University Press, 1991.

Naipaul, V.S. *A Bend in the River*. New York: Modern Library, 1997.

Neustadt, Richard. *Presidential Power and the Modern Presidents*. New York: Free Press, 1960.

Nielsen, Kai. "On the Ethics of Revolution," *Radical Philosophy* 6 (1973): 17-19.

———. "Violence and Terrorism: Its Uses and Abuses," in B. M. Leiser, eds., *Values in Conflict*. New York: Macmillan Publishing Co., 1981.

———. "There is No Dilemma of Dirty Hands," *South African Journal of Philosophy* 15:1 (Fall, 1996): 1-7.

———. "There is No Dilemma of Dirty Hands: A Response to Stephen de Wijze," *South African Journal of Philosophy* 15:4 (Nov. 1996): 155-8.

———. *Marxism and the Moral Point of View: Morality, Ideology, and Historical Materialism*. Boulder, CO: Westview Press, 1989.

———. *Naturalism Without Foundations*. Buffalo, New York: Prometheus Press, 1996.

Noddings, Nell. *Women and Evil*. Berkeley: University of California Press, 1989.

Nozick, Robert. *Anarchy, State and Utopia*. Oxford: Blackwell, 1974.

Nussbaum, M. *The Fragility of Goodness: Luck and Ethics in Greek Tragedy and Philosophy*. Cambridge: Cambridge University Press, 1986.

O'Brien, Conor Cruise. *To Katanga and Back: A UN Case History*. New York: Simon & Schuster, 1962.

O'Neill, O. *Towards Justice and Virtue*. Cambridge: Cambridge University Press, 1996.

Pitkin, Hannah. *The Concept of Representation*. Berkeley: University of California Press, 1976.

Pound, Roscoe. "Law in Books and Law in Action," *American Law Review* 44 (1910): 12-36.

Raiffa, Howard. *The Art and Science of Negotiation*. Cambridge: Belknap University Press, 1982.

Raz, Joseph. *Political Reason and Norms*. London: Hutchinson Press, 1975.

———. *The Authority of the Law*. Oxford: Oxford University Press, 1979.

Rawls, John. *A Theory of Justice*. Cambridge, Massachusetts: Harvard University Press, 1971.

Ross, W.D. *Foundations of Ethics*. Oxford: Clarendon Press, 1939.

———. *The Right and the Good*. Oxford: Oxford University Press, 1963.

Ruddick, Sara. *Maternal Thinking*. New York: Ballentine Books, 1989.

Sartre, Jean-Paul. *Les mains sales*. Paris: Gallimard, 1948.

———. *No Exit: And Three Other Plays*, Lionel Abel, trans., New York: Vintage Books, 1955.

Scharfstein, Ben-Ami. *Amoral Politics: the Persistent Truth of Machiavellism*. Albany: State University of New York Press, 1995.

Scheper-Hughes, N. *Death and Weeping: The Violence of Everyday Life in Brazil*. Berkley: University of California Press, 1992.

Scruton, Roger. *The Meaning of Conservatism*. Harmondsworth: Penguin, 1980.

Sears, David and Carolyn Funk. "Self Interest in American Political Opinion," in J. Mansbridge, ed., *Beyond Self Interest*. Chicago: University of Chicago Press, 1990.

Shugarman, David P. "The Use and Abuse of Politics," in Don MacNiven, ed., *Moral Expertise: Studies in Practical and Professional Ethics*. New York: Routledge, 1990.

Shumpeter, Joseph. *Capitalism, Socialism, and Democracy*. London: Allen and Unwin, 1976.

Simpson, Evan. "Rights Thinking," *Philosophy* 72 (1997): 29-58.

———. "Between Internalism and Externalism in Ethics," *The Philosophical Quarterly* 49 (1999): 201-214.

Sinnott-Armstrong, W. *Moral Dilemmas*. Oxford: Basil Blackwell, 1988.

Sophocles. "Antigone," in E.F. Watling trans., *The Theban Plays*. Harmondsworth: Penguin, 1947.

Sorell, Tom. *Hobbes*. London: Routledge, 1986.

———. *Moral Theory and Anomaly*. (Aristotelian Society Monographs Series.) Oxford: Blackwell, 1999.

Stocker, Michael. "Rightness and Goodness: Is There a Difference?," *American Philosophical Quarterly* 10 (1973): 87-98.

———. "The Schizophrenia of Modern Ethical Theories," *Journal of Philosophy* 73 (1976): 453-66.

———. *Plural and Conflicting Values*. Oxford: Clarendon Press, 1990.

——— and Elizabeth Hegeman. *Valuing Emotions*. Cambridge: Cambridge University Press, 1996.

Sumner, L.W., *The Moral Foundation of Rights*. Oxford: Clarendon Press, 1987.

Sutherland, S.L. "The Al-Mashat Affair: Administrative Accountability in Parliamentary Institutions," *Canadian Public Administration* 34 (1991): 573-603.

———. "The Problem of Dirty Hands in Politics: Peace in the Vegetable Trade," *Canadian Journal of Political Science* 28:3 (September 1995): 479-508.

Thiele, Leslie Paul. *Thinking Politics*. Chatham, New Jersey: Chatham House Publishers, 1997.

Thompson, Dennis F. *Political Ethics and Public Office*. Cambridge: Harvard University Press, 1987.

———. "Mediated Corruption: The Case of the Keating Five," *American Political Science Review* 87 (1993): 369-81.

Trotsky, Leon, John Dewey, and George Novack. *Their Morals and Ours: Marxist versus Liberal Views on Morality. Four Essays*. New York: Pathfinder Press, 1973.

Tyler, Tom. "Justice, Self Interest and the Legitimacy of Legal and Political Authority," in J. Mansbridge, ed., *Beyond Self Interest*. Chicago: Chicago University Press, 1990.

Walzer, Michael. "Political Action: The Problem of Dirty Hands," *Philosophy and Public Affairs* 2:2 (1973): 160-80.

———. *Spheres of Justice: A Defense of Pluralism and Equality*. New York: Basic Books, 1983.

———. *Just and Unjust Wars: A Moral Argument With Historical Illustrations*, 2nd ed. New York: Basic Books, 1992.

Wasserstrom, Richard. "Lawyers as Professionals: Some Moral Issues," in Tom L. Beauchamp and Norman E. Bowie, eds., *Ethical Theory and Business*. New Jersey: Prentice Hall, 1979.

Weber, Max. "Politics as a Vocation," in H.H. Gerth and C. Wright Mills, eds., *From Max Weber: Essays in Sociology*. New York: Oxford University Press, 1973.

Webster, Paul. "Touvier Trial Goes Easy On Vichy," *Manchester Guardian Weekly* April 10, 1994, 4.

Weinsheimer, Joel. *Gadamer's Hermeneutics: A Reading of Truth and Method*. New Haven: Yale University Press, 1985.

Williams, Bernard. *Problems of the Self; Philosophical Papers 1956-1972*. Cambridge: Cambridge University Press, 1973.

———. "Politics and Moral Character," in S. Hampshire, ed., *Public and Private Morality*. 1978.

———. *Moral Luck*. Cambridge: Cambridge University Press, 1981.

Williams, Bernard, and J.J.C. Smart, eds. *Utilitarianism: For and Against.* Cambridge: Cambridge University Press, 1973.

Wolff, Jonathan. *Robert Nozick: Property, Justice and the Minimal State.* Oxford: Polity Press, 1991.

Yeo, Michael. "The Ethics of Public Participation," in Michael Stingl and Donna Wilson, eds., *Efficiency Versus Equality: Health Reform in Canada.* Halifax: Fernwood Publishing, 1996.

Young, Hugo. "If this is the New Ethical Order, It Stinks," *Manchester Guardian Weekly* Jan. 17, 1993, 5.

Contributors

John Allett teaches in the Division of Social Science at York University. He is the author of *New Liberalism: The Political Economy of J.A. Hobson* (1981) and has published several articles on the social thought of Bernard Shaw. He is currently preparing a comparative study of the works of Bernard Shaw and H.G. Wells.

Arthur Isak Applbaum is a professor of Public Policy at Harvard University's John F. Kennedy School of Government and Director of Graduate Fellowships in the Harvard University Program in Ethics and the Professions. Among his recent publications is *Ethics for Adversaries: The Morality of Roles in Public and Professional Life* (1999).

Ronald Beiner is a member of the Department of Political Science at the University of Toronto. His recent books include *What's the Matter with Liberalism?* (1992) and *Philosophy in a Time of Lost Spirit: Essays on Contemporary Theory* (1997). He is also editor of *Theorizing Nationalism* (1999).

Leah Bradshaw is a professor in Brock University's Department of Politics. She is the author of *Acting and Thinking: The Political Thought of Hannah Arendt* (1989) and of articles on Plato, Aristotle, and George Grant. She currently is working on a book on tyranny.

Wes Cragg is the Gardiner Professor of Business Ethics in the Schulich School of Business at York University. He has published widely in the fields of applied ethics and moral theory and is editor of *Contemporary Moral Issues* (1992). He is currently president of the Canadian chapter of Transparency International.

Ian Greene is associate dean of the Faculty of Arts at York University, where he also teaches public law in the Department of Political Science. He has recently co-authored *Final Appeal* (1998), *Honest Politics* (1997), and *Judges and Judging* (1991).

Michael McDonald holds the Maurice Young Chair of Applied Ethics and is the director of the Centre for Applied Ethics at the University of British Columbia. He has published widely on applied and theoretical issues in ethics and political philosophy. His most recent research has been on cross-cultural approaches in health care ethics and in the use of human subjects in medical research.

Kai Nielsen is professor emeritus at the University of Calgary (Philosophy) and is now teaching at Concordia University. He has published extensively on ethics and philosophy including *Equality and Liberty: A Defense of Radical Egalitarianism* (1985), *Marxism and the Moral Point of View* (1989), and *Naturalism Without Foundations* (1996).

Paul Rynard is a doctoral candidate in political science at York University. He has written on the political ethics of Herbert Marcuse. His current research and upcoming publications concern public policy and First Nations' land rights, including an essay in G. Todd, *Landscapes of Political Economy* (forthcoming).

David P. Shugarman is the master of McLaughlin College at York University where he also teaches in the Department of Political Science and is director of the York Centre for Practical Ethics. He has edited and co-edited several books including *Federalism and Political Community* (1989). His writings include *Honest Politics* (1997).

Evan Simpson is vice-president (academic) at Memorial University. His recent writings include "Prudence and Anti-Prudence" *(American Philosophical Quarterly,* 1998) and "Between Intemalism and Externalism in Ethics" *(The Philosophical Quarterly,* 1999).

Tom Sorell is professor of philosophy at the University of Essex. He has published extensively in moral theory and applied ethics, the philosophy of science, and the history and historiography of early modern philosophy. His *Moral Theory and Anomaly* will be published in 1999.

Michael Stocker is the Guttag Professor of Ethics and Political Philosophy at Syracuse University. For the last several decades he has been working on moral psychology, especially the emotions. In 1996 he, along with Elizabeth Hegeman, published *Valuing Emotions*.

S.L. (Sharon) Sutherland is a professor of political science in Ottawa, Ontario. Her research and teaching interests include political psychology, democratic theory, executive-legislative and executive-civil service relations, and the ethics of public office. Her writings include "The Canadian Federal Government: Patronage, Unity, Security, and Purity," in Langford and Tupper, eds., *Corruption, Character and Conduct* (1993).

Michael Yeo is acting director of Ethics at the Canadian Medical Association. He has published extensively in the area of bioethics and his main current interest is privacy and health information. His writings include "The Ethics of Public Participation" in Stingl and Wilson, eds., *Efficiency Versus Equality: Health Reform in Canada* (1996).

Sources

John Allett, "Bernard Shaw and Dirty-Hands Politics: A Comparison of *Mrs Warren's Profession* and *Major Barbara*," first appeared in the *Journal of Social Philosophy* 26:2 (Fall 1995), 32-45. Reprinted by the permission of the *Journal of Social Philosophy*.

Arthur Isak Applbaum, "Democratic Legitimacy and Official Discretion" is abridged from Arthur Isak Applbaum, *Ethics for Adversaries: the Morality of Roles in Public and Professional Life*. Princeton, N.J. © 1999 by Princeton University Press. Reprinted by permission of Princeton University Press. It first appeared in *Philosophy and Public Affairs* 21:3 (Summer 1992), 240-274.

The selection from Niccolò Machiavelli in the appendix is taken from Niccolò Machiavelli, *Selected Political Writings*, David Wooton, ed. and trans. Indianapolis: Hackett, 1994. Reprinted by permission of Hackett Publishing Company, Inc. All rights reserved.

Kai Nielsen, "There is No Dilemma of Dirty Hands," first appeared in the *South African Journal of Philosophy* 15:1 (Fall, 1996), 1-7. Reprinted with the permission of the *South African Journal of Philosophy*.

The selection from Jean-Paul Sartre in the appendix is taken from J.P. Sartre, *No Exit: And Three Other Plays*, Lionel Abel, trans., New York: Vintage Books, 1955. Copyright 1946 by Stuart Gilbert, Copyright renewed 1974 by Maris Agnes Mathilde Gilbert Copyright 1948, 1949 by Alfred A. Knopf Inc. Reprinted by permission of the publisher.

Index

This index lists the theorists and other names mentioned throughout the articles and notes. It does not cover the introductions to the two parts of the text, although the general introduction is included.

Acton, Lord 242
Adams, R.M. 42
Aeschylus 104
Anderson, Charles W. 226
Andrew, Edward 99
Anscombe, Elizabeth 144, 150, 154
Arendt, Hannah 87-99
Aristotle 31, 33, 35, 39, 93-96, 245
Armstrong, David 42
Atkinson, Michael 205
Austin, J.L. 57

Baier, Annette 193-194, 197
Barry, Brian 141, 145, 154
Bayles, Michael 197
Benn, Stanley 16, 19, 209, 226, 231, 247
Bentley, Eric 64
Blais, André 205
Bok, Sissela 54, 64-65, 202, 205, 243, 249
Boland, Edward P. 114, 126, 128, 131
Bourgault, Jacques 205
Branch, Taylor 131
Brandeis, Justice Louis D. 239
Brandt, Richard 29, 42
Braybrooke, David 208, 210, 213, 225-226
Brecht, Bertolt 142-143, 153, 224, 227

Broad, C.D. 143, 150
Brown, Bryson 225
Bush, George 219

Califano, Joseph A. 131
Cameron, Ewan 241
Camus, Albert 54, 226, 236-238
Carr, David 214, 226
Carter, Jimmy 241, 249
Carter, Stephen 200, 205
Chavez, Cesar 112-113, 124
Chrétien, Jean 227
Churchill, Winston 217-218
Clinton, Bill 199ff.
Coady, C.A.J. 225, 246, 248-249
Cohen, David K. 225
Collins, Anne 248
Connolly, William 95
Conrad, Joseph 174
Cunningham, Anthony P. 226

Dahl, Robert 248
Dancy, Jonathan 110
Danielson, Peter 190ff. 197
De George, Richard T. 185-186
Deigh, John 226
Dewey, John 19, 247-248
Dion, Stéphane 205
Donagan, Alan 144, 150, 154, 226

Draper, Theodore 131
Duplessis, Maurice 203
Dworkin, Ronald 119, 121, 122, 125, 132, 200, 205, 248

Eichmann, Adolph 94
Elkin, Stephen L. 227
Elshtain, Jean 87, 98
Engels, Friedrich 249

Foley, Michael 227
Ford, Gerald 219
Foucault, Michel 95
Frost, David 219
Funk, C. 86

Gadamer, Hans-Georg 214
Gandhi, Mahatma 232
Ganz, Arthur 65
Gewirth. Alan 101, 104, 110, 248
Gilligan, Carol 96, 104, 110
Goldwater, Barry 16
Goodin, Robert 84, 86, 173
Gottlieb, Sidney 241
Greene, Ian 8, 19, 197, 205, 248-249
Greenspan, Patricia 33, 42
Gutmann, Amy 132

Haber, Joram Graf 155
Habermas Jürgen 130
Haig, Alexander 242
Hampshire, Stuart 16, 19, 49, 77-80, 86, 174
Hare, R.M. 29, 42, 186
Hart, H.L.A. 197
Hegeman, Elizabeth 42
Held, Virginia 54-55, 64
Hitchner, Stephen B. 131
Hitler, Adolf 92
Hobbes, Thomas 68, 75-77
Hollis, Martin 16, 19, 154, 189, 197, 208-209, 216-218, 221, 225, 227, 230-231, 247

Holmes, Oliver Wendell 131
Holroyd, Michael 64
Howard, Kenneth 248

Ibsen, Henrik 59

Jackson, F. 42
Jagger, Alison M. 64
Johnson, Lyndon B. 112, 242
Johnston, Michael 205
Jones, Paula 199, 203
Judt, Tony 242, 249

Kant, Immanuel 11-12, 17, 35, 61, 72-73, 85, 88, 94, 98-99, 143, 163-164, 173, 236
Kennedy, John F. 203, 239
King, Anthony 212, 226
King, Martin Luther 101, 109, 232, 247
King, W.L. Mackenzie 188
Kissinger, Henry 242
Kleist, H. 154
Kohlhaas, Michael 141
Kolakowski, Leszek 141, 150
Korsgaard, C. 42
Kundera, Milan 88

Lane, H. 179, 185
Lax, David A. 132
Levi, I. 42
Lewinsky, Monica 199ff.
Lindblom, Charles E. 208, 210, 213, 225-226
Lukes, Stephen 16, 19, 46, 48-49
Luther, Martin 53
Lycos, Kimon 42
Lynd, Robert 247
Lyons, David 110

Machiavelli, Niccolò 12, 13-15, 16-18, 32, 45-48, 52-54, 61-62, 68, 75-77, 85, 89, 91-92, 141, 176, 181, 185, 187, 209, 230-232, 236-237, 243-245, 247, 251-252
Macpherson, C.B. 248
Mancuso, Maureen 205
Marcus, R. 42
Marx, Karl 55, 95, 143, 245, 246
Merleau-Ponty, Maurice 42, 46, 245, 249
Mill, John Stuart 130, 243
Miller, Richard 154
Moore, G.E. 144
Moore, Mark H. 131
Morris, H. 42
Murdoch, Iris 31

Nacht, David 247
Nagel, Thomas 16, 19, 29, 33, 35, 42, 140, 144, 146, 154
Naipaul, V.S. 186
Neustadt, Richard E. 131
Nevitte, Neil 205
Niebuhr, Reinhold 19
Nielsen, Kai 154, 155, 226
Nixon, Richard 203, 218-219, 239, 242
Noddings, Nell 96, 99
North, Oliver 114-115, 118, 124, 128, 229
Novack, George 19
Nozick, Robert 226

O'Brien, Conor Cruise 43-48
Olivier, Sydney 62
O'Neill, Onora 86
Orwell, George 173, 204

Parmenides 91
Pilate, Pontius 101, 107, 109
Pitkin, Hannah Fenichel 132

Plato 12-13, 19, 52, 60, 89, 91-92, 245
Pound, Roscoe 131
Purdom, C.B. 51

Rachels, James 65
Raiffa, Howard 132
Rawls, John 42, 103, 110, 118, 129-132, 248
Raz, Joseph 116-117, 131-132
Reagan, Ronald 112, 124, 126, 128, 219
Robertson, Emily 42
Robertson, John 42
Rorty, Richard 95
Ross, W.D. 42, 143, 150
Rubin, Ken 227
Ruddick, Sara 104, 110

Sartre, Jean-Paul 14, 32, 140, 142, 162-163, 207, 237-238, 246, 258
Schotch, Peter K. 225
Schumpeter, Joseph 132, 233, 247
Scruton, Roger 110
Sears, D. 86
Sebenius, James K. 132
Sellers, Peter 240-241
Shaw, Bernard 51ff., 55-62
Shugarman, David P. 8, 19, 99, 173, 181, 184-186, 197, 205, 247-249
Shultz, George 114, 124
Simpson, D. 179, 185
Simpson, Evan 223, 227
Smart, J.J.C. 186
Smith, J. Percy 54, 59, 64
Socrates 11-13, 60, 90, 92
Sorell, Tom 86
Sparrow, Malcolm K. 131
Stalin, Josef 92
Starr, Kenneth 199ff.
Stocker, Michael 42, 93, 96, 99
Stone, Oliver 220
Styron William 33-34

Sugden, Robert 197
Sumner, L.W. 110
Sutherland, Sharon 172, 227

Thiele, Leslie P. 95, 99
Thompson, Dennis F. 81-82, 86,
    132, 208, 215-216, 224-225, 227,
    249
Tinder, Glenn 52, 64
Trotsky, Leon 16, 245-246, 249, 254
Trudeau, Pierre 202
Turner, Stansfield 241
Tutu, Desmond 230

Valency, Maurice 58
Vance, Cyrus 249
Vincent, Tony 227

Walzer, Michael 14-16, 19, 27-29,
    32-33, 39, 42, 46, 48-49, 51, 53-54,
    57, 73, 86, 98,   119, 121, 132, 139-
    141, 144, 146ff., 154, 157ff., 172,
    176, 185, 197, 226, 230,   234ff.,
    243-244, 247, 260
Warwick, Donald 131
Wasserstrom, Richard 189, 197
Weber, Max 14, 46, 48, 53, 61, 233,
    247, 255
Weil, Simone 31
Weinsheimer, Joel C. 226
White, Theodore 19
Williams, Bernard 16, 29, 42, 46,
    49, 86, 140, 144, 146, 154, 174,
    186, 226, 248
Wolin, Sheldon S. 64
Wooton, David 247

Young, Hugo 227